Political Development

This book fills a growing gap in the literature on international development by addressing the debates about good governance and institution building within the context of political development.

This accessible volume returns the key issues of human rights and democratization to the centre of the development debate and offers the reader an alternative to the conventional approach to, and definition of, the idea of "development." Discussing political development in its broadest context, it includes chapters on democracy, institutional-building, the state, state failure, nation, human rights and political violence.

Damien Kingsbury, a leading expert on development and Southeast Asia, argues that "good governance," in its common usage, is too narrowly defined and that good governance is not just about ensuring the integrity of a state's financial arrangements, but that it goes to the core social and political issues of transparency and accountability, implying a range of social structures defined as "institutions."

Providing new insights into political development, this comprehensive text can be used on advanced undergraduate and postgraduate courses in international development, comparative politics, political theory and international relations.

Damien Kingsbury is Director of the Masters in International and Community Development program and Associate Professor in International Development Studies at Deakin University, Victoria, Australia.

Political Development

Damien Kingsbury

Routledge
Taylor & Francis Group

LONDON AND NEW YORK

First published 2007
by Routledge
2 Park Square, Milton Park, Abingdon, Oxon OX14 4RN

Simultaneously published in the USA and Canada
by Routledge
711 Third Ave, New York, NY 10017

Routledge is an imprint of the Taylor & Francis Group, an informa business

© 2007 Damien Kingsbury

Typeset in Garamond by
RefineCatch Limited, Bungay, Suffolk

British Library Cataloguing in Publication Data
A catalogue record for this book is available from the British Library

Library of Congress Cataloging-in-Publication Data
Kingsbury, Damien.
   Political development / Damien Kingsbury.—1st ed
      p. cm.
   Includes bibliographical references and index.
   ISBN 978–0–415–40187–6 (hardback : alk. paper)—
   ISBN 978–0–415–40188–3 (pbk. : alk. paper)
   1. Political development.   I. Title.
   JA66.K56 2007
   320.1—dc22
                              2006039495

ISBN 10: 0–415–40187–9 (hbk)
ISBN 10: 0–415–40188–7 (pbk)
ISBN 10: 0–203–94708–8 (ebk)

ISBN 13: 978–0–415–40187–6 (hbk)
ISBN 13: 978–0–415–40188–3 (pbk)
ISBN 13: 978–0–203–94708–1 (ebk)

For Fiona
and my friends in Aceh

Acknowledgements

I would like to thank Michelle Miller for her valuable and insightful comments on a draft of this book, with the proviso that I retain sole responsibility for its remaining shortcomings.

Contents

Figures

Introduction

Political development, as an idea, is not new. The period of the Enlightenment in particular engaged with notions of political development, and despite some more recent criticisms of that era for its foundational modernist tendencies, the legacy of the Enlightenment's ethical reason continues to inform the core debates about political principals and the direction of political practise. The legacies of the Enlightenment, in particular liberalism and socialism, reflecting the core principles of freedom and equality, remain the point of departure for contemporary debate about "the good," or that which has the greatest social benefit.

That there has been an active debate on the application of these principles of freedom and equality, including their global diminution in the latter part of the twentieth and early twenty-first centuries, only reinforces that these ideas are central to political development, if not wholly agreed upon. As this book will discuss, however, claims against the more broadly applied notions of freedom and equality reflect narrower interests, even if they are themselves sometimes disguised as just these principles; the freedom and equality of opportunity to dominate others appear to be malignant forms of the original ideas.

The idea of a rational "good," of course, goes back much earlier than the Enlightenment. In one sense the idea is as old as politics itself, or at least as old as competition within politics over differing visions of the "good." The idea can be seen to apply to the general historical trajectory of political processes. This is not to say that this trajectory has been linear, as demonstrably it has not, and different criteria have impacted on what might be called political development from time to time. More importantly, though, political development is not an end in itself; it is a means to an end. This implies that rather than political development necessarily referring to a specified goal, it refers to the process itself. This is aimed at the betterment of human political relations, or those relationships between people that entail the application of aspects of power.

Necessary but sufficient?

In the realm of human need, adequate nutrition and shelter are necessary conditions for survival, but there remains a question as to whether they are sufficient. There are places that either strive to or actually do provide nutrition and shelter at a level necessary for survival. However, while some such places are organized along liberal democratic lines, others may be organized along formal and authoritarian lines, have a distinct top-down system of social organization and rule making, brook no questioning of their authority, or allow no appeals against their decisions. Freedom of expression may be curtailed, with no meaningful opportunity to change the status quo and attempts to do so may be met with a harsh and repressive response. This description could characterize a number of developing countries, including some of those that call themselves a "people's democracy"; it could also characterize a prison.

In the debate about development, there has been a case put that economic or material development must precede other forms of development, including "human rights," as they are sometimes pejoratively referred to. Indeed, from the 1960s to the 1980s, the backlash against "rights" was so virulent that a separate set of rights was developed, being "economic, social and cultural rights" (UN 1976) along with the "right to development" (UN 1986). There is no doubt that it is difficult to enjoy human rights when one is hungry or socially or culturally constrained. Yet it is difficult not to see the addition to the "rights agenda" as on one hand setting up a competing rights framework that privileges economic development, and rationalizes this "economic development first" paradigm by relativizing social and political conditions via "cultural difference." Indeed, from the 1960s to the 1980s, it was commonplace to not only assert that economic development must precede political freedoms, but that certain political freedoms were inappropriate to particular cultural contexts; that "democracy," for example could only function in a developed economic climate and that it reflected a particular cultural paradigm.

Ironically, the idea that political freedoms could only be gained after and as a result of economic development was a crude form of Marxist historical materialism. Yet few of the governments that claimed this logic were sympathetic to Marxism. It was, in most cases, a blind for the narrow distribution of resources; for the rich and powerful to become more rich and powerful. In that this logic suited the economic preferences of a number of developed states, it was easier for them to form strategic alliances with seemingly permanent rulers in developing countries. Few developed country governments were prepared to challenge this notion, at least up until such time that the international agenda determined that such implied authoritarianism was no longer convenient. As for avowedly Marxist governments, deep in the recesses of their ideology remained the idea that authoritarianism was also necessary to efficiently marshal economic resources in order to speed up their development, the ultimate purpose of which was the liberation of humanity. That they generally failed to deliver much efficiency and relatively little human liberation probably said more for the concentration of power in the hands of an authoritarian elite, as in non-Marxist authoritarian states, than it did about the aspirations that originally motivated such thinking.

In discussion about development, the theme "governance" recurs. Development concerns quality of life and the range of factors that impact upon this, while governance addresses the methods by which there is a process of accountability in relation to development. These issues go to the very heart of the way in which people live, be they in developed societies that enjoy relatively high standards of living or in developing countries in which standards of living are often inadequate to meet basic human needs. In either case, however, development and governance are usually applied to economic criteria. In so far as development refers to the "economy" or economic criteria, this is usually intended to apply to the broad range of material conditions of life, and not just the narrow "money" understanding that the term "economics" commonly implies. That is, while material conditions of living are dominated by access to money and decisions related to them (such as supply, interest rates, accumulation, distribution and so on), it is the concretely measurable things that money can buy, or allow (such as health, shelter, education and other material choices) that constitute the general understanding of development.

The World Bank, which has been the principal promoter of notions of governance, defines it by a range of inter-related criteria, including: "Voice and Accountability," "Political Stability and Absence of Violence," "Government Effectiveness," "Regulatory Quality," "Rule of Law" and "Control of Corruption" (World Bank 2005). While these criteria potentially imply more than an economic focus, it is important to note that each of the criteria refers to the conditions in which an economy functions. It is therefore widely agreed that development cannot take place if good governance is not first in place (see, for example Kaufmann *et al.* 2005; Kaufmann 2004; Kaufmann *et al.* 2003; Hellman *et al.* 2000; Kaufmann *et al.* 2000; Kaufmann *et al.* 1999). The issue, though, is that, while it can be acknowledged that a broad range of governance issues are necessary for economic development, governance can and arguably should refer to more than just economic development.

The proposal presented here considers an alternative to this conventional approach to and definition of the idea of "development" and "governance," considering the processes by which decisions are made about economic issues, such as allocation of resources, and the probity and accountability that can and should apply to decision-making processes. It will put the case that "good governance," in its common usage, is too narrowly defined. It will argue that good governance is not just about ensuring the probity of a state's financial arrangements, but goes to core social and political issues of transparency and accountability. This in turn implies a range of social structures that could be defined as "institutions." A focus on such institutional development has been considered by Huntington (1968) and Fukuyama (2004). However, in both these cases, institutions are also narrowly defined – more or less as bureaucracies – and in specifically instrumentalist terms. This book intends to adopt the idea of institutions, but expand it to the broader range of social and political institutions, including participatory and representative political processes, public democracy, political convention the role of civil and political rights, civil society, and so on.

The book will put the case that while there are levels of access to these social conditions, the extent of such access defines political development. Greater political development, it will be argued, not only facilitates other, more conventional material aspects of development, but along with the material capacity to live, is the principal development goal (for example, see Sen 1999). That is, there is little human value in providing food and shelter if the full range of human requirements, including some capacity to determine one's own affairs, to share and discuss such affairs freely, and to question various propositions about social organization, are not also met.

In this understanding of political development, there is a normative assumption about desirable states of affairs that comply more or less with conventional notions of human rights, broadly understood as preferred conditions of physical and social well-being, the minimum acceptable level at which those conditions can exist, and acceptance of a framework to ensure those conditions. Given that this state of minimum desirability has historically not applied to very many people and in a contemporary sense continues to not apply to many, the argument is that there is a process of development of those conditions, predicated upon political processes or the capacity of people to express their interests as preferences. This is a modernist view of politics that ordinarily complies with the description of "progressive" in that it assumes the capacity and the desirability of political progress, that it advocates a process in which there is greater public accountability to citizens, and in which the greatest good of the greatest number without discriminating against minorities is normatively desirable. That is to say, the idea of political "progress" from a less desirable state of being towards one that is more desirable, and the conditions that allow it, can be described as "political development."

Where this idea of political development has a corollary with economic or material development, it does not imply a cost or deficit as posited by material development (for example in a balance of trade or to the environment). In that a negative quality can be associated with political development, it is a reduction of narrowly conceived or top-down authority, which itself implies a greater control by a wider population. The idea of political development also privileges itself above material development and its associated "science" of economics, implying that there is no value-free process of economic accumulation or distribution, and that such accumulation or distribution is properly the prerogative of those who it primarily affects. In this, an advanced model of political development assumes a high degree of governance and accountability on the part of representative power holders and economic actors. "Governance" is thus not about the instrumentalist ensuring of financial probity or compliance with a "scientific" paradigm; rather, it is about a bottom-up process of accountability and responsibility, and the appropriate application of socially shared values codified as law. A further development of this line of thinking is that material development is not an end in itself, but the creation of material conditions that allow the more complete exploration and satisfaction of social and individual potential. This agrees with the purpose of development as outlined by Amartya Sen in his seminal work *Development as Freedom* (1999).

This model of political development further implies a contestation of authority, from a more authoritarian and autocratic to a more liberal and accountable model. It must therefore engage with the language of the debate that has characterized recent trends towards placing more power in the hands of technocrats and officials elected through a process of increasingly narrowly, challenge-worthy and in some cases quite inaccurate uses of the term "democracy." To this end, a discussion of political development cannot proceed without clarification of a range of key political ideas, and the rescue of a number of key political terms. "Accountability," for example, is not the sole preserve of creditors or share-holders, unless these terms are understood in a political and hence metaphorical sense, which they are largely not. Similarly, the idea of "reform" is not restricted to "economic reform," and even here it is invariably a code for shifting public control or ownership to private control or ownership. This certainly says nothing about "reform" in its political sense and arguably militates against traditional conceptions of social and political reform, or progressive change. Even in an economic sense, the debate is much less about "reform" than it is about a Hayekian transfer of control of material resources, which may or may not have any of the socially or economically progressive implications that the term implies (see Hayek 1960, 1976, 1988). In this sense, hegemonic frameworks have shifted meaning in subtle and sometimes unsubtle ways, which in turn influence the way in which language works and ideas are conceptualized. Any discussion about political development, then, must at least acknowledge this shift, and reclaim this lost linguistic territory, or a reduction in the use of what Watson (2005) has so accurately referred to as "weasel words" and "management-speak."

The question here is not just one of how the debate is shaped, and over whose territory the debate is pursued. The debate is also over the way in which ideas are shaped, how they are framed and communicated, what has its meaning cloaked and obscured and what is delegitimized or relegitimized as a site of public contestation. This then goes to the principle claim of freedom, which is to think, to communicate those thoughts, and to establish and accept the legitimacy of a plurality of expressed ideas. This lies at the very center of any meaningful claim to political development.

Political development, then, does not subscribe to the prevailing hegemonic order, or indeed to the idea of the legitimacy of hegemonies. Political development is about embarking down a path of liberation that is focused on a fundamental improvement of social relations within and across societies. In this, it addresses at least the basic aspects of political relations, and seeks to chart a dynamic course that assumes a capacity for improvement. Humanity has evolved a long way, if not evenly. There is much catching up to do, and there remains much scope for further evolution.

1 An outline of political development

In any discussion about politics or the organization of society, rather than launching into preferred styles and methods, or policies and ideologies, it is perhaps more useful to first ask what is the desired outcome of these criteria. That is, what type of social organization is regarded as normatively preferable and how does that imply a particular orientation towards political progress? This then raises two further questions, these being what constitutes the "good" and, assuming that ends should not predominate to the exclusion of "means," the processes and systems in which such "good" is manifested.

Regarding what constitutes "good," there will, of course, be almost as many answers to such a question as there are people to answer it. Despite these many answers, there is also likely to be coherence around sets of values that embody common conceptions of the common good.[1] In this, "good," or positive, can range in focus from particular personal benefit to the widest social benefit. The points at which the personal and the social converge or separate underpin most of what is understood about politics and the various political systems and processes by which we understand it.

If a case can be made for some basic principles concerning the widest possible articulation of such a "good" – and this assumes that there are available some universals predicated upon the common human condition – this then raises the necessity of identifying systems and processes that are consistent with, and conducive towards such a good. Such an approach does not necessarily imply a utilitarian answer to this type of question, even if aspects of utilitarianism help define a possible framework. What it does do, though, is take the idea of a first principle – the definition of a good – and seeks to manifest it through an appropriate process or processes, the existence of which constitute "good" in the act of becoming.

Within the context of this book, the principal of good can be identified as "freedom," both freedom to fulfill human potential and freedom from limitations upon that potential. This general idea contains within it a broad, if not fixed, series of claims. Perhaps the most important constituent claim within the idea of freedom is that of "equality," not in terms of any claim to absolute sameness, but in terms of the circumstances and opportunities for the realization of human potential within social contexts. That is, individuals might have more or less potential, but the basic conditions in which such individuals exist must make circumstances available to them which allow them to explore that potential, or not unduly limit them, concomitant without limiting the circumstances of others. Equality in this sense, then, means political and legal equality, in which the opportunity for a citizen to express political views is no more or less privileged than that of any other citizen, and that the rights of citizens are equally allowed and protected under a consistent and just rule of law.

That there is a tension within this idea which refers to the material aspects of equality, and the question of the relationship between such material circumstances and political equality. Within discussion about equality, there has been a claim – and in some cases a reality – that egalitarian processes imply limitations upon the freedom of some in order to support the freedom of others. This applies to pre-existing imbalances in power relations, but also to economic arrangements, in which economic advantage is viewed as providing a social and political advantage. The assumption, then, is that claims to equality necessarily imply some sort of limiting or social flattening process. However, this is a narrowly defined and simplistic understanding of equality. One view of the freedom-equality debate revolves around what has been characterized as the French-Anglo-American divide. In this, the French position is held to be that: "There can be no individual freedom short of some sort of deep seated equality that goes well beyond equality of rights to a kind of equality of opportunity and resources" (Spitz in Weinstock and Nadeau 2004: 54). The proposed dichotomy presents the Anglo-American view as being whatever is private is legitimate, and whatever is public requires apology and justification, However, Spitz recognizes that while this dichotomy exists, and is variously presented as existing on the part of particular interests, he claims that it is a fundamentally false dichotomy. "Mastering private domination through law," he says, "and trying to regulate and compensate unjustified inequalities through public institutions in order to create a fair equality of opportunity is not specifically French, since it is at the very heart of liberal political philosophy" (Spitz in Weinstock and Nadeau 2004: 59). That is, where private power is not consented to, if democratic forms are to prevail, such non-consensual power must be equitably regulated. Public institutions must have a primary concern for the widest possible interest, in order to ensure that least advantaged sections of society are able to understand that such institutions do not just facilitate their domination (Spitz in Weinstock and Nadeau 2004: 57). That is, "when politics is nothing more than the art of negotiating compromises [of interest], it is no longer the rule of right but the rule of might" (Spitz in Weinstock and Nadeau 2004: 58). It is at this point that there is an intersection between what is "right" and what is "good," which in turn provides a foundation for moral philosophy and consequent political ethics.

In this respect, in the fullness of its application, any equality which acts as a limitation upon freedom – which imposes a relationship that implies an imbalance of power – only describes a distortion of equality. This abstraction of a particular application of an equalizing principle can imply a loss of actual freedom through imposing the same requirements upon all. This "flattening" approach, however, does not address the substantive claims of equality, which apply in the first instance as the opposite quality of narrow power, or the delegitimization of unfair advantage. In its positive and more complete sense, equality is the foundation upon which freedom is constructed, and it is the negotiated tension between equality and freedom that provides the political space in which the debate over what constitutes political development takes place.

The first principles of "good" are, then, freedom based on equality, which can most suitably occur through a broadly participatory, representative and accountable process. The question then becomes how can this best be realized, and what conditions must prevail in order for this to happen. This then raises the further question of how this good relates to less favorable pre-existing circumstances and what are the criteria needed to progress from one to the other.

This approach contains within it an explicit assumption and an implicit assumption. Explicitly, there is an assumption that many, perhaps most, people live in political circumstances that are less than ideal and that there is a common aspiration to live under a better set of social and material circumstances. That is, there is not just a possibility but a desire for "progress" and that progress exists, or can exist, not just as an idea but as a social reality (the corollary of this is that actively pushing for such progress is, by definition, "progressive"). It is important to note at this point that "progress" does not have a particular or permanently fixed definition and certainly cannot be solely allied with the modernist economic understanding of progress as industrialization, or perhaps even post-industrial economic development. Similarly, it does not imply a single deterministic outcome for social affairs. It means advancement in the state of human affairs, most important among which is how people organize their relations with each other and how they manifest and concentrate or share power.

Implicitly, there is an assumption that there is a method by which such progress can be achieved, and that this identifies a path or a confluence of paths, developing from the particular (or a number of particulars) to a normative universal. It is important here to note that discussion of "universals" does not imply a flattening or deadening quality or the suppression of difference (the imposition of power to achieve a minimalist sameness). Rather, it implies commonality, the capacity for shared experience and the potential for shared understanding of that experience. This might not apply in every circumstance, but it can apply in many circumstances, and, perhaps those that are most basic and hence important to the conditions of human life. Moreover, recognition of key universals does not logically imply a totality, much less an institutionalized totalizing capacity (totalitarianism). Indeed, taking into account certain specific conditions that might apply from place to place (although not allowing for an imposed cultural relativism),[2] it should normatively imply the opposite of totalitarianism, that shared universals are the principle counterpoint to totalitarianism. This occurs through a commonly shared understanding creating the social space necessary for the genuine and non-restrictive expression of the social particular, or the greatest possible freedom. This, then, is the process of "political development."

Approaches to political development

As a term, "political development" was explicitly used in the 1960s as a means of describing the process of what might be called "political modernization" by then recently decolonized and other developing countries. In the period following decolonization, the primary concern of political analysts was to see the development of stable political communities that would more or less follow the path set by developed (and often formerly colonizing) countries. The purpose of this was generally twofold: to allow the stable material development and participation of these newer members of the international community, and, particularly from a Western perspective, to ensure that development occurred along politically acceptable (that is, non-communist) lines. Having asserted a claim to independence and often backed this with militant political activity, many newer states found there was a prevailing concern over "too much politics" and not enough capacity. From a perspective that was more favorably inclined towards the communist model, or aspects of it such as central economic planning, the view from developing countries was that these new political societies needed to establish structures in which to allow such planning and, it was hoped, consequent material development to take place. Viewed from an historical-functionalist perspective, Jaguaribe noted at the time that political development constituted "a shift from the former ethnocentric and static position, which tended to measure the development of any political system by its resemblance to a fixed standard – that of Western democracy, particularly in its current British or American versions. Political development is now regarded as the process of adjustment of a political system, at any historical stage of the overall development, to the functions required by this system as they arise from the economic, cultural, social, and political structural conditions" (Jaguaribe 1968: 53, nb2).

If one could characterize the above approaches, they reflected "institutionalism" on one hand and "political economy" on the other. What both had in common was a primary focus on the state as the main instrument to manifest social political will, and the principle framework within to construct newly emergent "nations." As largely legatees of the colonial experience, most postcolonial states employed the territorial boundaries set for them by their colonial masters, which in turn rarely took into consideration pre-existing ethnic or national boundaries. Rivers, by way of illustration, often became markers of territorial divisions, whereas in most pre-colonial societies they were the main means of transport within those societies. The idea of "nation," therefore, did not always come naturally or easily to post-colonial states. It had also not come easily for the original formally demarcated states of Europe that were recognized under the Treaty of Westphalia of 1648, although perhaps more so for those states that emerged as expressions of collective identity in the nineteenth and early twentieth centuries.

The concern, then, in the post-colonial period was around establishing a reliable basis for consistent social organization. Added to a natural, or naturalized, tendency for those who can achieve power to accrue it to themselves, particularly in societies that retained significant vestiges of pre-colonial political conceptualization, this led to the proliferation of strong state institutions *vis-à-vis* frequently weak political societies. One manifestation of this was a low level of political participation and consequently little democratization or accountability. As a further consequence, there were often high levels of corruption, incompetence and the employment of means of state repression against dissent from these establishing orders. In some cases, the strength of a particular state institution, such as the army, was at the cost of other, more socially focused institutions. This led to institutionalized violence against the state's own citizens, and the quasi-permanent establishment of a predatory class. In this, the function of the citizens of the state was to provide the source of enrichment or aggrandizement for an elite of corrupt politicians, military officers and businessmen (or robber barons), all of which could be and often were and too often still are interchangeable.

Not surprisingly, this period produced little development of any type (although with a few notable exceptions), and saw a number of states actually go backwards in economic terms, with an overall widening of the gap between rich and poor states. In searching for an explanation(s) for this common "failure" of development, the World Bank and other observers and analysts began to focus on what they termed "governance," which was initially intended to imply the application and observance of rules of financial conduct, but which has come to be broadened to include a wide range of state institutional responsibilities.

To ensure that good governance is implemented, and that states and their institutions comply with at least the requirements for relative honesty and some degree of efficiency, they must be held accountable. The "international community," in this case meaning the IMF, World Bank and WTO, among other multilateral agencies, has some capacity to impose degrees of discipline and accountability on otherwise recalcitrant states and their governments. But real accountability, from those who are most intimately acquainted with its lack, derives from the citizens of such states. In order for citizens to exercise a requirement for accountability, they must be able to participate in the political process, to support programs that are in their interests (presumably including "good governance") and to oppose those that are not. This in turn implies that citizens should have a guaranteed capacity to hold their government accountable, which means that they have the "right" to do so, and the specific supporting rights that buttress such a general political right.

This then, is the point at which the social "politics" comes back into the equation with institutions, or where agency or the interest and capacity of individuals is balanced against the state, the state's institutions, and the collective or communal interests they claim to represent as legitimizing their political existence. Political development, in this sense, is both about redressing the imbalance between the state institutions and collective or communitarian interest and the constituent members of the state, as citizens, and their more direct concerns, interests and allegiances as individuals.

The balancing act implied in this must raise the further question of to whose benefit is this process about. In this respect, development generally and political development in particular should have some socially beneficial function, and that they should contribute towards the betterment of the lives of the people at which they are aimed. In Sen's view, the goal of development, including political development, should be to enhance "freedom," including freedoms "from" and freedoms "to." If this is the goal and purpose of development, the issue of constraints on such "freedoms" arises. It has been said, in relation to human rights, that they cannot be guaranteed by their abrogation. That is, one cannot deny human rights or freedoms in the present on the pretext of allowing them at some later time.[3] Assuming the validity of this claim, this means that the maximum possible allowance must be made for guarantees which secure freedoms "from" and freedoms "to." This in turn puts political power back into the hands of the people on whose behalf it is supposed to be exercised – the political constituents, or citizens – to ensure the accountability of their political representatives that they are working as honestly and efficiently as possible in order to protect and enhance their collective and individual interests and rights.

In this sense, then, the gap in the debate about political development between the 1960s and the early twenty-first century indicates a gulf between two perspectives on political development; one institutional and collective or communitarian, the other rights-based and socially plural. As with "rights and responsibilities," it is neither practical nor desirable to suggest that one could or should exist without being balanced by the other. To date, however, the balance has been in favor of the former rather than the latter. The tendency is that there was a brief respite from a communitarian focus, the economic challenges of "efficiency" and the security challenges of "terrorism," state failure and a range of decreasingly important but none the less manipulated "fears." These have worked to shift the balance further towards the communitarian position – the power of which, as human agency would have it, rests in the hands of a few. In all societies, however, this is both materially counterproductive and, perhaps more importantly, constrains those freedoms to which the full expression of the human condition aspires.

There is also another counter-point in this understanding of political development, which comes about as a consequence of the collapse of Soviet-style communism and economic central planning in most places that it existed. On the one hand, the collapse of the Soviet system ushered in an era of creation of new independent states, in the former Soviet Union, the former Yugoslavia and in the division of Czechoslovakia. This liberalization of the global political climate also spurred a number of local groups to assert claims to autonomy or independence, though generally, to date, with much less success, East Timor and Eritrea being the primary exceptions. On the other hand, in moving away from one-party political systems, the assumption was that where there was increasingly political competition this comprised democracy, as broadly understood in previously democratic countries. This begged the meaning of the term "democracy," and the various degrees and types of democracy which might be available. But it did not stop a type of triumphalism from developing, particularly in the US, which perceived itself and was largely perceived by others, to be the "winner" of the cold war.

Ideologues such as Frances Fukuyama (1992) argued that the triumph of a particular interpretation of political liberalism, and what he (and others) claimed was its necessary economic corollary of economic neo-liberalism, constituted the "end of history." In this, Fukuyama borrowed from Hegel the idea that there was an ideal end point in political development and it had been reached, at least in some places, and that this demonstrated a political finality. This "end of history" was predicated upon the legitimacy of state power was not lost on the capacity for increasingly unilateral US decision making, especially in relation to foreign policy. As the world's sole super-power, the US perceived that it had both a responsibility and a right to act as the "global policeman." Fukuyama's ideology dove-tailed with that of Huntington (1993, 1996) who argued that the world was divided along lines demarcated by "civilizations," in this way providing a pretext for US interven-tion in particular states characterized by cultural dissimilarity (particularly those characterized by Islam).

There are elements of Fukuyama's claim that are supportable within a political development debate, notably his favor for what are distinctly American understandings of political liberalism. Where this book finds itself taking a different position to such an otherwise unilateral view of liberalism (and its claim of a necessary corollary with economic neo-liberalism) is on the claim that there is, or can be, an "end of history" (and an attendant "last man"). Since Fukuyama's triumphal political self-congratulation, the paradigm to which he was referring – the collapse of the Soviet Union and the end of the cold war – has markedly shifted. Since then, the world in general and the US in particular have discovered, or invented, a new global enemy: militant Islamism. The Western strategic environment which in the early 1990s seemed to find security was, within ten years, no longer secure. State budgets changed, priorities shifted, and new, often draconian laws that undermined conventional notions of the rule of law were passed within liberal democra-cies. Indeed, there was a common view that "the world changed" as a con-sequence of events on 11 September 2001, when two hijacked aircraft crashed into and destroyed the iconic twin towers of the World Trade Center in New York City, and a third crashed into the Pentagon in Washington.

Both normatively and in historical fact, politics and the political evolution of humanity does not and cannot have an end point. Just as Hegel was in error to assume that the introduction of the Napoleonic Code in Prussia indicated an "end of history" for political development, so too any claim made in the present cannot by definition have the benefit of some future hindsight. It may be that we (or Fukuyama, or Hegel) cannot conceive of a future different that's much less better than our own, if we happen to be so lucky as to live in what we regard as an ideal world. The majority of the world's people are clearly not so fortunate, and this is a consequence not of their failure to achieve "our" ideal but because of a structural inability to do so. "We" have in large part built our own ideal on their misery, despite modernist and pro-foundly environmentally ignorant claims that economic growth can continue endlessly and will solve all problems.

In so far as we can imagine the future, as Marx tried to do, we may envisage a utopian end point. The problems here, though, are that one person's utopia may be another person's hell, that utopias are, by definition, not as accessible as the imagination that conceived them, and that in the struggle to bring forward this utopia (why delay if it is known to be out there waiting?) the costs of its attainment may be vastly greater than any putative rewards it may be able to offer. That is, the means of achieving utopia can, and to date has, fundamentally compromised its end.

Another view, then, and that which is presented here, is that there is no end to human politics, history or evolution, nor short of global annihilation can there be one. What is important is not that societies should aspire to, or fight for a particular end of political development, or jealously guard and maintain such an end to political development should they believe they have achieved it. What is important is that the focus be placed on the process of political development, and that the process itself be understood as defining the type of future into which it leads. This is not to suggest a fixation with the present, but a fulsome regard for the lessons of the past and a continuous and critical reappraisal of the present in order to facilitate its progress.

Political development and post-colonialism

Earlier characterizations of political development often confused it with the politics of development, in part reflecting the preoccupations of the immedi-ate post-colonial period. This comprised the creation of "national" identities (and the attendant resolution of proto-national pluralism), the establishment of political stability and civic order, and the ideological assumptions that underpinned ideas about "development" in the economic sense of the term (for example, see Anderson *et al.* 1967). No doubt newly emerging post-colonial states struggled with an uneven colonial experience and inherited colonial borders that very often failed to correspond to coherent ethnic groupings and which, as such, resurfaced as competing vertical (ethnic) claims. The assumption was that such vertical claims could be resolved by them being subsumed by a created or an imposed "national" order, in tandem with or as a consequence of modernization (for example, see Gellner 1983). However, this neglected the frequent failure of the modernization project and, assuming at least some linkage (although not a structural determinism), the lag between material or technological and cultural change (see Ogburn 1964), often of two or three generations. That is, political development was seen as being available only or primarily by buying into the modernist "nation-building" project, which was primarily identified with economic development (see Chapter 3, The nation). This in turn required political stability and order. Such stability and order tended to exclude the principle focus on freedom and equality, and thus the civic virtues that derive from such goals. This meant that in the focus on order, the development project in many post-colonial countries turned authoritarian.

The claim for and emphasis upon political stability as a feature of political development is supportable if it refers to orderly political processes, including (sometimes frequent) change. The claim that frequent political change undermined, for example, Indonesia's political order in the 1950s is challenged by the retention of political order during Italy's own experience with frequent postwar political change. Change and its frequency are not a problem for political development; a lack of respect for and adherence to political rules is. Too often, however, in post-colonial states, the claim to political "stability" was supported by political compulsion, in many cases completely rewriting or throwing out the "political rules." Compulsion does not resolve inherent tensions; at best it temporarily subsumes them, usually by repression. This in turn closes down the public space for a free determination of ideological preferences in the pursuit of economic development, however that might be defined, and leads to lesser rather than greater political development. That is, orderly political processes and an adherence to political rules are the guarantors of equality-based freedom.

This emphasis on an imposed nation-building and order in turn reflected not so much a desire for political development, but an understanding of development as being overwhelmingly defined in material or economic terms. "Development," defined as such, has frequently been the overriding rhetorical concern of the governments of developing countries, and the point by which governments have attempted to legitimize their rule and policies. The goal of "development" defined as economic development, has thus been predicated upon order and stability, which has in turn been the major rationalization for the employment of authoritarian methods of political control, as well as for democratic processes.

For much of the three decades after the Second World War, the term "development" was not just defined in material terms, but in narrow economic terms that were almost exclusively understood as meaning growth in per capita gross domestic product (GDP). This ratio of how much money a country earned in a year from local production divided by its population – potential average income – was viewed as the primary indicator of development. Within the broad category of per capita GDP is the further economic indicator of Purchasing Parity Power (PPP), or the purchasing power of a country's currency relative to a "basket" of goods and services that can be bought in another, denominated currency, usually US dollars (for example, a dollar will buy a different quantity of rice in Laos than in the US). Given that income is not distributed based on an average, but unequally, the distribution of income, referred to as the Gini coefficient (that is, the ratio of rich to poor in a given country), was a further refinement of the per capita GDP model. Importantly, since per capita GDP is so blunt a measurement as to be of limited use, from the 1970s the idea of "development" has been expanded to also refer to nutrition, literacy, health care, sanitation, education, housing, environmental degradation, fertility, infant mortality rates, average life expectancy, and causes of death. This expanded material measurement of development is generally referred to as the Human Development Index (HDI), with the formal HDI as used by the UNDP having 33 categories with each having several further sub-categories (UNDP 2005: 219–329).

The HDI begins to get to the real purpose of development, which is improving the quality of people's lives, and in this is an increasingly useful indicator of the success or failure of particular policies or other changes in material circumstances. Human development is thus about much more than the rise or fall of average national incomes; it is about creating an environment in which people can develop their full potential and lead productive, creative lives in accord with their needs and interests. Development is therefore about expanding the choices people have to lead lives that they value. As such, it is about much more than economic growth, which is only a means – if a very important one – of enlarging people's choices. It is the fact of choice, though, that constitutes freedom, not the automatic provision of the goods that might be chosen. As Sen implies, there is a definite link between freedom and rational processes (Sen 2002). But Sen might also have taken the further step of considering that rationality is a defining quality of freedom; that without rationality, that which is defined as freedom – a freedom to act blindly or to limit the freedoms of others – becomes a functional "unfreedom."[4] Without rationality, decision-making processes are bound by dogma, ritual and power. Logic ceases to be an informing principle of decisions, which consequently have little chance of producing good outcomes and which will much more likely fail without being understood why.

Fundamental to enlarging these choices is building human capabilities, or the range of things that people can do or be in life. The most basic capabilities for human development are to lead long and healthy lives, to be knowledgeable, to have access to the resources needed for a decent standard of living and to be able to participate in the life of the community. Without these basic human capabilities, many choices are simply not available, and many opportunities in life remain inaccessible. This way of looking at development, often forgotten in the immediate concern with accumulating commodities and financial wealth, is not new. As Aristotle offered on the matter of "good": "Wealth is evidently not the good we are seeking, for it is merely useful for the sake of something else." In seeking that something else, human development shares a common vision with human rights. The goal of development is human freedom, and in pursuing capabilities and realizing rights, this freedom is vital. People must be free to exercise their choices and to participate in decision-making processes that affect their lives. Human development and human rights are mutually reinforcing, helping to secure the well-being and dignity of all people, building self-respect and respect for others (see Chapter 5, Civil and political rights).

More than this, though, ideas of development have increasingly begun to take into consideration non-material qualities, such as notions of human dignity, personal fulfillment, self-determination, and access to political participation and representation. These somewhat more nebulous or less formally quantifiable areas are not yet fully accepted in debate about development, but increasingly there is disquiet about a purely material focus on what constitutes "development." It is the point at which such "nebulous" categories manifest as the political that there is increasing movement towards widening the development index, to consider aspects of "human welfare" as well as more conventional concerns such as governance, transparency and accountability.

Within this context, and putting aside the idea that political development equates primarily to order, this general field has only recently begun to be discussed, and then usually in the instrumentalist terms of "governance" – bureaucratic rule-following – and "institution building," or creating bureaucracies that embody government functions. However, at one level, political development is the most fundamental aspect of "development," if that term is understood in its wider and more complete sense as Aristotle's "something else." That "something else" equating to both positive and negative rights, is not just freedom to explore one's potential, but also freedom from restrictions upon such exploration; Hutchcroft noted that in the Philippines, political under-development was the prime cause of continuing economic under-development (Hutchcroft 1998), as also discussed by Evans in relation to sub-Saharan Africa (Evans 1995), and, more recently and broadly, by Fukuyama (2004).

Political development can be thought of as reflecting a process of change away from archaic political forms, such as single-source (prebendal) patrimonialism (patronage that is ensured through payment) or feudalism, through to oligarchic, authoritarian or oppressive political systems, at the most extreme end of the scale a parasitic, predatory and totalitarian type of government. A more developed or mature political system at the opposite end of the political scale could be typified by being benign, inclusive, participatory and accountable, accurately reflecting the aspirations of most citizens. The particular emphasis on political development via institution building by more conservative proponents such as Fukuyama (2004) and Huntington (1968) has not adequately noted that successful institutions tend to correspond not just to a narrowly conceived (procedural) "democratization" but to the full range of social and political values. Similarly, limited institutional existence or failure tends to correspond more closely with lower order social political development. The idea that institutions can be constructed somewhat apart from, or prior to their pre-existing primary political context (that is, the rights and other political circumstances of constituent members of the state) separates institutional development from political development in ways that leave it immediately vulnerable to bureaucratic authoritarianism or to collapse, and thus unable to fulfill the material requirements for which it was established.

Without popular legitimacy, institutions are or quickly become meaningless. That is to say, for institutions to function properly, there need to be checks and balances, in some cases as competing elements which nevertheless find an equilibrium between the institutions and the system of checks and balances (Smith 2003: 109). Overwhelming, this implies the need to have a vibrant civil society, which can be said to include a free and questioning media, an active intelligentsia, non-government organizations and trade unions, and independent arbiters such as ombudsmen.

Democracy

Often discussion about normative models of government defaults to notions of "democracy" or "democratization." It is generally assumed, at least in Western societies, that "democracy" is the single most effective means of ensuring that the wishes of a society are most suitably represented and supported. Where the idea of democracy is spelled out, it is usually the "minimalist" democratic model, which assumes that unhindered voting for representatives constitutes the full democratic experience. It also assumes in its broader application that a model of democracy as practiced in the West, usually by the US, constitutes an ideal aspiration, not taking into account that there is no single Western democratic standard; nor is the US seen as an ideal political or social model by many developing countries. Even Huntington noted that America's political "modernization" was "strangely attenuated and incomplete" (1968: 98), and based on voter participation it has become more so since Huntington's observation. Nor is such a particular Western orientation necessarily applicable to countries in which illiteracy is high, communication is poor, patronage is dominant and consensus is preferred.

While it can be argued that "democracy" is indeed generally the single most effective form of government, at least in principle, there are a number of qualifications to such an assertion. These can include what is meant by the term "democracy" (see Lijphart 1999), the multiplicity of types of democracies (representative democracy, social democracy, liberal democracy, "guided" democracy, people's democracy, etc.), their institutional or constitutional ideologies (left versus right, authoritarian versus liberal, central versus decentralized, statist versus social, etc.) and their respective efficacy. There is also debate over distinctions between political and economic democracies, which in practise has resulted in different political and usually mutually exclusive systems. It must also be noted that some governments' attempts to appropriate the word "democracy" for what are clearly non-democratic systems of government tends to imply the need for some particular definitions for meaningful application of the term. Similarly, illiteracy, poor communication, patronage and consensus need not preclude democratization; the catch here is that the only way for a people to reject a particular political model in ways that can adequately reflect the genuine nature of such rejection, be it "democracy" or some other form of governance, is through a free and open decision-making process, that is, democracy!

For the purpose of this exercise, the term democracy is taken to mean a form of rule in which citizens either act as the policy-making authority (direct democracy) or are represented by others to make policy on their behalf (representative democracy). In both cases, as argued by Lane and Ersson, democracy is, or should be "the political regime where the will of the people *ex ante* becomes the law of the country (legal order) *ex post*" (2003: 2). The former tends only to exist in small or closed societies, while the latter is the more widely applicable model. The issue of participation might also be included in such a definition, allowing citizens opportunities to both stand for election as representatives and to express their views outside the formal policy-making or representative-election process. In the case of representative democracy, which is exclusively the type practiced at the state level, citizens must have the capacity to vote for candidates of their choice, without fear or hindrance, and their vote must be weighted equally with all other votes. Attendant to this, citizens must have free access to information about and from candidates and other sources of relevant information, the freedom to speak or otherwise communicate on issues they deem relevant, and the freedom to assemble with others to discuss such matters, to form associations or to non-violently protest decisions or situations they regard as objectionable. In all of this, not only must these conditions exist, but negative conditions, such as fear of arrest, punishment, torture and must not be present. While these criteria are not especially controversial in democratic theory, they rarely exist in pristine form in even the most democratic of countries (although they do largely exist in functional form in such countries). The problem here arises that even in such a functional democratic system, there is the capacity for a majority – "fifty per cent plus one" – to assert its will over the minority, which may preclude inclusive decision making and thus preclude models of democracy that are more complex than the simple majoritarian model (Lane and Ersson 2003: 3–9)

As an institutional manifestation of political development, the equitable and consistent application of a broadly subscribed to law, support for access to that law, guarantees of civil and political rights and the capacity to participate in free and fair elections are all key markers of political development. Such civil and political (first order human) rights are generally divided into "positive" and "negative" rights, or rights "to" (for example, freedom of expression, gathering, political activity) and rights "from" (such as, arbitrary arrest, detention or torture), and between natural (implied) rights and positive (codified) rights. These correspond to the capacity for, and potential restrictions upon agency. In this, they reflect the wide potential capacity of the quality of being human; that is, to determine within or to choose to act beyond the constraints of structure. In this, human rights cannot be qualified by structural exigencies, including economics, political institutionalism (institutions, parties, systems) or "culture" (assuming this can be understood as a static, reified and universally accepted, or imposed word view).

Finally, a strong argument has been put claiming that economic development precedes political development and that a "strong" government is a necessary pre-condition for the economic development of the state. There is some (though far from overwhelming) evidence to suggest that this proposition could be at least partially correct. This idea of economic development before political development has been referred to as the "Full Bellies Thesis," or the idea that people need and want to have material security before considering other, more esoteric, issues such as political participation (Howard 1983). This has been nowhere more clearly stated than in a major regional statement on human rights, the Bangkok Declaration of the World Conference on Human Rights (1993), which said that civil and political rights, which are the pre-conditions for political development, are conditional on economic development. The declaration agreed to "Underline the essential need to create favorable conditions for effective enjoyment of human rights at both the national and international levels" (World Conference on Human Rights 1993: 3.2). Such "favorable conditions" usually include limitations on political activity and censorship of the media. Such an approach has been suggested to be in keeping with the "Asian" experience. Yet not all "Asians" accept such conditions.

More recently, institutions such as the World Bank have accepted the positive link between political and economic development (for example, Stiglitz 2003). The World Bank itself has increasingly focused its concerns on issues of governance, accountability and transparency, which it recognizes are most effectively achieved through an open political framework. Also against the argument in favor of authoritarian government is the fact that a representative government is less prone to corruption (Lane and Errson 2003: 222) and is less likely to spend vast sums on an unproductive "security" force. A representative government is also more likely to offer "soft" political changes rather than the more abrupt, often violent changes that occur when an authoritarian leader is finally dumped and their usually tainted bureaucracy requires a fundamental overhaul. Further, the free flow of ideas in such a system is more likely to invigorate market development, as opposed to a culture of silence in which original ideas are not encouraged, and indeed are sometimes regarded as dangerous (see Howard 1983: 478; Donnelly 1984: 258; Goodin 1979; Lane and Errson 2003: 194). Finally, as Lane and Errson note, while democracy is not always good for development in straightforward ways, it still reflects "a number of intrinsic values, which makes it preferable to non-democracy" (2003: 65).

Political "stability" is, no doubt, a preferential environment for investors to instability, and policy consistency is preferred to a political environment in which policy can change from year to year, depending on the whims of the electorate or the influence of pressure groups. However, in this sense "strong" should be underscored as "consistent and capable," with a capacity to resist undermining influences and tendencies, rather than exhibiting strength in the more authoritarian sense of political order. Further, it does appear that economic development will moderate the extent of radical oppositional political programs, as well as reduce the real political tensions that can accrue as a result of relative material desperation.

Somewhat ironically, the argument in favor of economic development ahead of political development is usually put forward by political conservatives, not least including authoritarian leaders in many developing countries and their supporters and apologists in developed countries. Yet the structurally determined idea of economic development providing the foundation of political development comes directly from the revolutionary Karl Marx. Despite these competing ideologies supporting a similar proposition, there have been exceptions both for and against democratization reflecting economic development. For example, Singapore has become less democratic even though it has become more economically successful. On the other hand, the Philippines and Indonesia have both become more democratic, relative to the authoritarian Marcos and Suharto eras, despite both being relatively poor and dealing with continuing economic difficulties. Similarly, Cambodia and East Timor have engaged in a number of elections and continue to embed democracy, with varying degrees of success, despite achieving not only very low levels of economic development, literacy and communication, but in each case being burdened by histories that would otherwise tend to militate against relatively open and contested political processes. So, while the argument of political development being built upon economic development might have some validity as a general tendency, it is far from a rule of politics and other factors can also influence political outcomes. That is to say, structures are important in determining political outcomes, but they are not absolute, and human will, or agency, can also shape political events. There is no cut-off point at which wealth allows democratic outcomes and poverty does not.

To recap, the first definition of political development is that it is intended to produce the greatest amount of freedom most equitably shared, in which there is an increased capacity by individuals and social groups to determine their own affairs. The second definition, then, characterizes it as a political process rather than an instrumentalist goal. In that there is an instrumentalist function in political development, it is in the mechanism by which it is manifested, which is principally by the state representing and supporting the plurality of interests of its citizens. Further, the institutions of state should be the primary vehicle for the implementation of this support, but for such states to remain accountable to both larger (multilateral, universalist) and more local (specific, individual, community) claims. Political development is an end or a good in itself, and its ultimate goal is the liberation of humanity from the limitations over which it has volition.

2 Structure and agency

The issues of structure and agency at first glance have a rather abstract relationship to ideas of political development. Yet these issues are fundamental to how one understands the competing forces that shape political processes and, consequently, how one chooses to act and upon what grounds. Despite the claims of some political theorists, it is not possible to establish a single rule or theoretical model that adequately explains all conditions that might prevail, what the available options might be or how people might react to them in their many and varied ways. That is to say, despite the claims to, neatness of, and preference for "grand uniting theories," none are in fact universally applicable. The countervailing tendency in the latter part of the twentieth and early twenty-first centuries has been towards more specific and local theorizing.

The distinctions between the related dichotomies of the global and the local, the universal and the particular, objective and subjective, positivist and relativist and between structure and agency shows them as metaphors for each other. These dichotomies are essentially about different approaches to the same subject: about how to interpret reality. In simple terms, those in favor of a structural analysis might argue that the world is shaped by its material conditions, as are human relations, that these have explicable and logical relations with each other, and that the structural relationship between them can be understood as operating in fairly consistent (and sometimes deterministic) ways. A competing view is that the link between the material conditions of life and behavior are tenuous and that there are far too many differences between people to draw general or over-arching conclusions about their consistency. That is, agency demonstrates a capacity for activity in spite of externally opposite conditions and indicates that human will is a greater force for producing outcomes than claims to underlying conditions. Interestingly, the debate over the competing claims of these two perspectives has shifted pendulum-like in a clearly identifiable manner since the mid-nineteenth century and, arguably, long before that. The claims of one, often supported by an unreflective acceptance of the argument, has commonly invited a similarly opposite reaction from the other. The most recent demonstration of this was the "structuralist" tendency in social "sciences" of the 1950s and 1960s being challenged by the post-structural/deconstructionist turn of the 1980s and 1990s.

In favor of a structuralist case, Acemoglu and Robinson (2006: Chapter 3) argue that there are material conditions that can be seen to correspond more or less to particular outcomes, and it is likely that the social organization that is required of particular industrial forms will lend itself towards particular cultural outcomes. For example, the extended family fitted less neatly into early industrial society than it did into the preceding rural society, and the slimming down of the family unit had implications for how societies ensured that each member was adequately cared for, introducing aspects of welfarism. It appears that there is a proportionately similar change underway as industrial (manufacturing) society transforms into a service-based society, with particular emphasis on increasing communications and potential worker autonomy. At the higher end of this "post-industrial" scale, the outcomes can be quite materially rewarding and individually empowering. At the lower end of this scale, the outcomes tend to produce isolation, powerlessness and economic marginalization. This has been reflected in the creation of an industrial underclass, not to mention the role of developing countries in relation to developed countries. For such societies, the contrast between these positions has the capacity to produce new social and political outcomes as interests change and gel, inequalities are enforced or challenged, and societies reconsider either through altruism or necessity the options that open before them. In this respect, despite the lag of cultural change, the material conditions in which people live do have a profound effect on the broad outline of their lives.

Within this structure, however, remains the capacity for individual and collective action, and will. Setting aside a Nietzschian "will to power" (1968), the willpower required to overcome difficult odds or to take significant risks might not seem "rational," but it does appear to be a human characteristic and one which is often widely admired. Failure is quickly forgotten, but success against the odds is considered of worth, and altruistic success against the odds is often considered heroic. Even altruistic failure can be considered heroic if it demonstrates sufficient will. There is also the will of martyrs, who consciously sacrifice themselves for a perceived greater good. While it might be argued that some deliberate martyrs sacrifice themselves on the promise of the hereafter, martyrdom is not only known as sacrifice for some metaphysical outcome, but also as an act of social commitment. Assuming the primacy of self-interest (the motivation of "rational" economic actors), it is difficult to consider self-sacrifice to be a rational act. Another act that may be conceived of as not rational is revolutionary will, where the zealotry of the actor extends a particular cause beyond immediate or contingent circumstances to a future and absolute goal. It may be that revolutionary activity could not succeed if its participants were half-hearted, especially given the opposition they would likely face. But the will to succeed, or to die trying to succeed, cannot easily be explained as a rational response to particular material circumstances. In such cases, material circumstances might provide the platform and even the motivation, but the will takes over and drives events through to their contested conclusion. What constitutes rational motivation, therefore, may vary not just according to materially determined self-interest, but may be informed by what might be termed "rational altruism." Conversely, "rationalism" as it has been applied to economics does not mean rational as such, but rather is management-speak for short-term profit-making efficiencies.

How the debate between material (economic) rationalism and rational altruism (enlightened self-interest) plays out in politics varies, based on the distinction between authoritarianism, which supposes a singular legitimate view, and liberalism, which supposes a plurality of legitimate views. Within a more authoritarian framework, one might categorize this debate as the distinction between corporatism (a highly structured, bureaucratic and conceptually constrained political model) and a libertarian social Darwinism, a political free for all in which the "strong" flourish and the "weak" perish. Within a more liberal or progressive framework, such a debate might constitute the distinction between emphasis on the structural basis of inequality and its resolution at the price of limits on freedom, or an emphasis on freedom at the price of limits to resolving inequality.

Structure

This book subscribes to a qualified political economy view of the world, in which politics tends to reflect economic or material interests or the capacity of economic actors to assert their self-interest in the political sphere. Conversely, it does not subscribe to the "rational economic actor" model, in that volition can account for "non-rational" or rationally altruistic choices. In this sense, it agrees with Acemoglu and Robinson (2006) that political action is largely determined by preservation of economic interest, or the gradual sacrifice of parts of economic interest to preserve other (and more commonly greater) parts. However, it disagrees with Acemoglu and Robinson in that they predicate their assumptions upon "game theory," in which actors with competing interests behave "rationally" in a narrowly conceived sense of the term. It may be that such interest-driven actors do often behave rationally in a formal sense, but they may also not do so for a variety of reasons, and may have varying conceptions of what constitutes the rational according to subjective criteria. As Sen notes, "rational" economic interest, that is self-interest, may indeed be rational, but it might also be morally or politically bereft (Sen 2002: 4–7, 7nb4) and hence irrational from other, longer-term or more socially sustainable perspectives. Moral or political emptiness can have social implications which may potentially or actually negatively impact upon oneself, one's loved ones and the community in which one lives. That is, what is "rational" in the short-term, or what might be construed as rational self-interest, might not be so if the criteria for the "good life" extends beyond oneself, to those who contribute to life's meaning. Moreover, if the defining criteria of self-interest is to enhance one's freedom, there are two further problems. The first is that one's freedom in some areas might be constrained as a consequence of self-interested decisions. For example, the accumulation of great wealth might lead to resentment by others and attempts to "redistribute" that wealth, possibly with the result of violence to oneself that may require defensively limiting structures. The second problem is that even if one can exercise self-interest without potential or actual negative personal consequences, the likely implications for others may act as a constraint on their capacity for freedom (see Rawls 1971).

There is, of course, also sharp disagreement about what constitutes a rational response to areas of competing material interest, not least when viewed from the perspective of hegemony or coercion. It is a common hegemonic argument that people often make decisions that are not rationally in their own material best interests, and yet they do so because they are led to believe their interests are best served otherwise. That is, what is portrayed as "rational self-interest" is not only sometimes not that, for most people it only constitutes perceived, rather than actual, self-interest, which reflects the establishment of a successful hegemony. What is "rational," therefore, is often other than what it is presented to be.

Beyond this distinction between "rational actors" (and hence game theory) and hegemony, the position taken here broadly derives from a "soft" Marxian view that economics ("modes of production") are reflected in respective political systems that best suit their organizational needs, but which incorporate more overtly subjective responses, or expressions of will or social altruism. In a normative sense, the system of political analysis should refer to an internally coherent and largely regularized method of political organization that generally produces consistent political results, but which may also allow for a range of non-material concerns, the variability between them constituting "freedoms."

In political systems in which there is a correspondence with economic organizational needs there is a tension between the self-serving interests of its primary beneficiaries and those who contribute to it but receive closer to a survival-level income or subsistence. In so far as the former group is able to manage the tensions created by the more marginal situation of the latter, this is achieved through a type of "social contract," in which there is agreement between social groups about their respective roles and the extent of costs and benefits to be ascribed to each in such an arrangement, or other methods of reciprocal relations, with regulated "freedoms." Such reciprocal relations may be less than ideal, but lest a ruling elite seek revolution, they must either concede to certain pressures from below or use repression to counter them, which is not especially productive in the short-term and is unsustainable in the long-term. In that this acceptance is encouraged, the state usually employs a range of mechanisms to positively reinforce acceptance through a system of rewards and incentives. States also negatively reinforce acceptance through a system of limitations and punishments, via its claimed monopoly on the use of violence. All of this is framed within an almost classical Gramscian hegemony, in which the extent of the state's control of information, the law, and administrative processes, enable it to shape acceptance, desire and a subtle but clear appreciation of the willingness to employ sanctions against malcontents.

Having noted there are linkages between economic and political structures, these linkages are not deterministic. Rather, they act as types of frameworks that apply influence, exert pressure and create possibilities. It is at this point that the balance between structure and agency and the various considerations that affect judgment come into play. There is little doubt that the available data shows that societies that have a higher economic standard of living, greater distribution of income and higher education levels are more likely to be democratic and able to sustain democratic processes than those that are poorer, more unequal and less educated (Acemoglu and Robinson 2006: Chapter 3). Yet such a statistical assessment in part speaks not just to the conditions that allow or confirm democracy, but which democracy assists in producing. It is not clear that societies that have developed materially could have done so or sustained such development without concessions to democratic reform along the way. Similarly, there are statistically contradictory states, such as Singapore, which would appear to have the material pre-conditions for democracy, and yet continue to steadfastly refuse such a transition. On the other hand, the number of states that do not appear to meet the material criteria, and yet which have made the transition to procedural democracy, has grown substantially in the post-cold war era. While the states of Eastern Europe have to varying degrees successfully democratized, this was not a consequence of their prior economic liberalization (see Van Brabant 1990).

Agency

The manner in which decisions are taken about how societies politically organize themselves reflects some degree of "will," or agency. Within the range of possibilities created by a particular set of circumstances, the decision to choose one political method over the other reflects judgment and the will to manifest such judgment. That is, if capitalism requires a type of representative government to best function (representing the interests of capital), yet the state is ruled by an autocracy, there may be pressure to change. This tends to explain the seventeenth- and eighteenth-century processes of political change in England, France and the US. It also helps to explain more recent political change in places like Thailand,[1] Indonesia and a number of other developing countries.

However, despite its potency, agency alone cannot determine outcomes. Societies that remain in mixed stages of economic evolution may respond unevenly to political pressures. Hence, there could be urban revolution but rural reaction, or, in cases where rural exploitation has continued despite political movement elsewhere, there may be rural radicalization and urban conservativism or reaction. For example, the Philippines democratized while retaining a highly exploitative rural economic system, leading to a renewal of rural radicalism, China's rural population was radicalized before most of its urban population, while Cambodia's rural-based Khmer Rouge was far more radical than its urban counterparts.

Culture

In that societies do respond to changing material circumstances, they may do so more slowly than the material circumstances would suggest if there was a more definite or deterministic structural link. That is, political systems or political modes of social relations become "habituated" and are accepted as the natural order of things. For example, many Americans cannot understand how the world does not conform to their self-evidently and "naturally" superior political system. Yet what is "natural" to Americans is not "natural" to many others; nor are the circumstances that gave rise to that sense of cultural ownership the same or similar in many cases.

Embedded in culture (or world view), which is a key determinant of agency, such political "naturalization" is slow to change, and may lag behind material or economic change (or be encouraged to lag behind, such as in Vietnam and China where there is little correspondence between capitalist economic development and central authoritarian government). Alternatively, culture or world view or agency may progress ahead of economic change, or may press for a variation of the social contract within a particular structural environment, such as through greater equity, more accountability, justice, and so on. In this sense, culture can and often does shape responses to material conditions, as an act of agency, even though it does not directly reflect those conditions.

Social will is manifested in communication between people through the exchange of thoughts and ideas. Indeed, it is the capacity for complex communication that not just shapes or contributes to how we understand our world, but communication more than any other quality defines us as human. In this, social "will" can significantly exceed its apparent material circumstances, again for example in the high voter turn out in the Cambodian and East Timor elections, and the relatively high degree of political awareness in both cases. This was despite there not having been a "culture" of democracy in either place, and also despite low levels of literacy. These cases and many others have disproved the structural determinism that it is necessary to have economic development before, or at least alongside, political development. Ideas, assisted by the midwife of opportunity, can and do correspond to circumstances that are not just economic, but which are also human (that is, people have a range of needs that correspond to and buttress their material security, including various rights "to" and rights "from").

Communication

Between economic push and political pull, the capacity of agency appears to be most variable, as it has the greatest scope for reflecting variable need or desire, as opposed to the internally referential logic of particular sets of economic relations (for example, markets). That is, human capacity and human desire can as an act of will or volition alter circumstances, regardless of or despite pressures that derive from other sources (such as the logic of markets). In this, the notion of reciprocal relations or social contract recurs, lest the contradiction between economic "rationality" and human need become too great, requiring radical (revolutionary) "correction."

The single biggest asset in communication is literacy. Literacy assists communicant in two fundamental ways. First, it communicates more widely and more consistently sets of ideas (regarding nation formation see Anderson 1991). Second, it changes the way people conceptualize towards a more structured, analytical and ultimately critical means of thinking, which is capable of being built upon like so many blocks into complex intellectual structures (see Ong 2002). The proposition here corresponds to the work of Brazilian educational reformer Paulo Freire (1973), who proposed that literacy was the means of ending oppression and the gateway to development. This proposition was, for this observer, initially informed by an experience in Nicaragua in 1983. Prior to the Sandinista revolution in 1979, Nicaragua's literacy rate had been in the order of 10 to 15 per cent. After the Sandinista's literacy (and health) campaign, it was over 80 per cent. At that time, Nicaragua was under attack from US-backed "Contra" (counter-revolutionary) rebels, and there was real fear that the Sandinista revolution would be lost, as indeed it eventually was. However, as one small shop-owner told the author, even if an autocratic or oligarchic government returned, it could never take away the people's capacity to read and write. That is, they could never take away their capacity to receive and disseminate political ideas. This, he said, was the lasting legacy of the revolution (personal communication, Managua, December 1983). In this sense, literacy empowered agency.

Following from this, then, are the questions of censorship, freedom of expression, and control over the flow of information and ideas, and thus restriction of the capacity of agency. Assuming literacy (which, in its wider sense, includes an ability to make sense of other, non-literal symbolic messages), restrictions on the free flow of ideas are by definition imposed limitations on, or repression of a capacity to exercise agency. It is a restriction upon or repression of the most fundamental human quality; communication. This then leads directly into issues of "human rights," and the capacity to protect them via political participation and representation.

A sliding scale

Any model illustrating a complex point will inevitably fail on detail or exceptions. Similarly, the use of models is itself a default acceptance of understanding a given reality in more or less structural terms. Conversely, a more fully developed version of the opposite position would counter that it is not so much the exceptions that undermine the use of models as it is that the model should be primarily, if not exclusively focused on exceptions, for which no model is possible. This in turn raises the specter of deconstructionism, in which no one set of conditions can be understood without first unpacking its component parts and, in turn, unpacking and exploring their component parts, in theory *ad infinitum*. The practical consequence of this theoretical position, if pursued to its logical conclusion is that because one is focused on the composition of the constituent parts (itself a form of structuralism in reverse), one cannot focus on the subject at hand. Not only would this make modeling impossible, it would also deny the validity of writing in this or any other book that lays some modest claim to dealing with reality.

The real difficulty in the structure-agency debate, assuming that many real political issues comprise elements of both structure and agency, is working out the relationship between the two, the extent of the impact of each, and the multifaceted and sometimes seemingly kaleidoscopic ways in which such impact can take place. There is no single or absolute answer to this dilemma, and the common approach is to work from existing theoretical frameworks, test them against the evidence and assess the results against what is known. An alternative method is to learn about the subject under investigation in his or her own setting and to establish principles from their patterns of behavior. This requires if not what Geertz called "thick (highly detailed) description" (1993: Chapter 1) then at least a thick knowledge, or an awareness of the context in which actions take place.

Assuming the modesty of its claim, then, the proposed model is one way of approaching and perhaps understanding the relative positioning of the competing claims of structure and agency or, more precisely, positivism (that which is or which is claimed to be for itself) and relativism (that which exists only in relation to the other).

The intention of Figure 2.1 is to indicate that at one end of this scale, concrete and hence measurable reality tends to comply with a more structural understanding of its relationship to like qualities. Conversely, at the other end of the scale, will, values, tastes and other preferences tend to comply with

Positivist/Structure   Relativist/Agency

Material measure   Will and Values

Figure 2.1 The positivist-relativist or structure and agency sliding scale, indicating parallel relationships with materiality and values.

the qualities of agency. It is at this end of the scale that there is much greater capacity for variation and interpretation and where, in correspondence with each other, there is considerable capacity for distinction. Along this scale there will be, of course, circumstances that lend themselves to either greater or lesser positivist or relativist interpretations; material quality of life would tend to exist towards the positivist end of the scale, while value systems about what to do about it might occur further towards the relativist end of the scale. The relative positioning of circumstances and the balance of positivist and relativist conceptions, or structure and agency, is the basis for understanding the types of influences that play upon events of fact and the extent of their interpretability.

Conceptions of human rights, for example, might be claimed to represent a particular value judgment or cultural location, yet the physical reality of being in jail is quite concrete, and the indignity or despair that accompanies it may be subject to the variables of personality but must, in almost all cases, be understood to have a broadly universal applicability. So too, the crime of extra-judicial killing might be understood as a greater or lesser offense in particular cultural environments in which people have been habituated or acculturated to accept the appropriateness or inevitability of such an out-come. But its material reality in the case of the victim is not only absolute, it is also universal. This then locates the act of extra-judicial killing at the far end of the positivist scale. The relationship between an employer and an employee, or a landholder and a land worker, however, might fluctuate from the middle ground, depending on degrees of conditionality, compromise, agreement and mutual contract. There can still be argued to be a structurally definable and possibly repetitive aspect to their relationship that no amount of agency short of objective force can remove or resolve. But the combination of elements from both ends of the scale add a complexity that is not simply reductionist, and which does not, other than in extreme circumstances, benefit from simple perspective available at both ends of the spectrum. For example, claims that employees or land workers are necessarily exploited to the absolute maximum may be, but are not necessarily, correct while employer or landholder claims that employees or land workers have free choice in the place and conditions of their work may be similarly incorrect.

People and events

The debate about structure and agency is often seen to revolve around the site of the "great person" versus the circumstances that allowed that person to achieve "greatness." On one hand, there is strong argument in favor of the idea that it was the personal qualities of Julius Caesar, Napoleon Bonaparte, Otto von Bismarck, Adolph Hitler, Mahatma Gandhi, Nelson Mandela and Suharto, among many others, that made them dominant figures in their own time and place. Conversely, Caesar entered life as an aristocratic patri-cian, while Napoleon came from a relatively wealthy noble family and rose on the back of a fortuitous battle at a time when the state required a military leader, who in turn had little choice but to attack neighboring states or see his own state lose the gains of its revolution, Bismarck began in a socially elevated position as the university educated son of a Prussian military officer at a time of nationalist ferment, while Hitler rose on the back of exploiting a deeply divided polity, itself pushed to extremes by severe economic hardship and resentment. Similarly, Ghandi rose on the singularly practical policy of non-violence at a time of declining British imperial fortunes within the context of a more generalized shift towards post-colonial settlements, while Mandela's fortune was being on the side of history as it turned away from institutionalized racism, and Suharto rose on the back of the murder of his senior colleagues to lead an already planned military-backed consensus on a state struggling to become a nation. It seems reasonable to assume, at the very least, that each of these "great" leaders would have required considerable personal qualities in order to be able to exploit or develop the circumstances in which they found themselves. It seems equally reasonable to assume that they did not create their circumstances, but rather read them correctly or, in some cases, found themselves in the right place at the right time and with the opportunity to act upon a fortuitous confluence of events.

An arguably more serious question arises, however, in analysing what influences or shapes events, and why things turn out the way they do. The claim that culture is the principle influence on the success or failure of states, the political systems they employ and various responses to issues that come under the broad headings of "equality" and "liberty" cannot be dismissed out of hand. In relation to Latin America, there was the strong suggestion of

> a reciprocal relationship between political culture and political system. Democratic culture helps to maintain and press for the return of democracy, but historically, the choice of democracy by political elites clearly preceded, in many of our cases, the presence of democratic values among the general public or other elites.
>
> (Diamond *et al.* 1989c: 10)

The commitment to democracy by elites arose only because the cost of maintaining a repressive regime apparatus became unsustainable for economic or organizational reasons. Where democracy performed poorly, no deep commitment to democracy became embedded. *Ipso facto*, where democratic success has been demonstrated, there has been greater commitment to democratic values, and the acculturation of democratic norms. Democratic function, then, is seen to promote democratic values (Diamond *et al.* 1989c: 11–13).

There is no doubt that the acculturation, or *habitus*, of a people does shape the way they see their world and the way in which they respond to it. The psychological make-up of individuals is, if not a dominant factor in overall outcomes, still deeply influential in particular cases. The right time and place might create a possibility, but it takes a person or people to realize it, and to drive it to its furthest conclusion. Similarly, there is little doubt that a culture or world view is not immutable, that it changes over time according to its prevailing circumstances. People are motivated by many things, but the material conditions of life and the status pertaining to that both by way of accumulation and power are critical to how things work and why they work the way they do. At a more basic level, material desperation is a powerful motivator, or at least up until that point that it acts as a disincentive based on hopelessness.

Ideology

Ideologies have a particular place in the structure-agency debate, in that they are often claimed to reflect structural logic, but are frequently pursued as a matter of will. The term "ideology" has long been misunderstood, becoming an often abused (or abusive) term. The original use of the term, as coined by Destutt de Tracy, applied to the "science of ideas" as a means of offering insights into human nature, and hence providing a rational basis for the reordering of social and political structures to better suit human needs and aspirations. But in its more contemporary sense, the term "ideology" has a distinctly political overtone, following Napoleon Bonaparte's criticism of de Tracy and his colleagues as "ideologues," reflecting his criticism of ideology being an abstract doctrine, developing the term to include religious and philosophical ideas.

Since the early nineteenth century, "ideology" has, at its most favorable, come to mean a basic or first principle set of ideas through which an intellectual order is made of social and political experience. At its least favorable, the term refers to a particular and arguably limited, incomplete or biased view of political affairs. As such, the term has sometimes been negatively used to criticize competing sets of political ideas, the corollary of this being that one's own set of ideas are not highly structured and therefore artificial, but are "natural." But according to Gramsci, there is no such "natural" set of political ideas, and what seems unforced is the product of a subtle but totally pervasive system of influence (Gramsci 1971; see also Lukes 1974; Althusser 2006, 2003).

In the general contemporary sense, an ideology should ideally be coherent and internally consistent, and is sometimes characterized by the suffix "ism," such as conservatism, communism, fascism, liberalism, feminism, and so on. However, some ideological propositions have lacked internal coherence. Hitler's Nazism lacked internal consistency, especially over time, moving in the space of a few years from socialist foundations to one that embraced large-scale capital, and was coherent only in that it relied on a logic of power. Japanese imperialism was perhaps more internally consistent, but being out of chronological step with the earlier, main period of colonial expansion, also relied on a logic of power, in particular colonial expansion, which lacked coherent correspondence with the global environment. In a post-colonial context, Sukarno's "Nasakom" (combining nationalism, communism and religion) lacked both coherence and internal consistency. Indeed, it was logically at odds with itself, and was hence both unstable and ultimately unsustainable.

Ideology's main transformation from a "science of ideas" to a political proposition arguably arrived with Marx and Engels (1970), in which they critically characterized the views of the "Young Hegelians" as "the German ideology." In this, Marx and Engels broadly followed Napoleon's criticism of de Tracy and company by arguing that this "ideology" was too abstract and disconnected from the lives of ordinary citizens. The countervailing set of ideas as proposed by Marx and Engels was that society was divided into classes which had conflicting interests and claims. This was taken up by subsequent Marxists as an alternative "ideology."

Not only Marxism, but all political systems represent ideological assumptions, even where such assumptions are not explicit. That is to say, political leaders might claim to be pragmatic, to assert the good of the state or the nation above ideology, or to not represent contemporary ideologies but traditional patterns of political behavior. But in each case, they are usually representing ideas that derive from classical or neo-classical economic theory, from Leninist interpretations of Marxism, from nationalist claims or from resurrected feudal or pre-feudal traditions, all of which are ideologies. Such has been the case where political rhetoric, say on land redistribution (the Philippines), free markets (Singapore), socialism (Vietnam), the role of the armed forces (Burma, Indonesia) or human rights, has not necessarily been matched by corresponding political practise.

As noted, "ideology" was originally the study of ideas, yet its more contemporary meaning has it as a coherent and largely internally consistent system of first principle ideas through which an intellectual order is made of social and political experience, or a set of ideas that inform a particular political perspective. Ideologies that have received general recognition are specifically identified, with the names given to them intended to convey (if not always accurately) their core values and goals. Better known examples of ideologies include Marxism or communism, liberalism, capitalism and fascism, although religious beliefs such as Christianity or Islam (theocracy), or ideas about the nation ("nationalism") or the state ("unitarianism," "federalism"), can also function as ideologies. As a consequence of the role of the military, in some instances, in both the liberation and state-creation process, military thinking has also come to exhibit characteristics of an ideology. This is especially relevant in terms of the relationship between the state, its institutions and individual citizens, and in terms of broader conceptions of power, hierarchy and authority. Military ideology can be clearly seen in a number of developing or recently independent countries. In some places the role of the military in political affairs has declined (Nigeria, Argentina, Venezuala, Indonesia), while in others it has increased (Sudan, Burma), and in others simply changed (Vietnam, Laos, Thailand). The lessening of military involvement in political affairs has usually been regarded as a sign of the political maturity of the state, a sign that the state is capable of assuming responsibility for its affairs (Dodd 1972: 50–4), reflecting an ideological framework in transition.

It is necessary to note that it is a logical error to ascribe to a political system a particular ideological label, regardless of the claims made on behalf of that system, if its practise does not comply. That is to say, a state that calls itself "socialist" but which practises free market capitalism is not socialist at all, but rather a single-party state usually employing aspects of authoritarianism (for example, Vietnam). Similarly, claims to "nationalism," which most often find themselves reflecting a romanticized, organicist claims to people's unity, may reflect an aspiration but may not necessarily represent reality (such as the "Unitary State of the Republic of Indonesia"). To determine the ideology of a state, it is first necessary to consider the rules of operation of a state and how these are put into practise. Only then is it helpful to compare the reality of ideological practise with the claims of ideological rhetoric.

In that there is commonly a gap between ideological rhetoric and lived political reality, the ideological assumptions that underpin each state might claim to be in the interests of most people, but may not be the most accurate representation of the interests or wishes of most of the people of such states. Such interests tend to be most accurately represented where there is a high degree of political accountability and, as such, rhetoric tends to be reflected, even if imperfectly, in reality. As a consequence, one must ask of the extent to which the political interests of state constituents – the citizens of the state – are represented, or to what extent such constituents are satisfied that their interests are represented. That is perhaps the surest indicator of what ideology actually prevails.

As ideologies are presented, they usually claim a link to organizational necessity, and hence to structure. How they are presented and pursued, however, more often reflects agency. And if ideologies do not accord with practise, there is a degree of discordance between the structure and the idea. Issues of structure and agency, therefore, are not simple or fixed, and vary according to a range of competing circumstances and requirements. However, it is by keeping in mind these varying contributions to outcomes that better sense can be made of social circumstances, in this case of political development.

3 The nation

The idea of "nation" is the framework around which bonded political communities cohere, define themselves and build other political structures. Further, the expression of nation as an ideology of social and political unity ("nationalism") is probably the most fundamental issue in relation to the state, which is the geo-political institution through which most issues concerning political development are manifested. The idea of nation, then, is central to political development.

The idea of the nation as a central theme in political development returned in the latter part of the twentieth century, after having declined due to an increased postwar focus on states, institutions and the modernization project on one hand, and local ethnicities on the other. The study of nations in the traditional sense were regarded as somewhat passe, retaining a faint whiff of some nationalist claims of the 1920s and 1930s, in which nationalist exclusivity culminated in the late 1930s and 1940s in war, genocide and other gross violations of human rights. However, as the postwar, post-colonial era settled, localisms emerged to challenge the assumed certainties of existing states. This was exacerbated by the failure of the modernization project in many developing countries, which encouraged their peoples to think of themselves not as some latter-day European copies in the nation-state sense, but with identities that did not always conform to a state-centered understanding of "nation." Further, the collapse of communism, the break-up of the USSR and Yugoslavia and the end of the cold war meant that there was less support for regimes that held states together in spite of "nationalist" claims within them. Thus, as such, the idea of "nation" was given a new lease of life, not least in claims to self-determination.

In common parlance, "nation" has been used interchangeably with "state" or "country." So usual is it for most people to refer to the nation as also encompassing other, usually institutional or spatial qualities that the term has come to be unreflectively used as synonymous with them. Yet this broad use of the term "nation" makes the idea of political identity ambiguous, especially where it relates to the state. The state is a specific geographic area, which is comprised of citizens and in which generally continuing institutions manifest claims to sovereign authority.[1] By contrast, the nation is the bonded political group, which may or may not conform to the state but which understands its political identity and its internal unity as being its principle marker of external relationships. In that the "nation" might not conform to the state, using the terms interchangeably assumes a bonded political unity where what is being described is a spatial organizational quality. Claims to "nation," therefore, are claims to recognition of the status of group identity. Such claims may be powerful, but may also be aspirational or ambit claims which are unable to be sustained for a variety of cultural, logistical or institutional reasons. A nation, therefore, may be claimed to exist but, beyond internal recognition by its members, perhaps only does so through its capacity to externally assert that existence.

Nations traditionally have tended to reflect ethnic (and less commonly religious) unity, particularly through the medium of language in relation to specific and usually contiguous and demarcated territory. However, multi-ethnic or multi-religious nations, in particular those comprised of immigrants and their descendents, can also exist by adhering to non-ethnic/religious forms of identification, such as particular civic values, for example around methods of government, rule of law, and social reciprocity. This might be referred to as "civic nationalism." Further, even those nations that originated as largely single ethnic polities, where they have been most successful have also exhibited the qualities of civic nationalism. Nations, then, may take various forms and comprise single or various ethnicities, religions, cultures, and so on. Ultimately, what makes a nation is the commitment to it as an idea by those individuals who claim to comprise it and who are recognized as such. Where there is little or no commitment to such an idea, the nation cannot be said to exist, or can exist only under serious internal challenge or external imposition.

In understanding how nations have come about, the process of national identification may further include a range of factors that develop from an underlying unity. These include but cannot be adequately explained by the determinism of historical materialism, the simple ideology of nationalism, the effects of the free market, or by claims to self-determination. Other significant factors in nation formation also include ethnic political mobility or the capacity to organize geographically, the process of assertion or re-assertion of nationalist claims, conscious nation building or nation re-building (Taras in Bremmer and Taras 1997: 687), or indeed simple "invention" (see Hobsbawm 1983, 1990: Chapter 4). These factors have been demonstrated in the formation of more recent states, such as the 15 former Soviet states, which are each significantly multi-ethnic in their make-up, and which have each come to represent "national" aspirations in a variety of formats (Taras in Bremmer and Taras 1997: 706–7).

What a "nation" is, then, depends on different quantities of the above-noted qualities. No two nations are exactly alike (see Weber in Hutchinson and Smith 1994: 21–5), not least because they find forms of separate identification.

Nationalism as ideology

The claim of the nation to a particular political identity, and especially the active or programmatic assertion of that identity, is usually referred to as "nationalism." In that the nation is actively asserted, usually as a particularly defined political entity, it has been suggested that "nationalism" is an ideology (for example, see Smith 1986b: 11). This ideology was most pronounced in the nineteenth century, particularly around related claims to states based on national identities. If one accepts this period as marking the beginning of modern nationalism, it is possible to see nationalism in three, or possibly four phases. The first phase was the "classical" nationalism of the late eighteenth and nineteenth century, which gave rise to most of the states which now comprise the countries of the developed world (often characterized by membership of the Organisation for Economic Cooperation and Development, or OECD). In this, the early establishment of a cohesive nation appears to have assisted economic development or, conversely, economic development assisted early nation formation. A second phase of nationalism can be said to have begun in the period following the First World War, reflected in the Wilsonian principle of self-determination.[2] One view might be that this principle flowed over into the self-determination struggles of colonized peoples, especially following the Second World War and up to around 1980. Another view is that this phase of decolonization was substantively different to Wilsonian self-determination and constitutes a third phase of nationalist assertion. A further, fourth, phase of nationalism can be said to have arisen from around the late 1980s with claims for self-determination being made from within existing states, including Yugoslavia, the Soviet Union and Ethiopia/Eritrea, but also including many claims by nationalist groups that have not yet been (and may not become) successful.

   The idea of nationalism reflects a desire for, or affirmation of, nation, and generally manifests as support for the creation, continuation or strengthening of an idea of a common bonded identity, an assertion of independent unity and, usually, self-determination (see Connor 1994; Anderson 1991; Smith 1986a; Smith 1986b; Smith 2003; Gellner 1983). Means of creating or attempting to create such a common political identity are various, but usually revolve around a (sometimes manufactured) common language, more broadly shared (or imposed) cultural values, world view (*weltanschauung*) or ideology, and sets of myths or (actual or manufactured) history, often involving a common hero or heroes as the national archetype and, not infrequently, in response to a commonly perceived threat. Other qualities of nation can include the criteria of size, historicity, reasonably compact territory, a capable and energetic intellectual class: all help but not all are absolutely necessary (Gellner 1983: 46). As put by Jaguaribe: "The nation is a particular form of society, characterized by the objective solidarity binding the nation to its individual members, founded on common characteristics and interests, and the subjective solidarity binding these members to the project of nationhood founded on common aspirations for political integration" (Jaguaribe 1968: 33). Further, while the idea of nation can be relatively passive, involving an acceptance of the state of affairs one might be born into (that is, membership of a community), "nationalism" implies a more active or assertive understanding of national identity.

The detailed form of the ideology which informs movement towards nation creation varies from place to place, for example, from the organicist (proto-fascist) origins of the Indonesian state and consequent assertions of national identity, or the Leninist model of the Vietnamese state which implied an imposed civic identity, to ethnic claims of national assertion such as those by Sri Lanka's Tamils or Indonesia's Acehnese, in which the political code that the nation adopts is less important than the establishment of the nation's distinct political identity, manifested as a separate nation-state. What these examples feature in common, however, is not just a desire for independent national unity and, consequently, self-determination, but the creation and recognition of an idea of a common bonded identity. Within this category, it is necessary to distinguish between "organic" nationalism (or that which evolves more or less naturally in relation to its environment), and "artificial" nationalism, or that which is more clearly constructed or imposed.

As a manifestation of the nationalist program, according to Gellner (1983: 44), the assertion of a nation to statehood is a principle form of state legitimacy, and *ipso facto* the main function of the state is to protect the nation's culture (Gellner 1983: 110). States can and do survive without being contiguous with a nation, although the nationalist tensions inherent in such an arrangement are frequently problematic. Similarly, nations that find themselves torn between states (for example, pre-unification Germany) have commonly sought unity as a means of redressing what is usually seen as an organizational distinction that does not reflect the reality of shared identification (in the case of Germany, such identification being ethnic rather than civic).

National identity as the basis for the assertion of nationalist claims can be characterized in two broad streams, or three according to some criteria. The most common and arguably necessary first quality of national identity is based on ethnicity or, gauging the confluence between the "historical record" of primordial and modern cohesive cultural identities, as *ethnie* (Smith 1986b: 22–46). A strong ethno-nationalist identity has been a common prerequisite for establishing successful states, as noted by Smith (1986b: 13–18) and Gellner (1983: 44). That is, proceeding from a common culture is usually the first form of nation formation. However, basing the national project solely on culture, without extending that to include wider civic values, raises the prospect of reifying a mythical "glorious past" (see Smith 1986b: 174–208). As such, it does not lay a foundation for national development, but in reifying itself becomes inwardly focused and reactionary. As noted by Sitrampalam in relation to Sri Lanka, the development of nationalist sentiment during the colonial era was based "on the foundations of the society's traditional past. They saw the modern phase of nationalism, not as a novel, essentially

different phenomenon, causing a break with the past, but rather as an extension of their past, a rebirth of the old society, its renaissance in a new form"
(Sitrampalam undated). In the case of colonial Sri Lanka, "Traditional cultural
nationalism" that had not yet developed as a civic identity led to an attempted
hegemony by the majority ethnic Sinhalese over the Tamil and Muslim
minorities, which in turn generated conflict as these minorities sought to
resist that hegemony. That is, a nationalism based solely on claims to cultural
specificity fails to provide a civil basis for inclusive citizenship, and thus
becomes exclusivist along ethnic lines. Structuring national participation on
non-civic lines can work for a majority in the short-term, through preferential
dominance. The logic of such a proposition is, however, that should circumstances change and some within that majority wish to seek redress, the
civic structures of, for example, equal access to a consistent rule of law will
not be available. In particular, as the characteristics of that dominance are
increasingly defined, individuals who would otherwise be members of that
national community are portrayed as "bad" nationals, or having betrayed
the nationalist cause. This narrowing of cultural identity as the only criteria
for national inclusion, then, constitutes a slide into a specifically defined
nationalist absolutism.

   This second equally necessary quality for continuing success in sustaining
national identity is based on concordance around shared values or the codification of civil values. The second idea of nationalism comprises what has
been termed "civic nationalism," or "civic nationality" (Miller, 1993, 1995; see
also Smith 1998: 210–13). This concept corresponds to a more inclusive,
participatory and open political society (for example, liberal democracy). In
this, national identity and hence citizenship are ascribed on the basis of
commitment to core civic values rather than ethnic origin. The idea of civic
nationalism can be traced back to the Roman state, in which citizenship
was allocated on the basis of being born the child of citizens, earning citizenship through outstanding service, being an inhabitant of a province that
was included as Roman or, from the third century, being a male inhabitant of
the empire. In this, civic nationalism can be equated with the civic values
of republicanism. While some Renaissance states allowed citizenship, the
idea more fully flourished as a result of the American and French Revolutions,
in which "nationals" were citizens on the basis of ascribing to the laws pertaining to the state and having passed other assessable criteria (see Smith
1998: 121, 125–6; Hobsbawn 1990: 9–10). In the case of the French revolution, the civic quality was formally linked to territory; in the American
situation the territorial basis was more imperial in scope, substantially
expanding from its 13 founding colonies. This civic nationalism has also
been described as "republicanism," in that it is a manifestation of a normative republican system based on equitable rule of law. However, this is an
inaccurate characterization of republicanism in that republics may allow or
encourage fuller civic engagement but may also preclude such engagement.
The criteria for civic nationalism under republican systems less reflects the

external political model and much more reflects the model's internal political qualities. The distinction is perhaps between a normative republican ethos, which implies civic participation and responsibility, and republican practise, which can range from highly participatory and accountable to autocratic.

In his proposal of a "socio-cultural definition," Michael Seymour (2000) adds what he sees as a political dimension to what he opposes as a purely cultural one. A nation is a cultural group, he says, which may be but is not necessarily united by common descent (more or less mythical ethnic commonality), but which has developed civic ties. This type of definition would be generally accepted as it broadly complies with the contemporary notion of how a nation normatively functions. In this respect, the idea of "nation" employs more than just an ethno-cultural quality and combines with it a civic category, which again echoes the Roman model. However, Seymour claims this identification of "nation" is still closer to an ethno-cultural orientation than it is to a purely civic function.

The difficulty with Seymour's definition is that while it complies with a common Western understanding of nation, it tends to conform primarily to developed countries and, even in this case, cannot be held as a universal. That is, a sense of nation, or the "program of nationalism" can exist with little attention paid to claimed civic virtues. In particular, the nation can quickly diminish existing civic virtues in the face of an actual or perceived common threat. In cases where the state exists but the nation is relatively weak or unformed, challenges to either the claim to nation or threats to the state can quickly see a retreat from the civic. This is often manifested as lapses in the equal and consistent application of law, or the redrafting of law so that it institutionalizes unequal or ethno-specific legal responses. Further, in seeking to allay (sometimes manufactured perceptions of) group-based fears, those with control of the levers of state power are able to manipulate both perceptions of threats and the responded rationalization of concentrated state power, which may be applied unequally or in a discriminatory manner. In this sense, the civic quality of nationalism may exist, but does not necessarily do so.

To extend beyond Seymour's definition, civic nationalism does not just imply equality under rule of law, although it must include that. It also reflects the common coherence of shared values of fairness, relative equal access to economic opportunity, a commitment to participating in, shaping and sharing public life, an active rather than passive communication on matters of common interest, support for public debate, and respect for its plurality.

Because of the implicit threats to citizens posed by a singular appeal to specific cultural identity, a culturally based form of nationalism must evolve to an identification with the state based on law and broadly shared civic values. That is, if "civic nationalism" (for example support for plural democracy, basic human rights, etc.) is to constitute a stable state form, it must be able to constructively engage with its future (see Plamenatz 1973). Citizens surrender elements of their cultural self to the law (with which, presumably, they agree) on condition that such law offers them protection, thus establishing a community of equality under agreed codes of behavior, or the acculturation of the civic. In this sense, civic nationalism can be seen to equate to the idea of a developed voluntarist nationalism, or a nationalism based the desire to belong because of continuing social equity under law, to which all other citizens similarly volunteer. A nationalism that remains inherently reliant on ethnicity is always on the verge of or actually realizing its exclusivity (Brubaker 2004). Consequently it defined itself along lines of increasingly specific cultural identification and hence fragmentation. This latter quality in particular defines the distinction between nation and nationalism. A sense of "nation" is an "impulse," but which can merge into nationalism as an idea and, in its final manifestation, nationalism as a program, and finally the capacity for such programs to become prescriptive (Walzer 1988: 66). The questions, then, are what form of ideas those impulses take, and, in what shape that manifests as a nationalist program.

A third idea that overcomes the singularity of ethnic nationalism yet provides a greater historicity and sense of community than pure civic nationalism, or Habermas' even more unrooted "constitutional patriotism" (2001a, 2001b), is that of "plural nationalism," in which ethnicity is not the sole criteria for national identity but the establishment of historical bonds does strengthen sometimes emotionally weaker (if intellectually stronger) claims to civic or constitutional nationalism. In this, the specific ethnic origins of citizens are less important than citizens from differing backgrounds having broad agreement on basic issues. The first of these issues would be the use of a common language, which in turn creates the linguistic framework in which other issues can be mediated. A close second issue would be that citizens have a commitment to each other's welfare, up to the extent that the political community is concerned for the affairs of its constituent citizens. It should be noted, however, that successful multicultural nationalisms are rare and exist principally in immigrant societies (e.g. Australia, Canada). Multiculturalism does exist elsewhere (e.g. UK, US, France), but with a lesser common national identity and, frankly, success.

Ethno-nationalism

Assuming the transition between the nation as an idea and nationalism as a program, and the aspirational correspondence between the nation and the state, the state as political unit is seen by nationalists as centrally "belonging" to one ethno-cultural group – or an agreed multicultural group – and is charged with protecting and promulgating the traditions ascribed to the national identity. This form is exemplified by the classical, "revivalist" nationalism that was most prominent in the nineteenth century in Europe and Latin America, in which antiquarian nations were "rediscovered," if often in a somewhat romanticized sense. This classical nationalism later spread across the world and still marks many contemporary nationalisms, as well as nation-alist claims to statehood.

For the ethno-cultural nationalist, it is one's ethno-cultural background which determines one's membership of the community; one must be born into the group in order to be a member (Kohn 1965). One cannot choose to be a member; instead, membership depends on the accident of origin and early socialization. However, absolute commonality of origin has turned out to be mythical for most contemporary candidate groups. Ethnic groups have been mixing for millennia, and claims to ethnic purity reflect more an assertion of an imagined defining identity than the fact of that claim.

It is easy to see that ethno-nationalism and group exclusivity based on claims to ethnic "purity" are only slightly removed from the most irrational chauvinism, or "intense, even hysterical nationalist enthusiasm" (Heywood 2003: 177). In cases of perceived grievance or political manipulation (or both), such ethno-nationalism can degenerate into feelings of rejection and then violence. Yet claims to group identity based on ethnicity do retain a strong hold on many, particularly for those who seek security in group identity in response to other feelings of insecurity in their wider socio-economic environment. As Heywood aptly notes: "National chauvinism has a particularly strong appeal for the isolated and powerless, for whom national-ism offers the prospect of security, self-respect and pride" (Heywood 2003: 177). Drawing on the emotional appeal of the group, but seeking a more "legitimate" means of its expression, more sophisticated nationalists tend to stress cultural membership only and to speak of "nationality," omitting the "ethno-" part (Tamir 1993; Gans 2003).

It is ethno-nationalist identity, being based around a relatively homogen-ous or linguistically focused cultural group, that informed the creation of the original "nation-states" of Europe, and which motivated the Wilsonian principles of self-determination, especially in relation to the post-First World War reorganization of Europe's borders. In its less enlightened forms, this ethno-nationalism is ethnically exclusive and hence implicitly racist. Yet a common bonded identity does appear to be a critical factor in successful nation-creation. In that there has been dissent, this has occurred either in those states in which national identities have been geographically mixed (for example within the composite states of former Yugoslavia), or at the margins (such as Alsace-Lorraine, the Basque region of Spain and France and in the reordering of the states and the national reach of Germany, Poland, Russia and Finland). While there remain these exceptions, and in part as a con-sequence of a conscious process of inclusion, there has increasingly become a relatively high degree of cultural coherence within European nations. There have also been challenges by distinct ethnic communities in states that have not succeeded in creating a sense of civic nationalism, such as Iraq, Indonesia, Burma and Sri Lanka. Conversely, state boundaries that do not include all members of the (ethno)nation are incomplete and reflect temporary boundaries established by a political struggle that similarly may not yet be complete (Bullock 1962: 315).

Constructed nationalism

Nations seem to be "natural" to most people, or at least to most people who do not live in a state where nationalisms are imposed or contest against each other. Yet no nationalism simply appeared, complete and fully evolved. The shape and orientation of the bonded political identity that generally describes the nation has been at the center of much practical political thinking since people first began to form into coherent groups and identified themselves in relation to "others." That is to say, ever since people first began to reflect on their common political group, they have also influenced, changed and manipulated it.

It can therefore be suggested that all nationalisms are constructed in that they are a consequence of a conscious and systematic building of common understanding or identity around shared core ideas. This is a common claim, particularly where the assertion of an *uber*-national unity is contested by competing claims. "Construction" implies the artificiality of the claim, and thus delegitimizes it. However, this assertion of constructed national identity is perhaps less helpful than understanding whether the "nationalism" in question is the product of local, voluntary (that is, organic)[3] conditions, or whether it is a consequence of coercion or compulsion, often external (artificial). This is not to suggest that there is not a high degree of artificiality in many nationalisms. Many of the states of Europe, for example, comprise non-core groups that have been obliged to share in the nationalist project, and indeed even the core group has been reinvented in many cases (see Smith 1998: 129–31; Hobsbawm 1990, 1983). However, the ordering of state borders, which in Europe are usually claimed to be contiguous with nationalisms (hence the term, nation-state), has usually been undertaken on a more or less voluntary basis. While there are exceptions, such as the Germanic speakers of northern Italy or the Basques of Spain, there is a relatively high degree of cultural coherence within European nations.

By contrast, the states of South and South-East Asia, for example, do not always correspond comfortably to assertions of nationalism, primarily because of the often arbitrary manner in which their borders were defined by external colonial powers. As such, they were much less a reflection of the will of local inhabitants, or even, as in the case of Europe, an historical trade-off that allowed borders to occur along approximately national lines, or along lines that corresponded to the political reach of core national groups. However, within the colonial context, the bond born of fighting against a common colonialist enemy has been a key component in the construction of national identities. In this last sense, the common aspiration and struggle for "liberation" has helped forge a shared identity through a common cause, often through shared hardship and through identification with the newly bonded group in opposition to a common enemy. As in the case of Europe, this common bonded identity has been regarded as the basis for an assertion of legitimate control over the "nation's" territory (see SarDesai 1997: Chapters 18 and 24) and can thus be seen as a basis for claiming the existence of a nation.

If it can be claimed that all nationalisms are constructed, they are the consequence of an historically increasing systematic building of common understanding or identity around shared core ideas. This may be even where the nation does not consciously question its identity or its cohesion – and there is usually an explicit endorsement of such identity and cohesion. There is, then, an unconscious system of self-reference and re-affirmation. There is also often a conscious if unofficial restatement of what it means to be one of "us," as "we" understand or imagine ourselves in common to be. The question is around the extent to which this national identity can be claimed to be unconscious or a product of occasional conscious reflection, or whether there is an external or overarching force at play which contributes to shaping the identity under consideration. That is, it might be that all self-understandings of "nation" in the final analysis are constructed.

Stating that all nations are to some extent constructed does not address the degree to which such constructions have evolved naturally, or as the product of more compelled sets of circumstances. The issue then, is whether the national identity in question is the result of local, voluntary, or organic conditions (for example common language or shared struggle), or whether it is a consequence of coercion, and hence artificial (such as incorporation into an arbitrary geographically defined region, an imposed "common" language, or both). Diminishing or deleting those aspects of history that do not accord with the idea of common unity or a shared struggle has been a common feature of conscious nation-building, even if this official version of nation papers over continuing local histories, myths and shared memories. As one Indonesian nationalist asserted in the face of a fractured national coalition, the construction of "nation" was not, successfully, a consequence of remembering. It was, he proposed, a consequence of forgetting (Goenawan 2002: 22).

The idea of "nationalism" in states based on traditional polities is also complicated by the fact that the modernist adoption (or imposition) of fixed borders clashed with the ebb and flow of such polities' authority, including the drift of migrants from one region to another. In the contemporary political world, the free flow of people is regarded as challenging the state's control of its borders, upsetting patterns of established land use and ownership, and threatening loyalty to the state. Historically, however, such migration was encouraged, as a means of strengthening the state in both economic and military terms, and might also be seen to have an echo in encouraging inflows of skilled migration to developed states with declining population rates. This had implications for pre-colonial state formation and how that has influenced contemporary states. The ideas that derive from the pre-colonial period also inform, sometimes consciously and sometimes subconsciously, the way political leaders look at their own country and those around them. For example, ideas around centralized control of the state can, on one hand, be seen to conform to conventional bureaucratic organization, but can also be seen to conform to pre-colonial court culture. Relations between the center of the state and its periphery, particularly in ethnically differentiated states, can also reflect pre-colonial approaches to state control. Groups on the periphery of the state, such as West Papuans in Indonesia, the Karen in Burma or Muslims in southern Thailand, for example, very often do not enjoy functionally equal status under uniformly applied laws.

With the establishment of European colonies in the region, colonizers sought to extend their authority either to or beyond the limits of the state as they found it, as a part of their empire creation. The Dutch included not just Java in their colony of the Dutch East Indies, but also islands which had only peripheral relations with Java, such as the archipelago's south-east islands (Nusa Tenggara). Similarly, Britain incorporated not only the core state of Burma within the Irrawaddy Valley, which it acknowledged as "Burma Proper," but also states that had conflicting histories in relation to Burma, which they acknowledged as the "Frontier States." The French correctly understood the connectedness of the three states of Vietnam, as they found them, as Cochin-China, Annam and Tonkin. However, it was only through the shallow establishment of a Vietnamese claim to suzerainty that they then annexed the Lao state of Luang Prabang, extended to incorporate the other Lao states of Vieng Chan (Vientiane) and Champassak.[4] That Thailand also claimed suzerainty over these states little worried the French, although the Thai claim to the northern Malay state once known as Pattani (which still exists as one of Thailand's four constitutive southern provinces) has caused continuing conflict. Further, to compound this lack of acknowledgement for what political arrangements did and did not exist, the French then chose to delineate their newly acquired Lao territory along the Mekong River, with the exception of small northern and southern sections. The Mekong had traditionally been the main artery *within* the Lao nation, and earlier within the Lao state of Lan Xang. This had little meaning for the French, but left a majority of ethnic Lao Loum in what was thereafter defined as Thailand rather than in territorial Laos. Similarly, the border area of Afghanistan and Pakistan has historically belonged to the tribes that live there, in particular on either side some 18 million ethnic Pashtuns, and little has changed since the drawing of the so-called Durand Line in 1893, which is claimed to have expired in 1993. The ethnically fragmented and geographically mountainous nature of the border region has had serious implications for state control, regional security and the capacity for global outlaws such as Osama bin Laden to hide with relative ease. In such areas, the concept of "nation" has a more localized meaning, and rarely one that neatly coincides with the state.

In the contemporary political world, polities have fixed borders and rarely voluntarily change them. Where strength and weakness have come into play, it has changed states primarily as a consequence of compulsion. Nations that have been identified with such states have variously been accommodated into the new state environment, absorbed or dissipated by the state (for example, forced internal migration), have been killed or become refugees. Immigration has also been encouraged in countries such as the US, Canada, Australia, New Zealand and South Africa, among many others. In the case of Australia, immigration was seen as a principle means of boosting what was regarded as an inadequate industrial population base, and in the immediate post-Second World War years was actively encouraged and in some cases assisted. As a nation of migrants, or their descendents, boosting population through immigration was a logical step. However, even in a "migrant country" such as Australia, the immigration of people from non-core (that is, non-Anglo-Celtic) nationalities has raised issues of social cohesion. Australia has largely accommodated ethnic difference, which has in turn enriched Australian cultural life. The US has had a similar policy towards immigration, particularly in the late nineteenth and early twentieth centuries. In both cases, "national" identity has come to be built on civic identification rather than on pre-existing ethnic origins. Where there have been exceptions to this, such as with sections of the US's African-American and Hispanic populations, the consequent alienation has resulted in occasionally high levels of inter-ethnic tension and violence.

History and myth

The role of history or myth in national identity has been developed by all successful nations and nationalist claims are usually predicated upon such history or myth. This is particularly the case where nations succeed by securing a state to represent the interests of the nation.[5] In particular, ideologies that have strongly promoted a sense of (chauvinistic) national identity, such as fascism, have emphasized not just historical unity but historical glories, some of which are invented and many of which are exaggerated to create a sense of national pride and superiority over other nations. In the wider form of social organicism, the "people" are posited as constituting a unity that has claimed to enjoy a special or privileged endowment. This perceived or claimed status has largely grown out of a romanticized understanding of national identity, embodying an idealized archetype as the model and, for many, the standard (see Berlin 1969). This was claimed by the "British" people, not least on behalf of the British Empire, even though what constituted a "Briton" during this time was more a consequence of education and acculturation than historical legacy. The history and myths of Britain have been celebrated out of proportion to their historical importance, but were central to the construction of a unified identity seeking to impose itself upon a less socially and militarily organized world. A common history and large dose of myth was also claimed for the German *volk* (people) under the National Socialist (Nazi) Party, identified as the supreme manifestation of the "Aryan race."[6] The corporatization and extension of national identity under the Nazis led to the singularization of associated options; *Ein Volk, Ein Reich, Ein Fuhrer* (On People/Nation, One Country/Empire, One Leader) (Wagner 1971).

Claims to national grace, however, are not limited to Europeans. The Jews have claimed a special relationship with their god as his chosen people, which via Zionism has been claimed to legitimize the state of Israel.[7] Some Americans of African descent have laid claim to a distinct national identity that has been extended by some in the Caribbean to a religious specificity (Rastafari). Japanese nationalists have claimed the "purity" of their nation to the extent that becoming a Japanese citizen remains barred to third generation Japan-born ethnic Koreans, while many Indonesian nationalists claim a unity explicitly based on the exaggerated and definitional imperial claims of unity under a thirteenth-century Javanese empire.

Unity through communication

As Anderson (1991) has noted, a common language is the principle mediator and conceptual definer of an "imagined community," in which individuals may not know each other but perceive themselves as having a common interest. That is, a shared language is the primary medium through which social association is made and common interest defined. Enhanced by literacy and the popularization of print (and later electronic) media, a community is thus able to communicate among itself, and is at least as importantly able to share ideas across a geographic range that would preclude direct communication.

It is because of the national bond born of common language that all successful states have implemented a policy of standardization of the "official" language or, in fewer cases, languages.[8] Indeed, where "organic" national languages have not existed, they have been invented, or standardized in such a way as to imply a considerable degree of conscious nation building. It might be argued, with a fair degree of legitimacy, that no official language is entirely "organic" and that all official languages have been standardized in ways that have moved them beyond "pre-national" usage. While languages continue to evolve, in the contemporary sense most often in relation to the effects of globalization, they also continued to be reified, through education systems, the media and, as a standardizing process, in dictionaries. Proto-national (that is, a potential or actual nation in the process of formation), sub-national or tribal languages, dialects and specific colloquialisms continue to exist and indeed assert themselves as markers of the "local." But the power of inclusion and exclusion, especially in relation to economic participation, as defined by language, does act as a compelling incentive to accede to standardized linguistic requirements.

This standardization can be seen, for example, in the public education system of the UK in terms of a standardized spelling, grammar and Received Pronunciation, applying not just to native English speakers but also to speakers of English dialects and to the Gaelic languages of Scotland, Wales and Ireland. It can be similarly seen in other European countries, particularly those that came to the idea of the nation and state being more or less contiguous relatively earlier (for example, France), rather than later (such as the constituent nations of the Austro-Hungarian empire). However, as a distinct marker of and contributor towards "national" identity, the standardization of language has also been a common feature of more recent states, such as Indonesia (Bahasa Indonesia), Malaysia (Bahasa Melayu) and the Philippines (Pilipino), or reiterated states,[9] such as China (Mandarin).

The issue of language is not absolute in the conceptualization of nationalism. It may be that for a nation to succeed it requires a common language, and that if a state (especially as the legitimate territorial manifestation of the nation) is to have a minimum functional capacity, it must also have a common language. As Gellner asserts, non-state politically bonded language groups also have a legitimate claim to "nationalism" (1983: 44, 140), although given the full range of markers of national identity perhaps in the first instance as "proto-nations." Yet the correspondence between such claims to nationalism and actual nations as marked by state representation are grossly out of proportion. Gellner measured the number of languages against the number of countries to show this discrepancy. There is greatest agreement on the number of recognized states being 195 (including Scotland, Taiwan and Puerto Rico) and some 6,000 languages that also have registered populations (a further approximately 500 languages are believed to exist but do not have populations registered against them). On this basis, there are a little more than 31 languages for every state, or for every language that is represented by a dominant culture and manages to establish statehood, there are around 30 that are left out in the unrepresented cold. This ratio looks even worse when one considers that some languages, such as Spanish, English, Arabic (though often counted as several languages due to its variations), and French, are the official languages of more than one country. That is, nations require a common language, but not all common languages are represented by a nation.

In that the idea of nation is manifested in a common understanding, this can be interpreted through wider social interaction than that implied by overt political considerations. Shared language is the most common marker of nation for the noted reason of specific communication. However, language has a more subtle function in national identity as the embodiment and means of expression of a particular culture or, in Gellner's terms, a pervasive "high" culture (Gellner 1983: 18, 142). That is, the use or standardization of a common language also complies with the idea of nationalism as a conscious program. In what can be described as a symbiotic relationship between language and circumstance, the language that is available and the range of meanings it potentially contains defines the range of conceptualization available to its speakers. Multi-linguists potentially have a wider range of conceptual meanings available to them, although even here there are few such speakers whose frame of conceptual reference is not set by one language or another. Even where there is such linguistic multi-polarity the capacity for conceptualization still remains within that wider than usual linguistic scope (for example, Indonesian speakers have their linguistic conceptual structures embedded in their speech even when they are speaking English, and vice-versa). Thus, national identity is in part built around not just a common language but common and sometimes contextually specific points of reference within that language.

In relation to politics, a common or shared experience of a particular political system might acculturate it as "natural," around which can be understood the idea of a political culture (see Weber on habituation 1948: 152–3). From this it is but a short step to understanding politics as culturally relative, that different cultures have different political perceptions and requirements. For example, rapid political transformations among pre-modern hierarchical societies tended to produce a reified version of traditional forms of authority (see Weber 1948: 341–58, see also Pemberton (1994) on Indonesia, Sitrampalam undated on Sri Lanka). "Cultural relativism" is the basis of the case against universal political values, and for the identification of such values as themselves culturally specific. This assumes, however, cultural stasis, or the "impossibility of translation" (Whorf 1956), also known as the "incommensurability thesis" (as rejected by Gellner 1983: 120). That is, in particular political environments there might be the popular acceptance of an official, often highly constructed and usually imposed culture. This, however, does not imply that such a political culture is necessary or somehow the only legitimate choice available. While the physical environment is directly experiential and largely set as the context within which other physical activity takes place, political culture is contingent upon social relations and the capacities and interests of individuals and groups to realize their interests, through the exercise of "power" (Weber 1948: 152–3; Blau 1970: 147–65). To this end, political cultures change if there is sufficient will and capacity to make them do so.

This sub-rational (intuitive) appeal to cultural specificity, or exclusivity, as the basis for nationalism and the claim to its incommensurability removes it from the realm of universal principles. As such it has been a common defense of regimes that practise conventional authoritarian methods or which otherwise preclude equal and consistent application of the rule of law as the basic criteria for citizenship. Such approaches can be seen under predatory regimes, authoritarian regimes that privilege a particular social hierarchy, and states in which there are structural distinctions based on ethnic identity. At its most benign, such an appeal might have a parallel quality of preserving local cultural traditions or providing a framework for relatively improved material development as the result of political "stability." However, appeals to cultural specificity or exclusivity are necessary for neither preserving traditions or political stability. The potential for cultural preservation or economic development to take place is more a factor of accountability under a government popularly chosen to be most competent for that particular job. At their more malignant, governments that base their existence on appeals to cultural specificity have been responsible for the subjugation of culture for narrow political purposes, economic decay due to closure and corruption, ethnic discrimination at times leading to pogroms and ethnic cleansing, and other gross abuses of civil and political rights.

Common defense

In addition to language, a further defining factor contributing to the existence of a sense of "nation" is a common response to a common threat. Threats can be both real and perceived, and both natural and deliberate. Natural threats, such as flood,[10] drought,[11] fire, and so on,[12] can bond communities together out of a common need for self-preservation. However, social responses to natural threats tend to be relatively localized and while they may contribute to the affirmation of community, they may not necessarily do so on a scale as to warrant understanding as "nation." There may, however, be instances where the response is commonly shared across more than immediately contiguous areas, via mass communication which may elicit a wider common response and identification.

More concretely, however, bonding is more likely to occur when a proto-nation faces a common, widespread and deliberate threat. The act of social volition that causes the threat to arise, for example, in the case of attack or an act of war, tends to elicit a similarly deliberate response, or at least a response that identifies a dangerous "other" and hence amplifies the apparent sense of "security" to be found among one's own group. Common responses to threats from "the other" can be seen as a major contributing factor to the formation of many nations (and the states that are claimed as their geo-political embodiment), notably among post-colonial societies. Indeed, the key legacies of colonialism are the territorial boundaries which largely define post-colonial states, and the bonding of communities in order to expel the colonial power (even if this latter quality has not always survived the immediate post-independence period).

Within the post-colonial context, the bond born of fighting against a common colonialist enemy has been a key component in the construction of national identities. The common aspiration and struggle for "liberation" has helped forge a common identity through a common cause, often through shared common hardship and through the identification of the newly bonded group in opposition to its common enemy. As in the case of Europe, this common bonded identity, then, has been regarded as the basis for an assertion of legitimate control over the "nation's" territory. This has been the case in East Timor, despite relative ethnic commonalities across the whole island. Following Dutch incursions, the eastern half of the island remained under Portuguese colonial administration while the west fell to the Dutch. Following the independence of the Netherlands East Indies territories in 1949, West Timor became part of the Republic of Indonesia. East Timor declared independence in 1975, but only days before a formal Indonesian invasion occupied the territory. With a brutal occupying army, a civilian death toll of 180,000 (or approximately a quarter of a population of around 650,000), a widespread resistance movement and even a separate trade and immigration regime, East Timor was like a different nation compared to the western half of the island. Despite relative ethnic commonalities and the widespread use of common languages (Bahasa Indonesia and Tetum Praca), East Timor was, and following independence remains, sharply divided from West Timor. A "nation," then, is what its constituent members want it to be.

Not surprisingly, the bond born of facing a common threat is often valorized as part of the story of the forging of the nation, and its heroes are transformed into national heroes. This has occurred even where their struggles might have occurred much earlier, been more locally based or have been concerned with issues other than nation creation. The militaries of post-colonial states often claim, with varying degrees of justification, a leading role in the defeat of the common enemy, which in turn assists in legitimizing their often extensive role in post-colonial governments. Vietnam's military can fairly claim to have played a leading role in the defeat of the common colonial enemy (France) neo-colonial enemy (the US), and subsequently of China. Its continuing influence in the political affairs of state belies the nominal supremacy of civilian authority. In Indonesia, on the other hand, the military has sought to enhance its status as the deliverer of independence well beyond that which is supported by historical evidence, but which during a period of relative military domination (1966–98) was able to suppress alternative interpretations of the independence struggle, as well as subsequent events that could have repositioned authority (for example, to the communist party or Islamic organizations).

A further motivating factor in the building of national identity focuses on the phenomenon of industrialization as a key social organizational quality. To illustrate, Gellner cites industrialization and the Protestant work ethic as a critical aspect of the nation formation process (1983: Chapter 3; see also Smith 1998: 79–82). The centralized and externally focused nature of industrial organization and the standardization of language it requires can indeed be seen as contributing or strengthening both the development of a national identity and providing a basis for subsequent statehood (Hobsbawm 1983, 1990). While industrialization may be a contributing factor to nation formation, notably in Western countries, it cannot be held as a necessary, much less a universal, criterion. It is difficult to argue that Italy, Spain or Portugal coalesced as nations because of either industrialization or Protestantism, and it speaks little to post-colonial societies that may derive from a range of religious and cultural backgrounds and various levels of economic development that have been successful in creating both nations and states. In this, one might think of Vietnam, which despite its artificial north-south division and the deep ideological cleavages that produced, has a distinct and pronounced national identity and a clear (even if at times quite corrupt) state organization. This is one example of cultural commonality added to an external threat being the primary bonding agent, and the efficiencies required of total war being more important than the efficiencies required of industrial production (not withstanding some common organizing principles between them).

Territorial nationalism

Communal bonding born of mutual defense is generally tied to a common territory. The territory will most commonly be shared contiguous land around which a community has established common interests, such as shared resources (for example, in the first instance water, farming land, forest), or engages in mutual assistance (such as in the first instance during hunting, planting or harvesting). A mutual challenge or threat, then, will apply to a people who share a spatial and geo-specific relationship as well as a social relationship, and may be directed at either the quantity of their territory (for example, loss of resources), the loss of the territory itself, or the loss of control over particular populations.

Territory can in the first instance be the site of sources of livelihood and investment, and thus has the capacity to produce a relationship between the individual or community and the land, usually manifested as ownership or regular use. The relationship may also be manifested as animistic belief systems or other forms of spiritual association, including defining elements of culture by the physical qualities of place (wind, rain, groundwater, field, forest, etc.). However, mutual territorial defense invests in the territory not just a quality of providing but, potentially, a quality of sacrifice which in turn places greater, not directly material, value on the territory. Out of this complex association arises notions of territory as having almost anthropomorphic qualities, which frequently develop into the parental ("motherland" or "fatherland").

Between physical proximity, shared resources and common threats, the bond of community is established, linguistically and culturally demarcated, socially established and territorially defined. The relationship between and across the wider community is similarly defined along broader but still common lines, with that relationship ending at the point of differentiated language, culture, common interest or geographic identification. Because of the physical limitations imposed by geography on other forms of association, this is most commonly the traditional point of national demarcation. River valleys may be sites of communal origination, but it is most often mountain ranges that divide communities from each other. So too, dense forests, deserts and oceans can act as initial barriers, while the inhospitability of certain regions, such as mountains (Swiss, Afghans, Bhutanese), deserts (Arabs, Aborigines) and sub-Arctic regions (Lapps, Inuit), can be sites of defense, refuge or displacement.

The association of nation with territory, then, is a primordial one, and along with language and perhaps religion, is generally the most common marker of national identity. Conflicts between nations, beyond securing resources or defense are, therefore, commonly over the regularization of the territory of the nation and the self-determination of the nation within a territorial entity. Where significant problems arise is when the claim to "nation" is not predicated on such commonalities and especially where there is no geographic contiguity. Nations that are divided across separate territorial entities have a history of difficulty in surviving, the primary exception being where the principle territory vastly outweighs the peripheral territories, such as where the principal territory has authority over local islands. However, nations that are more evenly divided across territories, where the territories are actually or relatively geographically distinct or where the claim to national cohesion is otherwise weak, have a history of instability, dissent and conflict. Examples of this can be seen between West and East Pakistan (Pakistan and Bangladesh), the enclaves in the states of former Yugoslavia, the former United Arab Republic, UK (Northern Ireland), Russia (Chechnya), Georgia (Abkhazia), Iraq (Kurdistan), India (Jammu-Kashmir, Assam, Nagaland), China (Tibet, Xinjiang, Inner Mongolia), Azerbaijan (Nagorno-Karabakh), the Philippines (Mindanao), Burma (which is numerously divided by mountains and ethnicity), Papua-New Guinea (Bougainville) and Indonesia (which comprises separate islands and numerous distinct peoples).

Voluntary nations

The issue of nation and national identity has become increasingly acute in the later post-colonial period as the result of a confluence of issues. Originally, the pre-colonial separateness of many peoples was largely never overcome, and even the establishment of new states in the period between the two world wars saw the creation of relatively artificial polities, some of which have since been deconstructed (for example, Yugoslavia and Czechoslovakia). Further, the failure of a number of post-colonial states to deliver on post-independence promises, usually of economic development and equitable representation, have tested polities that were united to oppose a common enemy and achieve a common goal. The former having been realized, the failure of the latter begged the purpose of the former.

The Wilsonian emphasis on self-determination – the right of a geo-specific nation to a state – was intended to apply primarily to the nations of Europe moving towards statehood in the post-First World War period. The end of the subsequent decolonization process by the 1970s, along with an increasing emphasis on difference, highlighted distinctions between groups whose relations were not always comfortable, or who achieved some measure of protection from traditional enemies under colonial tutelage. The "frontier" states of Burma are a prime case in point. Beyond the success or failure of the post-Wilsonian self-determination or post-colonial state building project, the experience of modernization has also alienated many traditional societies, encouraging them to seek meaning in pre-modern kinship or wider group bonds. Whereas modernization has forged "horizontal" social commonalities (that is, commonalities around shared or group interest, such as economic stratification), this has occurred most strongly in societies that already shared a basic common relationship, usually of language but also in relation to a common (pre-modern) "class" enemy, such as land-owners or a feudal aristocracy. States that bring together groups that share common economic circumstances but which derive from disparate backgrounds and forms of social relations (such as Indonesia) less easily form "horizontal" alliances,[13] and remain prone to vertical, or ethnic, cleavages.

Finally, the impact of economic and cultural globalization has tested the institutional predominance of states and set in place a further context for social alienation along modernist lines. Modernization had the effect of destabilizing and undermining established social patterns and encouraging its less successful subjects to seek externally inspired alternatives. The post-modernizing qualities of globalization has had the even further impact of not just placing out of reach global standards and requirements, and destabilizing not just local communities, but the verities that were believed to exist within national identities. These latter aspects have also become common features of under-classes in developed states. This has in part led to a reassertion of those national verities (especially in developed countries), often as an unsophisti-cated and introspective nationalism (which historically gave rise to various forms of organicism such as fascism). In developing countries, economic and cultural globalization has had the competing effects of propelling unsecured national members towards more global alternatives on one hand, while push-ing others away from the sometimes superficial certainties of globalized agendas on the other. That is, globalization has encouraged citizens to ques-tion their place in the state, and in cases where the bonds have been weak, to encourage the consideration of alternatives.

Where national bonds are historically weak, states tend to impose compul-sory "national" membership, following rather than preceding the creation of the state, and tend to preclude civic values. That is, not being able to allow the full expression of social plurality, the state rules *by* (often oppressive) law. By contrast, voluntary nationalism, in which members freely embrace their agreed commonality, appears to provide a more stable basis for social equality of difference under rule *of* law. This in turn allows for and, having begun on that self-fulfilling trajectory, encourages and increases, public identification of national identity based more around a common set of civic values than on ethnicity.

While there are exceptions to the European "nation complies with state" model, such as the Germanic speakers of northern Italy (or perhaps even between northern and southern Italy) or the French speakers of Belgium, there is a relatively high degree of cultural coherence within nation-states. By contrast, the states of many post-colonial states do not always correspond comfortably to assertions of nationalism, primarily because of the often arbitrary manner in which their borders were defined by external colonial powers. However, importantly and as noted above, within the post-colonial context, the bond born of fighting against a common colonialist enemy has been a key component in the construction of national identities. The problem with this form of "national" identification, particularly in post-colonial states that are otherwise arbitrarily defined, is that once the "struggle" has been concluded, the rationale for the bonded identity ceases to exist. Unless a new bond is formed, such as around further common cause or identification, in particular around the idea of a "civic nationalism," the nation will become prone to dissipation or fragmentation. Few post-colonial states, however, have been successful in developing a sense of civic nationalism, and many post-colonial states have consequently struggled to maintain a sense of coherent national identity.

The "nation," then, is not a simple or singular idea. There are core features which can be said to comply with most nations that identify themselves as such, and some would appear to be critical to successful nation formation and continued existence. However, the idea of nation has also taken hold as a political tool, and has been used or manipulated in a range of ways that have had negative as well as positive outcomes for political development. Perhaps the central idea of the nation is that, assuming it genuinely exists in a definite bonded form, is that it should be self-determining; that is, the nation should be accountable primarily to itself and its constituent members, and should not be subject to domination by others.

This then leads to the question of the relationship of the nation to its territory, and the relationship between the nation and the state as the embodiment of territorial sovereignty. Claims to self-determination, and to sovereign territory, are among the key factors in conflict and war, particularly in the post-cold war era. The formation of states as a consequence of post-colonialism has often ridden roughshod over claims to national identity and allowed self-determination, expressed as political participation, only as a factor within a larger political framework. Often over-arching nationalist claims have been used as a pretext for limiting or removing even that limited level of political participation, with its consequent implications for notions of political development.

The nation is then perhaps the most vexing of fundamental political issues because it appears as so basic to political formation, yet, assuming the necessity of civic nationalism as a prerequisite guarantee for political development, it is finally redundant. That is, appeals to national identity say much about the group, its identity and perhaps its insecurity, but very little about how the group wishes to conduct itself in its affairs. Assuming, then, that the group is able to transcend the purely ethnic identity and rise to the civic, its ethnic quality reduces in significance until it is irrelevant. In principle, then, in a world comprised of civic nations, ethnic distinction becomes no more than an interesting qualitative marker of social being, rather than as a barrier to cross-state social and political interaction. Assuming this civic quality as a point of commonality, in a world based on agreed global values and global citizenship, the state ultimately becomes less important. Such civic cosmopolitanism can indeed be viewed as a higher level of political development.

However, in order to achieve this higher political level, nations must first feel they are able to be represented, and to represent themselves. The struggle for civic cosmopolitanism cannot proceed without first the emancipation of peoples at a more subordinate, national level. The problem is, though, that the enlightened self-interest of civic emancipation will always be beset by the narrower self-interest of the group (and the self-interested manipulation of that group), its perceptions dimmed by a fog of hazy group consciousness, and an insecurity that only finds comfort in the mob and, consequently, a mob mentality. The nation exists, therefore, as something primordial and perhaps which people still struggle to rise beyond, should they acknowledge its capacity for redundancy.

4 The state

As the primary site of political organization, the state is central to any set of ideas about political development. The "state" is generally understood as the spatially defined territory under a single political authority which claims the compliance of its citizens for its laws up to the extent of its sovereign boundaries. However, the state as it is commonly understood to function in the West does not necessarily apply in all circumstances; it has only recently existed, and is potentially not immune to further change.

In international relations theory, the state is the basic building block of contemporary understanding. In the "realist" school of theoretical thought, the state is both the final arbiter of the claims of its constituents and the principal determinant in global affairs. A competing "idealist" understanding allows citizens of the state to appeal beyond it, as well as positing supra-state bodies to shape its international responses. The idealist position is criticized by realists as not being pragmatic, ignoring the basic principles of *realpolitik* and failing in practise when international bodies attempt to intervene in state agendas. Similarly, the idealist position criticizes realism for both ignoring the increasing prevalence of global bodies and their capacity to intervene in intrastate and interstate affairs, the universalization of certain political values, such as democratization and civil and political rights, and the moral emptiness of a global political system based solely on naked power.

In reality, and somewhat like Weber's idealized characterization of political legitimacy, neither Realism nor Idealism can or do exist in a pristine sense. Realism often neglects the reality of rule-making and intervention by international bodies, the impact of global norms and the necessity for global cooperation, while Idealism often neglects what is sometimes the inapplicability or incapacity of global requirements and the frequent failures of interventions. That is, the world is a more complex and shifting place than either of these diametrically opposed positions would allow, and often both are combined in the same project (for example, United Nations (UN) intervention in East Timor, the "Coalition of the Willing" in Iraq, or the EU in Aceh, Indonesia). Similarly, the state is also battered by the exigencies of neo-liberalism and globalized capital (including lack of state capacity for restraining the free capital flow), as well as by global communications, culture and the acceptance, and occasional imposition or abrogation of global political norms, such as political and civil rights. Despite the battering that the state might have taken since what might be described as its hey-day in the inter-world war period, the state remains the primary site for political activity, the primary political actor and arbiter in internal and external affairs, the determinant of the value of citizenship and the primary, if not ideal location of the contest over notions of political development.

It is tempting to see the state as not just the primary site of political activity, but the cause of much or all of that activity negatively defined. Negatively, there is a strong anti-state undercurrent that informs ideas of political development, primarily through ideas of internationalization and what might be called civic cosmopolitanism. An anarchist (or original communist) perspective might also regard the state simply as the vehicle for the imposition of class power and a mechanism for levering economic exploitation by extra-state actors. However, and more positively, as a method of political organization, states do exist, will most probably assert their right to exist, continue to be the primary aspirational form for claims to self-determination and, even in an internationalized, civically cosmopolitan world, retain the capacity to represent interests based on the specific distinctions of geography, culture and material circumstance, as indeed do territories within federated structures, and local administrative structures within such territories. Even in the extension from the global to the local, the state occupies a mid-point, and while particular state forms may not be absolutely fixed, its location certainly is.

Ideas about the state

The state, as it is generally understood in the contemporary sense, refers to a specific and delineated area in which a government exercises (or claims to exercise) political and judicial authority[1] and claims a monopoly over the legitimate use of force. The state is not just defined by its territory, but the spatial quality of the state "is integral to its functions and agencies" (Smith 1986b: 235). That is, the area of the state defines the functional sovereign reach of its agencies; it defines the geographic material quality and quantity of the state, and is that which is marked on maps as defined borders. In the modern sense, the establishment of borders implies a state's complete authority up to the limits of its borders, although in more "traditional" (pre-colonial or pre-Westphalian) societies the borders and the extent and capacity of authority within state borders was more ambiguous. This conception of the "state" is distinct from that of the "nation," which, as noted in the preceding chapter, refers to a group of people who regard themselves as a bonded political community.

Within a given territory, the state can be identified by the presence and activities of its institutions, which define the functional capacity of the state. Strayer (1970) notes that the development of state institutions in medieval times formed the origins of the modern state. Such institutions have come to include the state bureaucracy, armed forces, educational institutions, state industries, the judiciary, police and penal systems. It should be noted, however, that while these are typical contemporary state institutions, the size and role of the state at the beginning of the twenty-first century was under challenge from competing ideological influences, world bodies such as the International Monetary Fund (IMF), the World Trade Organisation (WTO), and from an increasingly globalized economy. In particular, state industries and government bureaucratic services were sold in a number of states to private providers. The state, however, has generally retained legislative responsibility for these institutions.

There is, in state theory, no single idea of the state, although there are some general guidelines as to what can constitute a state. In the most simple, anthropological sense, the state could simply be a shared agreement among a group of people about the rules under which they jointly live (Krader 1976: Chapter 2; see also Gamble 1986; Crone 1986). However, this view of the state does not include the more "explicit, complex and formal" agencies of government, which are the usual markers of state existence (Krader 1976: 13). Indeed, this understanding of statehood probably bears a closer relationship to the idea of culture, as a shared world view or set of values, or nation, as a group of people who so identify themselves.

Another marker of the state is its internal integration, which tends to apply more to modern (fixed boundary, post-colonial) states than to pre-modern states in which issues of integration were less clear. A further characteristic of the state is the degree to which it is established and, similarly, the degree to which it can operate independently of external agencies. This idea of the "embeddedness" of the state refers to the degree to which the state is able to implement its programs and policies within its given territory (Evans 1995).

Most, though not all, states are marked by a type of "social contract," in which the ruler and the ruled agree to conditions of participation in the state. This implies a *modus vivendi* connected with a sense of mutual consent (Plamenatz 1968: Chapter 1) or mutual advantage (Rawls 1991: 4), but might in fact be a non-jural consideration. That is, being born into a particular state and with few options for change or flight from the state, participation in and effective acceptance of state rules might be a *fait accompli*. There are even states that have been referred to as "predatory," in which state elites prey on their constituent populations (for example, as discussed by Evans 1995: 12, 43–7). Morris has noted that strong authoritarian states in particular have a greater tendency to engage in harmful behavior towards their own citizens or to others, and that democratic states do not have a record of going to war with each other (Morris 1998: 14–19).[2] The implication of this is that where the power of the state is not in balance with a duty to its citizens, it can act in ways that are contrary to their interests. Such a balance between the state and its citizens is most recognizably achieved through the agencies of the state being accountable to the government, and the government in turn being accountable to its citizens.

The issue of how the state is conceived and the relationship between the state and territorial integrity raises the further issue of sovereignty. The term "sovereignty" or "sovereign" is generally used to denote the political independence of a state or state institution to act fully within its spatially defined area of authority. A "sovereign" power therefore does not share authority within its defined area, and resists attempts to do so. This might apply to the "sovereignty" of courts to decide legal matters (that is, to enjoy a "separation of powers" from the executive and legislature), or of the state to determine domestic matters within its territorial boundaries.

The population of a state is usually defined as its "citizens," a citizen being a member of a political community. A citizen is a state member who is entitled to such political and civil rights that exist within the state, and who owes an obligation of duty as defined by the state. Citizenship has been, since modern times, regarded as universally available for all legal, permanent inhabitants of a state.[3] However, in the past, citizenship was conferred to select members of the state based on wealth, gender or status.

Citizenship implies that citizens enjoy the protection of the laws of the state, and this tends to be in principle a universal quality (although it may not always be followed in practise). The idea of citizenship initially arose in Greek democratic city-states and was a defining feature of the Roman era. However, the idea of citizenship lapsed, only beginning its revival during the Renaissance and the reformulation of Italian city states (see, for example, Macchiavelli 1963: 18–19, 40–4) and, later, in England, as expressed by James Harrington and John Milton (see, for example, Harrington 1992; Daems and Nebo 2005), finding its fullest expression in the American Revolution (see Continental Congress, 2nd, 1776)[4] and the French Revolution (see, for example, Rousseau 1973, 1953: Book 12; Grimsley 1973: 89–119, Wright 1974: 58–61;[5] Paine 1969).

The modernist term "citizen" therefore applies to the individual constituent members of the state, and implies political rights and obligations. These include rights to participate in state affairs, and the obligation to protect the state in both external and internal attack. In certain circumstances, these may also include rights "from" the state, as well as a duty to the state. In this, the state is identified as the spatially and institutionally ordered manifestation of the public will (which is often bound up with the idea of "nation").

However, while this is a fairly conventional idea of citizenship, and within the context of the contemporary state could be said to apply as a first principle of statehood, in some political contexts citizens' rights do not necessarily apply. States do not always offer their protection; nor do they always regard citizens as having rights in relation to the state, while participation in state affairs can be quite circumscribed. However, duty to the state, including compliance with its laws, tends to be a given. Being a citizen more generally, if in a more limited way, implies being a constituent member of a state, being subject to its laws, the rights under which might vary considerably, despite the internationalization of first order human rights.

The idea of a "citizen" did not effectively apply in colonized territories until decolonization in the post-Second World War period, as a large proportion of colonized peoples were colonial subjects and not recognized as citizens as such. Prior to the colonial period, the conception upon which the state was based often granted little political status to those other than the ruling elites and their functionaries, and constituent members of the state often had similar utility value as livestock, or as manifestly lesser on a scale of human value. It was only with the establishment of the modern state in place of colonies, in particular with delineated borders and (at least theoretically) full and equal legal authority up to those borders, that citizenship became available and in principle applied to the occupants of new states.

Where states differ in their relationship with their citizens is in the level of political activity or participation they allow, with some states reducing citizenship to nominal legal status only. The critical problem with this is that without the capacity for effective political participation, there is little guarantee that political leaders will respect the laws under which the remaining qualities of citizenship are supposed to be protected.

A more extended or complete version of citizenship incorporates the active participation of citizens as members of civil society, or as active civic participants. The varied positioning of civil society actors in turns implies the necessary acceptance of a plurality of political and social views, which in turn demands at least tolerance and hopefully the application of mutual respect. Competing with this view, however, is a more communitarian perspective, which proposes the idea of a collective citizenship "public good" as a civic model in which individual rights do not displace wider social rights, and which therefore precede the idea of an individual "good." As discussed elsewhere, while the rights of individuals must be balanced against wider social interests (the rights of others as a collective of individuals), the diminution of individual rights necessarily limits the rights of the individual rights expressed in group form. Implicit in this diminution of individual rights is the reduction of pluralism and hence tolerance, mutual respect, and the maintenance of social harmony through the establishment of a highly structured "rule by law" rather than "rule of law." This then returns to the question of finding a balance between rights and responsibilities, or the status of the individual as opposed to the status of the individual primarily (or only) as a member of a corporate group, and the distinctions and correspondence between economic and political rights. This in turn identifies the redistribution/concentration and liberal/authoritarian ideological orientation of particular political decisions, as well as the method of their application. The status of the citizen thus goes to the heart of questions about political development.

The claimed sovereignty of the state became increasingly open to debate in the late twentieth century, challenged by a changing global reality (see Ba and Hoffman 2005; Mittelman and Othman 2001; Weber and Bierstaker 1996: 282; Hinsley 1978: 285–6; Camilleri 1994: 130–1; Camilleri and Falk 1992; Kearney 2001; Keohane 2002; Stiglitz 2003). For example, the UN, the IMF and the WTO, use degrees of compulsion in requiring sovereign states to bend to their expectations. This capacity can perhaps be seen as a parallel to the capacities of the state itself, where the state can use compulsion in relation to its citizens, usually with their consent in principle, while the UN, for example, can use compulsion in relation to its members, also usually with their consent in principle. "Consent in principle" implies that the rules consented to apply to all members in principle but may be applied in a way that might preclude consent in practise to specific members. Further, a global trend towards the removal of restrictions to trade and the related growth of global capital has removed from many states their capacity to make independent economic decisions. The Thai, Indonesian and Malaysian governments noted this loss of "economic sovereignty" during the regional economic crisis of 1997–8.

While no contemporary states seriously challenge the idea of fixed and clearly defined borders, many do disagree about where such borders should be or whether existing states do or do not contain embryonic states. Examples of embryonic states included East Timor (realized 1999), Aceh (set aside) and West Papua within Indonesia, the Karen and Kachin states of Burma, Bangsa Moro in the southern Philippines, Eritrea from Ethiopia (realized 1993), the Basque region of northern Spain, the Darfur region of Sudan, Western Sahara in Morocco, Xinjiang in China, and so on (see Fowler and Bunck 1995: 1–62). There have also been disputes about the exact location of borders between sovereign states, for example between Thailand and Laos, Thailand and Burma, Malaysia and the Philippines, and over sea-bed boundaries (for example in the South China Sea in the Spratley islands region). Border conflicts over disputed demarcation also test claims to territorial sovereignty, such as in the Kashmir-Jammu region of India, and over the status of Taiwan within China.

The state and government

The question of the relationship between the government and the state is critical in any understanding of state function. In principle, the state has an existence independent of the government and, with its other institutions, continues while governments come and go. However, the distinction between the state and the government was historically less clear. In pre-modern states, the capacity of a government or ruler created, maintained or expanded the state. While some states continued across generations of rulers, in other cases the loss of government or ruler meant that the state was potentially prey to the interests of other states or vulnerable to collapse due to a lack of internal cohesion.

A state within the contemporary political context can be determined as having a number of characteristics that define it. As outlined by Morris

(1998), the defining qualities of a state include the following: the state and its institutions must have an enduring quality, in particular being able to survive changes of government or political leadership. In this sense, the state must also transcend both the rulers and the ruled, while the institutions of the state must be able to continue regardless of political change. These institutions must be differentiated from other non-state institutions or agents, and, if the state is to function with a moderate degree of efficiency, be coordinated with each other. The state must therefore also correspond to a clearly defined territory, so that its sovereignty is identifiable and its application specifically enforceable. Within that territory, the agents of the state must have full and equally distributed authority. The territory of the state must be sovereign, in that the state can legitimately dissuade external parties from entering the state without authorization or otherwise threatening the state. The state will also claim a monopoly on the use of force within its territory, and jurisdiction for the use of force as well as other functional criteria, must extend to the full extent of the territory of the state. As noted, the legitimacy of the state and its right to claim a monopoly on the use of force (or compulsion) should preferably be consented to and must be adhered to by members of the state, and in that the state is the ultimate authority (Morris 1998: 45–6; see also Laski 1934: 21–4). This adherence should be in the form of allegiance to the state, superseding all other allegiances. To ensure this allegiance, the state should function to protect and promote the interests of its members. However, as discussed, in some circumstances it can be claimed that the state does not do this, but that it still claims adherence to its right to the monopoly of force. In such circumstances the legitimacy of the state can be challenged, although invariably in doing so having to confront state authority.

In any discussion about institutions of state, the structural and organizational role of the state itself is paramount, as both the vehicle for the institutions and as an institution itself. There are two subsequent issues to be considered. The first is the nature of the state and its ideological orientation. The second is whether the state (and its representatives) sees itself as manifesting and existing to facilitate the wishes of its citizens, or whether the state exists in its own right and sees its citizens' primary purpose as subservient to the state.

In conventional terms, the state is considered to have an organizational structure that may be either centrally focused or operate within a federal structure to cover a territorially demarcated area, over which it exercises authority. The model of federal structures tends to apply best to physically or ethnically disparate states, or states that have come together as a composition of pre-existing states or territories and where local polities already exist. A federated or diffuse political structure tends to be more suitable for such constructs, although unitary (centralized) models are often imposed (and sometimes resisted) by way of asserting an otherwise uncertain sense of national unity.

One "zero-sum" view of state capacity, especially in relation to politically fragmented societies, is that state capacity tends to rise when social resistance declines or, similarly, that state capacity tends to rise by compelling a decline in social resistance. This implies that state and social resistance are oppositional, and the strength of one necessarily implies a weakening of the other. Another, related view is that high social resistance to state authority reflects a failure of political institutions to adequately address social claims which, in turn, indicates that state institutions are failing to function according to social needs and, as such, are in danger of losing their legitimacy (see Miller 2006 for discussion of state capacity relative to social capacity). However, a further view is that it is possible to have a high level of state capacity, understood as the embeddedness of institutions and their autonomy from sectional interests (Evans 1995) *and* a high level of social capacity, understood in this sense as strong civil society which is able to constructively engage with the strong state. A further alternative view is that state legitimacy is actually enhanced by a capacity for social resistance; that social resistance to the impositions or depredations, of the state is a legitimate function of citizenry. Implicit in this view is that the citizenry in itself constitutes an "institution," the institution of civil society.

The state and its citizens

The debate over the role and features of the state *vis-à-vis* its citizens and the balance of power between them has been a central feature of political debate in the modern era.[6] One interpretation of this debate is that the state and its institutions are the ideal manifestation of the social capacity for freedom, that freedom is best and perhaps only realized through citizens' membership of the rational, ethical state (Hegel 1967: 155–8). Conversely, Sen's view would be that it is the function and obligation of the state, as the guarantor of development, to manifest freedom. Hegel's view, although carefully nuanced and contextualized, represents a preference for communitarianism, in which the ethical "good" of the whole is greater than the claim of the individual (1967: 157). Hegel carefully constructed his rational state as a constitutional monarchy prefiguring common modernist lines, with a bicameral parliament and powerful state bureaucracy that included checks and balances. Hegel claimed an underdeveloped intellectual basis for the citizenry which precluded their meaningful participation in decision making. This claim presumed knowledge of what comprised sufficient intellectual capacity to vote, who has it, and whether or not formal markers of intellectual capacity, such as education, are determinants of political awareness. Assuming such knowledge, Hegel opposed open legislative elections on the basis of the intellectual underdevelopment of the masses, although allowed for the channeling of popular views via deputies to the lower house of the legislature. Looking back to Plato (1955: Part VII), with a passing nod to Hobbes' more starkly functionalist understanding of humanity (1962: Part I) and unyielding

authority of the sovereign (1962: 248), and forward to bureaucratic tech-
nocracy (for example, see Ellul 1964), Hegel also proposed that those with the
greatest knowledge or skill should, trained in "the universal" (or "objective"
good), occupy positions of greatest authority.

Assuming all social needs are met within a system such as Plato's *Republic*
and to some extent Hobbes' *Leviathan*, Hegel's ideal state appears to fulfill
many of the requirements of an ethical, functional political society and
hence fulfills some of the criteria of political development. The difficulty
with Hegel's system, however, is that it is idealistic in that it assumes a
"universal" good. Hegel's approach is also transitional in that it limits popular
participation and ascribes ultimate authority to the monarch in an essentially
top-down, functionally absolute political structure. In this sense, it fundamentally compromises and acts as a brake on notions of political development. Further, as an "ideal" communitarian system that relies on a benign
universal value system, it is not only easy to subvert to specific political
interests in the name of "rationality," but also establishes a foundation for
privileging some systemic aspects, such as top-down authority or bureaucratic exceptionalism. As such, rules are created in the name of efficiency
to the advantage of bureaucracies over the people they are supposed to
serve, placing restrictions on things such as differentiated interest, political
participation, a more thorough form of political representation, transparency
and accountability. Reduced from such an ideal form, Hegel's political
philosophy became the intellectual basis for both Fascism and Nazism, which
paralleled Hegel's spiritualism, emphasis on the state and the subsuming of
the individual to the greater social will (see Oakshott 1939). It also became
the basis of Leninist communism which, through "professional revolutionaries" or the "vanguard of the proletariat" (see Lenin 1961: 347–528),[7] subverted
Marx's inversion of Hegel's philosophy by proposing the masses take political
control (see Marx and Engels 1969: 43–5; Marx 1959, 1970). Perhaps the key
distinction between Fascism and "communism" as they have been practiced is
that Fascism and its variants have been based on an extremist vertical nationalist identity and were essentially anti-rational (Heywood 2003: 218). By
contrast, Marxism is based on horizontal or class interest and could therefore
be argued to be "rational," especially if accepted in its "scientific" sense (for the
classic exposition, see Engels 1989). Fascism and its variants have directly or
indirectly been reflected in a number of military-dominated states seeking
"order," including Burma and New Order Indonesia, as well as several Latin
American states at different times. Leninism has influenced or dominated a
number of (especially post-colonial) states seeking an explanatory model,
revolutionary ethos and political method. In this "order," military intervention in politics defaults to a Hegelian-type position in that militaries are
highly structured, top-down hierarchies, in which the capacity of individuals
is realized through subordination to the collective, expressed as *esprit de
corps* or other such collectivist military codes (de Tocqueville's "inherent evil"
2003: Book 2, Chapter 22). Leninist imposition implies an over-bureaucratic

"polar night of icy darkness" (Weber 1948: 128), in which the revolutionary elite assumes its own greater wisdom and absolute authority, any questioning of which posits the questioner as an "enemy of the people," the will of the "people" being conflated with the perspectives and interests of the revolutionary elite.

At this point, each having departed from a common point in opposite directions, these models describe an arc where the domination of the state reaches a common point. Here these seemingly opposite ideologies cohere around the idea of absolute authority. This usually manifested in the person of the leader although with a coterie of administrative retainers, and in the singularity of the state. In that this absolute authority of the state confers capacity, it creates a "strong state," which may otherwise mean a state with a high degree of capacity as well as tolerance (a benign state) but which more commonly implies a high level of (often malign) authority to impose order, in contrast to a poorly organized or otherwise weak civil society (see Dauvergne 1998; Migdal 1994; Kohli and Shue 1994).

There are a number of ways of measuring modern state capacity, with one view, applying in particular to developing countries or countries where state capacity is less effective. This is where the relative compliance of a citizenry to government goals and objectives varies according to the capacity of the state to achieve compliance, which in turn reflects the state manifesting the wishes of its citizens, or compelling its citizens to accept its own determinations, or a mixture of the two. Legitimacy in this context, then, denotes a citizenry's relative acceptance of the conventional capacities of the state, including its provision of the institutional context for government, the capacity for that government to exercise authority, and for the state to hold the monopoly on the use of force within its borders. Assuming a normative correspondence between the function of the state and the interests (expressed as wishes) of its citizens, the greater the correspondence between the two then the greater the internally (and usually internationally) recognized legitimacy of the state.[8]

In an ideal sense, the state claims to exist as the pure embodiment of the will of its citizens; hence, all citizens should willingly subscribe to its dictates. This in turn implies a unity of thought among the citizens, usually around some idea of an idealized political community. This is usually identified as a form of "organicism," in which the "people" are as one in an idealized sense. That is, the "nation" (the commonly conceptualized political community) is viewed as at one with and manifested in the state, with the idea of "nation" often being constructed as both static and exclusive. In such an approximation, the state identifies itself as the "nation-state," and its political claimants refer to it as such in a usually uncritical and non-reflective manner, as though the nation-state was both the norm and the universal. Depending on definitions of "nation" and regardless of their actual claims, a minority of states can also meaningfully claim singular national status. Where nations claim self-determination as being legitimately manifested in the institution of the state, and where there are no meaningful competing claims within the territorial boundaries of the state a nation-state can be said to exist.[9] Similarly, where a national identity has cohered around common core civic values as represented by the institution of the state, there can also be reasonably said to be a nation-state. In circumstances where neither of these two criteria exist, a nation-state cannot be said to exist.

The most notorious application of the idea of the state being the sole legitimate representative of the nation was in Nazi Germany, although such an idea also found favor in the 1930s and 1940s in Italy, Spain, Portugal, Japan and, more recently, in some post-colonial states including Indonesia, Burma and other states attempting to construct "national" unity out of diverse groups. In cases where there are self-conceptualizing and largely exclusive political communities ("nations") within the state, tensions may arise between the interests of such political communities and the interests that are asserted on behalf of the state. Such tensions arise in particular where there are claims to separate state status by political communities, which claim national self-determination. This is where the state is seen to be the logical manifestation of the nation as a functional political community within a given territory. However, it is possible for multi-national or multi-ethnic states to function with a relatively high degree of internal political harmony if they are able to fairly balance the claims of their constituent groups and recognize the value of group members as more or less equal in terms of civic status and material opportunity. This most commonly arises in states comprised wholly or largely of immigrant communities and their descendents, in which few can claim "original" status.

Similarly, if ethnicity reflects a primordial interest and should be accommodated to ensure a functional, viable state, then other interests should similarly be accommodated such as between specific interest groups. That is to say, common recognition of a plurality of interests and the accommodation of the most basic requirements of these interests are necessary to ensure a successful, cohesive state (see Aristotle 1905: Book 2). There will necessarily be specific points around which agreement cannot be reached, but if these can be accommodated within a broader framework of agreement, with each interest being represented according to popular preference, then the state can coexist within itself. To illustrate, a society might be divided over whether there is one official language or two, but agrees on the framework within which to make decisions about such issues. However, if a basic common interest is precluded – that is, if there is no overarching framework – this necessarily establishes grievance and friction, and potentially discord and conflict.

The common problem with ethnic separateness within state borders is that where there is political organization, it tends to cohere around ethnic identity and thus cause vertical political fault lines. Where political identity is constructed on the basis of ethnicity (and usually patronage), and where such communities live in concentrations of like people, the wider state-related sense of "nation" is challenged, implying the potential for localized nationalist assertions in relation to the relevant territory. That is, a particular ethnic group that identifies itself first and foremost in common in relation to a given territory could potentially establish a claim to that territory based on its ethnic specificity.

The implications of ethnic political organization rather than political organization around economic or other interests is that motivating factors have generally been reflected in systems of patronage and personal rule, embodying "national" sentiment, rather than leadership on the basis of accountability and transparency. In multi-ethnic states, in particular post-colonial states (for example in sub-Saharan Africa), this has led to the formation of political parties that reflect ethnic rather than economic coherence. Where one ethnic group is dominant, this often leads to specific ethnic domination of state institutions to the detriment of minority communities. However, multi-ethnic states are not exclusive to Africa, and can be found in most post-colonial environments.

An illustration of this broad problem is in Sri Lanka, where the majority Sinhalese ethnic group has dominated government and state institutions, and where government policy on issues such as language has discriminated against the Tamil minority. Seeking redress, and in response to inter-ethnic conflict, Tamils formed separatist organizations, the most dominant being the Liberation Tigers of Tamil Eelam, which seeks to establish a new, breakaway state (see Phadnis, in Diamond *et al.* 1989a). From 2002, a de facto separate Tamil state existed as a manifestation of Tamil's claims to self-determination. Its future, however, was uncertain, given that the government of Sri Lanka continued to assert the primacy of the unitary state and appeared unwilling to countenance a compromise such as confederation (a federation with a less dominant central structure). A similar claim to separate statehood also existed in the Indonesian province of Aceh, which was resolved with an agreement to grant functional self-government (except in areas reserved to the Republic of Indonesia), despite Indonesia also having a unitary constitution.

Further problems of multi-ethnicity have also been key issues in Iraq, many of the post-Soviet states (with large Russian and other ethnic populations), and in countries such as Burma, the Philippines and Thailand, where claims to localized self-determination have continued. Conceptions of self-determination based on ethnic identity are often put as rationale for the establishment of new states. However, such claims face three key problems. The first problem is that the originating state is rarely willing to allow its unity to be challenged and its territorial sovereignty to be reduced. As Packer notes, claims to territorial sovereignty are intended to apply to the status of a state in relation to other, external states and not in relation to claims by a state's own citizens. But states generally do not regard separatism with equanimity, and are usually hostile to such claims. Further, while claims to national self-determination may be supported in principle in international law and appear to reflect the claims of civil and political rights, they are not specifically supported. There is no international legal mechanism for redress of separatist claims, and if there was it would probably have little binding capacity given the relative weakness of international political institutions (for example, the UN) when compared to the power of states (see Packer 1998, 1999, 2000a, 2000b).

Models of the state

In the post-Second World War period there has been a general acceptance in principle of the idea of separation between the government and the state (see Morris 1998: 21–2). However, the practise has in some cases been different. In part, this has been a consequence of the role played by certain agents, especially armies, but also by political parties or individuals, in the creation of the state. There has also been a tendency in post-colonial states to draw on or re-invent pre-colonial traditions that characterize the state as being embodied within the army, the party or the person of the political leader. The distinction between the army and the state in Burma, for example, is effectively non-existent, while the separation of the party and the state in Vietnam or Laos is similarly difficult to discern. In Indonesia under Sukarno's Guided Democracy and Suharto's New Order, and to a lesser extent in Singapore under Lee Kuan Yew, the state has been reflected in the person of the president or the prime minister. In recent cases where the state has been reflected in the person of the leader, the state has shown itself to be greater and more permanent than the leader. However, in each case the independence of state functions, especially the judiciary and the electoral system, has been seriously compromised.

The idea of the state with clearly delineated borders and sovereign authority within those territories is relatively new. This idea was only initiated in Europe at the time of the Treaty of Westphalia in 1648, which oversaw the diminution of authority of the Holy Roman Empire, and it only assumed the nation-state sense from the early nineteenth century. As an idea, state borders are still disputed in areas where the authority of the state is challenged by assertions of the nation. The most obvious examples of this are the former USSR, Yugoslavia, Czechoslovakia and Iraq, and, to a lesser extent, in Belgium, Italy (see Putnam 1993: Chapter 2) and Canada. Indonesia, Burma, the Philippines, Thailand and Morocco have all had localized "nationalist" rebellions against the spatial-functionalist claims of the state. In spite of protests against incorporation into established states, these rebellions have not opposed the idea of the state as such and, indeed, have aimed to create their own new states. As a borrowed, if useful, model then, the modern idea of the state is uniformly accepted by governments and other political movements, regardless of their post-colonial or other status.

Most developing states were at one stage colonies. Hence, the physical characteristics of many developing states were defined not so much by geography or national cohesion, as they tended to be in more developed Western countries, but by the methods and requirements of colonial powers. Further, most of these states had their traditional or indigenous models of political authority dismantled or emasculated, which required the establishment of new forms of state authority, in some cases drawing on reconstituted, reified or blended "traditional" models, as well as variations of models encouraged or imposed by former colonial powers.

Prior to colonialism or the Treaty of Westphalia in Europe, there were few states that had clearly delineated borders or which ruled with any permanent authority over their outer regions. Almost by definition, pre-colonial/pre-Westphalian states were in a constant state of expansion or retraction, with all, or almost all, authority located at what was often seen as an "exemplary center." In an idealized condition, it was from this center that a monarch ruled, his authority radiating outwards. Acknowledged in practise but less so in rhetoric, that power receded the further it traveled from that expemplary center. At or near the center, authority was greatest, while at the periphery it was dispersed, often through local rulers of increasing independence (Tambiah 1976: 114; see also McCloud 1995: 93–7) and increasingly doubtful loyalty, until the power of the center ceased to exist. At this point the authority from another center would begin to resonate. Where two centers of authority came into contact, other than through truces, suzerainty or marriages of convenience, conflict was almost inevitable. A state that could not maintain or continue to expand its authority was by definition in decline and, given the quasi-magical or metaphysical qualities associated with a ruler's power, once that loss of power was manifest, decline was inevitable. Without wishing to overstate the point, aspects of this model continued to be reflected in the post-colonial period in states that often relied heavily on the authority of an individual ruler and thus concentrated state power within themselves.

A further elaboration of this idea is that with the power of the pre-colonial state strengthening towards the center, the highest source of authority within the state was the individual who resided at its center: the monarch (or absolute ruler). Through patronage, as opposed to bureaucracy or feudal obligation, the monarch dispensed favor or otherwise balanced competing forces within his or her sphere. In a practical sense, the monarch might also have been required to enter into arrangements with other powerful individuals, or sub-states, diminishing the purity of this centralizing model. However, there remains not just a parallel but also a direct relationship between the central patrimonial system of monarchy and the notion of a centralized state. The centralization of power and distribution of patronage continue to be hallmarks of political models throughout post-colonial and developing countries, and elements can also be found among a number of less organized "developed" countries.

This idea of state organization has, in an Asian context, been referred to as a mandala, the Buddhist model of the universe in which all matters radiate from and revolve around the discussed exemplary center (Wolters 1999; Stuart-Fox 1997: 2–4; Moertono 1981: 71, nb207; Wilson 1969: 7). In its original cosmic sense, the mandala was intended to be a metaphorical rather than literal interpretation of the universe. It reflected a desire for order and balance as much as it did a method of explanation. Particular models of mandalas, like other forms of cultural expression, varied from one cultural environment to another, and, while retaining the same basic characteristics, said as much about their makers as about the thing they were supposed to represent. The idea of the mandala as a political model derives from India and has been used to describe the construction of early Buddhist and Hindu states. However, a similar model for political authority applied to China and the states it directly influenced, including Korea, Vietnam, and Japan as well as its own western provinces. It has also been suggested that the mandala political forms which, until the period of colonization, dominated much of Asia were in fact similar to those which had dominated Europe until the end of the Middle Ages or later (Steadman 1969: 26–7). In this respect, these mandala states reflected a particular stage of economic and related political development. A parallel idea of the mandala, that the universe revolved around the earth (and that the state was centered on the court), was dominant in Europe until at least the mid-seventeenth century. Weber discussed a similar idea in his model of "patrimonial-prebendal" states, in which the ruler dispensed with patronage and ensured loyalty from a central point (Weber 1958, 1968; see also Bakker and Ferrazzi 1997). In that sense, as is often the case, the idea of the mandala reflected and rationalized a pre-existing state of affairs or corresponding world view, rather than helped to shape them. As Kevin Hewison (2006: Chapter 1) has noted, however, the use of the term "mandala" can also be seen as deterministic, setting up a fixed view of political relations that was both differentiated and variable.

Wolters (1999) and Stuart-Fox (1999, personal communication) have suggested a distinction between traditional, pre-colonial or pre-Westphalian states as mandala (or non-bounded states) and imperium. An imperium is regarded as being relatively static and hence does not exhibit the expansion and contraction of a classic mandala (Wolters 1999: 144). Further, an imperium has more clearly defined boundaries and its authority is complete up to that clearly defined boundary. Wolters has also claimed that hereditary forms of government that reflect dynastic succession are not in keeping with a mandalic rise and fall of individual rulers in that they retain a constant political focus (in this case, Vietnam, on Hanoi) (see 1999: 143–54). The idea of an imperium, therefore suggests immutability. However, like most political models, the idea of an imperium (or a mandala) are somewhat like Weber's types of power, being idealized, with the reality being a variation on a diluted or combined form of the two models.

Empires

In so far as the above discussion can be applied as a model for pre-colonial or pre-Westphalian states, it can also be used for pre-colonial or pre-Westphalian (traditional) empires (super-states). The empire is but an extension of central authority: in the traditional format the greater the power of the central authority, the greater its reach. Within a single linguistic or cultural group the reach of central authority can be regarded as encompassing the state as a nation (see Motyl 2001: 13–36). However, once the state uses force to encompass other linguistic or cultural groups – other nations of peoples – it becomes an empire. Traditionally, empires encompassing diverse nations of peoples were not only common but were seen as a logical, perhaps necessary, extension of the successful state. But in the modern (or post-colonial) period, empires in the classical sense are almost universally regarded as illegitimate, and the term "imperialism" has found its most common expression as a pejorative term in colonial and post-colonial discourse.

Characteristics of empires have been various, but the above-noted central authority is a commonality. This did not preclude, however, a significant degree of local decision making on the part of officials recognized by the central authority, and some empires brought benefits as well as costs to their colonized peoples, including technology transfer, greater trade opportunities and in some cases greater literacy and communications skills. Empires have also been characterized, however, by allegiance and tax or tribute to the central authority, the presence of members of the imperial population and the presence of soldiers or other enforcers of central political will.

In that empires can be said to have had a "golden era," it was arguably from the late eighteenth century until the period just prior to the Great War (First World War), during which time European states competed to establish colonies that were primarily exploited for the economic benefit of the colonizing state, as well as establishing their own proximate empires (for example, the Austro-Hungarian and Russian Empires). There was some colonial expansion in the post-First World War period, primarily by Japan and Italy, and also Germany's expansionist policies in this period, especially for *lebensraum* ("living space")[10] which could be characterized as such. In the post-Second World War era, empires were generally regarded as either having dissolved or being in the process of dissolving, with the major imperial powers decolonizing willingly (for example, the UK and eventually Portugal) or, in some cases (such as France and the Netherlands), unwillingly. The Soviet Union was also characterized by some as an empire, in part because of its imposing character but, more accurately, because it was largely the successor state to the Russian Empire and included a number of states that were clearly identified as such (for example, in Soviet Central Asia). However, two issues arise from the legacy of empires and the decolonization process; the geographic quality of decolonized or successor states, and the continuation of empires as states.

There are two common claims among post-colonial states to justify their contemporary borders. The first is that the post-colonial state should generally equate to the territory occupied by the colonial power (see Clapham 2001; Marker 2003). However, this common claim has been as much in breech as in observance. British colonial occupation or mandated authority of contiguous territories from Egypt to South Africa ("Cape Town to Cairo") in the immediate post-First World War period, subsequently divided into 12 distinct political entities. Similarly, Latin America was largely (with the major exception of Brazil) occupied by Spain, but divided into 18 separate political entities, Indochina under the French, claimed as seven political entities, divided into three, while the Indian sub-continent under British rule divided into five (later six). Hence, claims to the legitimacy of the state being based on former colonial borders seem to be at odds with the experience. The second claim is to self-determination by "nations" that continue to embrace a separate pre-colonial identity from the states into which they have been incorporated. This claim raises the issue of whether, assuming the legitimacy of that claim, the states into which they have been subsumed equate with empires.

The general claim put by Burma is a case in point. The contemporary state of Burma (or Myanmar, according to its unelected government), comprises territories that are recognized as "divisions" most of which are based on earlier states. Historically, these states have from time to time been under the political sway of a central Burmese authority, but in an imperial (or mandalic) relationship. Under Chapter 10 of the Burmese constitution, *Burma pyinay* (subordinate Burma, formerly known as "frontier territories") were to be given the option of independent separation from the central state (*Burma pyima* – Burma proper) in 1958. However, based on a clear pre-existing wish to separate through open rebellion, the central government disallowed this constitutional provision and the state has since then exhibited many of the characteristics of the pre-colonial Burmese empire (Htin 1967).

Having less pre-colonial claim than Burma to the territory it now occupies, but basing its claim on colonial boundaries, Indonesia also tests the definitions of "post-colonial empire," bringing as it does numerous language and cultural groups from non-contiguous territories under a single – and unitary – political authority. Despite its disparate pre-colonial history, Indonesia has never held a ballot on voluntary inclusion of territories within the state and has used military force on a number of occasions to compel reluctant regions to stay within the state. If Indonesia does lay one claim to pre-colonial unity by which to buttress its post-colonial reach, it is through its primary school texts which present somewhat overstated claims to the thirteenth century Majapahit Empire, which is said to have had suzerain relations with most of the territory now occupied by the state. However, regardless of the validity of the extent and character of Majapahit's reach it was, *prima facie*, an empire, and the legitimacy of its claim is akin to that of the Holy Roman or Austro-Hungarian Empires of Europe.

As noted by the Melbourne consul-general for Indonesia (Supriyadi 2006) during a debate over the status of West Papua in Indonesia, the claims of multi-national or multi-ethnic post-colonial states rely on the principle of *uti possidetis juris* ("possessed by law") under which their boundaries are fixed at the time of their gaining independence. This was the conventional claim in Latin America (originating in the 1820s) and has also been used in Africa and Asia, although with dispute about the legitimacy and accuracy of colonial boundaries. However, in the case of Indonesia, its claim to West Papua may have existed in 1949 (as indeed did a claim in 1945 to what is now Malaysia and the Philippines), but Indonesia did not reach agreement to occupy the territory until 1962 (effected in 1963, formalized in 1969). That is to say, the claim of *uti possidetis juris* is posited primarily as a defense of the status quo – legal possession – but which in this case is actually *uti possidetis de facto* – possession in fact. In this case, the legality turns on the UN's acceptance of what is widely regarded as a sham vote by a little over 1,000 Papuan tribal leaders for incorporation into Indonesia, and that fact turns on the stationing of the largest per capita military and police presence in the country. Technical legality and fact of occupation, however, do not address the question of a genuine expression of self-determination.

Within states, often quite distinct ethnic groups can be amalgamated or brought together under a single political structure, usually under the tutelage of a dominant ethnic group that controls the administrative and military mechanisms. Faced with competing historical interests, conceptions of national or tribal identity and a requirement to forge a unified state which more or less complies with contemporary requirements to be self-administering, viable and independent, post-colonial states often draw on their respective local histories and political styles as well as many of the organizing principles of government derived from the West. Just as many newer states have sought to model themselves on the relatively recent European idea of a delineated sovereign territory, they have often also sought to implement political institutions that correspond to administering that territory. This has become especially important to those states that have engaged in increasingly complex interstate relations, including trade and diplomacy, which, within the modern context, traditional political forms are unable to adequately provide for.

This form of political organization then implies a government which is normatively capable of exercising full sovereignty to the limits of its borders (Morris 1998: 21) and which acknowledges citizenship of the permanent residents within those borders, as well as having independence from external powers (Morris 1998: 174). In a formal sense, sovereignty is, or should be, absolute, inalienable and indivisible (Morris 1998: 178), at least by external powers. Sovereignty can be limited, however, when governments are constitutionally deprived of certain juridical powers (for example, making state religion) (Morris 1998: 205).

Federalism

In response to internally competing claims over territorial authority and overarching commonalities that are still divided by local specificities, the idea of federating or confederating groups of otherwise autonomous states or regions has become a common solution. At the time of writing, there were around 21 federated states with a total of around two billion people, or 40 per cent of the earth's population. While there is no necessary link between federalism and democratization, federalist solutions have been adopted in a number of cases to encourage or enhance democratic participation, primarily by ensuring that local people have greater access to participation in local matters. This is especially relevant in states comprised of distinct pre-colonial polities or states, or where otherwise geographically specific ethnic minorities mean that claims to separate statehood are unsustainable. Under such conditions, inclusion in a unitary state is likely to see specific minority interests subsumed into a broader interest claim. For example, this could be through the imposition of ethnic majority cultural hegemony over the issue of language, which constitutes a limitation on substantive democratic practise. Hence, the devolution of political authority, or the combination of political authorities under a differentiated structure, is widely seen as an appropriate state response (see Kaldor 2004). In this respect, federation or autonomy has contributed to greater democratic participation, for example, in states such as Argentina, Brazil, Venezuela and Spain.

It would appear that most claims to self-government, self-determination or separation from states succeed or fail based on the relative capacity of the state to compel a particular outcome, through economic, military, or political means. The case of "self-government" for Aceh in Indonesia, as a resolution to an almost three-decade old claim for independence, is a case in point and reflected in large part the incapacity of government forces to militarily defeat the separatist Free Acheh Movement (*Gerakan Acheh Merdeka* – GAM) and for GAM to expel government forces, the high economic cost to the government of sustaining the conflict (including direct cost, corruption and lack of foreign investment), and a stated requirement to bring the military under full government authority. That is, GAM had some capacity to force concessions from the government, if not enough to claim full independence.

During the Helsinki peace talks aimed at achieving a settlement to the conflict in Aceh, representatives from both the Government of Indonesia and the GAM agreed not to use the terms "autonomy" and "federalism," which might otherwise be thought of as central to any negotiated position between absolute unity and absolute separation. "Autonomy" was unacceptable to GAM because it denoted the status quo, while "federalism" posed a direct challenge to the unitary construction of the Indonesian state. The ideas that inform both terms, however, were manifested in the peace agreement signed on 15 August 2005. In a country in which political appearances are often more important than reality, what is said in Indonesia does not necessarily correspond to what exists.

Broadly, federalism (or confederation) is held to be the most appropriate model for polities in which there is a relatively high degree of pre-established local political identity, but also a wider developing political commonality.

Indonesia spans eight major island groups (and some 13,000 inhabited islands), with more than a dozen major languages and 350 or so minor ones. Its main point of commonality was its colonial history. Although appearing as an ideal candidate for federalism and starting that way in 1949, in 1950 Indonesia was reconstrued as a unitary state. In this, Indonesia was recast not just as a unitary state but, in a sense, reflecting claims to the existence of the Majaphait empire. But there is little room in empire for a relationship between equals.

But reverting to a federal structure would require most of Indonesia's provinces to press for a new political arrangement, based on concessions to claims of devolution or separatism. Such claims are heard in Indonesia, but rarely with much conviction and even more rarely with any capacity, relative to a military that insists on the state's unitary structure.

The idea of the state, then, is not immutable. Localisms challenge existing states from within, while global tendencies challenge them from without. Even the management of states can present a challenge to their cohesion, while many states only partially fulfill the requirement regarded by Morris as standard for their legitimate claim to existence. Yet each state continues to assert itself, assuming in some cases an existence beyond that of the group or area it claims to represent. In this assertion of statehood, there is a morphing of the institutions of state with the state itself, and the role and ideology of government as defining the style and scope of the state. States may reflect older conceptions of statehood, or more universalist ones. There was little guarantee that the states that existed at the beginning of the twenty-first century, or even what was understood to be meant by the term "state," would continue in the same precise form indefinitely. The idea of the "state" has been fulsomely adopted throughout the world but, like other political forms, how it has been and would continue to be interpreted has been shaped by local desires, values, requirements, and impositions.

5 Civil and political rights

The link between political development and civil and political rights is a basic one. At one level the presence of and respect for civil and political rights indicates that the political community in which they exist also respects its citizens as valued members of political society who should be free to participate in political life and who should not be restricted from political participation. This society also offers certain guarantees to its citizens, especially in relation to the application of law. Similarly, if the application of democratic principles is understood as a political "good," then civil and political rights are fundamental to the application of that good and in a number of respects comprise part of it. At another and somewhat more complex level, in that a political community in which such rights exist acknowledges and supports them, its society has probably engaged in discussion and debate around their value and necessity and, through a rational process, has concluded that such rights should exist. That is to say, the political society in question has engaged in and advanced its own thinking about difficult if also fundamental political issues, concluded that the application of civil and political rights is appropriate to its own citizens, and in principle to all others. Both of these exercises are themselves significant markers of political development.

In relation to democracy and processes of democratization, recognition and acceptance of civil and political rights are perhaps the key marker of liberalization, and demonstrate the extent to which transition from an authoritarian or non-democratic regime has taken place. It is possible to respect civil and political rights under an authoritarian or non-democratic regime. But to do so, such a regime would necessarily be benign to the point that it could potentially comply with the will of the majority and would in any case be highly unlikely. Beyond this, conceptions of civil and political rights are a reliable marker of the extent of consolidation of democracy via the necessity of their application to allow basic democratic conditions. In that there can be claimed a standardized understanding of the meaning of "democracy" and that variations of it do not undermine its key principles, democracy can be said to have a potentially universal quality. That is, democracy might not obtain universally or be universally the same in its application, but its key principles are universal. Otherwise, it is not democracy in any meaningful sense of the term.

Assuming a high degree of potential capacity for political activity in any system that claims for itself the title of "democracy," the prevalence of political and civil rights are both the method and guarantee of such potential activity. The "positive rights" of freedom of speech, communication and assembly are fundamental to political organization and the development of and contest between political ideas, which in turn provide the basic building blocks of a democratic society. Similarly, the "negative" freedoms from arbitrary arrest, detention and torture are the means by which, having exercised "positive rights," political participants are not intimidated or otherwise restricted from continuing such activity.

Commonality

Contrary to some claims, conceptions of human rights (of which civil and political rights are seen as the "first generation")[1] are neither culturally specific nor especially recent. Moreover, while the codification of human rights ensures there is a specific set of criteria by which they can be measured and applied, human rights do not necessarily rely on codification in order to retain validity. The conception of "natural rights" applies here, parallel to natural law (for example, see Hobbes 1962; Locke 1960; Rousseau 1973), as those rights which pertain in a range of circumstances in which each are interpretations of the same or a similar original first principle. Such rights are claimed to exist as a consequence of freedom in a state of nature, which implies a natural moral order under God, whose human creations are equal in a state of nature, as the application to others of self-regard (moral coherence and consistency) or, most forcefully and without reference to God, as a practical consequence of human reason which implies a capacity for ethical reason (for example, see Kant 1997).

The earliest debates about or claims to human rights were not codified, and where codification began to exist, it often did so in an indirect or incompletely articulated sense. Religion was a principle area in which conceptions of rights were largely indirectly codified, but which categorically required adherence to particular responsibilities. This in turn implied rights for others, as did some of the earlier formalized philosophies. The Decalogue (20: 1–21) of the Bible and the Torah, for example, imply the right to protection from arbitrary killing, adultery, theft or defamation, while Exodus requires justice (22–26) and fairness (22: 20–27, 23: 6–7), as does Levicticus (19: 13–19, 33–37). Buddhism requires good works for others, with the Bodhisattva (person who has attained living Buddhahood) being infinitely compassionate, while those striving for such attainment do so through earning "merit" or good deeds. According to the Qur'an, Islam requires its followers to show mercy, undertake good deeds, respect the rule of law and place limitations on warfare. In less metaphysical terms, the Greek Stoic philosophers Epictectus and Hierapolis promoted the idea of "universal brotherhood," which implies equality of treatment among humankind. Socrates similarly advocated a common good, Plato promoted justice (1955: V) and democracy, which in a way that echoes to this day he defined as liberty and equality (IX: 6), while Aristotle promoted the "virtuous mean" (1953: IV). In *Antigone*, Sophocles (1947) advanced the idea of a "right," while Cicero promoted the conception of the citizens' republic and rule of law (1998). Further afield, Confucius' Analects arguably oppose the claims made for them by apologists for contemporary authoritarian governments (see Leys 1997). Confucius formulated the Analects in response to the political turmoil of the Chou Dynasty period in which he lived (circa 551–479 BCE). Within the *Analects* can be found a prevailing humanist theme (Ping-chia Kuo 1965: 19–23; Shurmann and Schell 1977: 10–11, 48), which was noted by scholars of Enlightenment Europe such as Voltaire (1979: 78–95). Confucius has been regarded as a social reformer (as illustrated by Confucius 1979) who was in favor of dissent (Leys 1997) and hence the legitimacy of plurality, rather than a supporter of an authoritarian status quo.

In contemporary society, the competing claims against human rights are many, with each reflecting assumptions about an ideal social organization. Utilitarianism supports rights on the basis of their majority utilitarian value, but may reject rights where they impede utility (or, with technocrats and bureaucrats, degrees of administrative convenience), broadly defined as the "greatest good for the greatest number." Communitarians assume a bonded identity, opposition to which is less tolerated, or which may be tolerated by way of an overarching, community-centered relativism that can include the abrogation of individual rights.

Tensions within rights

Civil and political (first order human) rights are generally divided into "positive" and "negative" rights, or rights "to" (for example, freedom of expression, gathering, political activity) and rights "from" (such as arbitrary arrest, detention or torture), and between natural (implied) rights and positive (codified) rights. These correspond to the capacity for and potential restrictions upon agency, although it is easy in a theoretical discussion to overstate the practical implications of the distinction. Freedom from limitations creates the practical opportunity of freedom to engage in activity. Noting this value of protection from (negative rights) to allow the opportunity to (positive rights), Weinstock noted that "citizens need a bundle of rights that ensure that their freedom will not be encroached upon [negative rights] in ways that make the realization of their projects [positive rights] impossible" (Weinstock in Weinstock and Nadeau 2004: 2)

These rights reflect the wide potential capacity of the quality of being human, to determine within or to choose to act beyond the constraints of structure, and the compulsion of oppression. In this, human rights cannot be qualified by structural exigencies, which may vary from place to place and time to time according to the preferences of power holders. Such variables may include, but not be limited to, economics, political institutionalism (institutions, parties, systems) or "culture," assuming that this can be understood as a static, reified and hegemonic – or imposed – word view.

It has been a basic assumption of democratic government, in which the interest of the majority prevails (if not at the absolute expense of the minority) that it should pursue policies that produce the most favorable outcome for the greatest number of people. This position of pursuit of broadly favorable outcomes, or "public good," assumes the existence of an overarching political unity, usually understood as "nation," which is intended to secure and preserve the interests of the nation (that is, the "national interest") within the context of a bounded and institutionally capable territory (the "state").

Such good can be construed in purely material terms, such as economic benefit, security of economic conditions, strategic (sovereign) security and access to the benefits of the state, such as a consistent and equitably applied law, infrastructure and social services such as education and health. This good may also be construed in terms of security of political benefit, including political participation and representation, and the associated rights to freedom of speech and communication, and assembly, and from arbitrary arrest, detention, torture and so on. However, in a generally open society, the public good of rights that secure political goods may be in tension with the public good of rights that secure utilitarian goods. That is, political debate in favor of some economic redistribution might potentially limit absolute economic growth. The two may coexist and indeed in most rights-based societies do so with relative equilibrium between them, but they do so only in an unending contest for supremacy based on orderings of individual and group interest.

The fundamental assumptions underpinning utilitarianism are that there is a political cohort to which its value applies and that the utility applies to most of the people in a given community most of the time. This in turn assumes a unity of purpose, which in a fully realized form may constitute a nation within the institutional context of a state. This is not to suggest that the nation, the state or the "nation-state" are a political ideal or absolute political ends in themselves. Rather it suggests that the fully realized form of a bonded political community may be called a "nation," but may potentially be less or greater than contemporary conceptions, being less than represented by a state or by being spread across states. A nation may be a devolved or relatively evolved political community, either less or greater than the rather static interpretations of nation (and also state) that tend to currently apply. By way of illustration, the Russian Empire (1721) evolved to become the Soviet Union (1917) but later devolved to become the Commonwealth of Independent States (1991), while Yugoslavia (1918) devolved to its constituent parts (1992). Conversely, the evolution of groups of nations has tended to be in primarily economic organizations such as the European Union (EU) (informally from 1951, and formally from 1992), although with a popular rejection of the EU constitution, curtailing its political organization (2005). Other examples include the North America Free Trade Agreement and the

Association of Southeast Asian Nations. The greatest example of an evolved political community, however, is the UN. For all its failings, the UN has been held as the principle arbiter of global affairs since its inception (1949). The general tendency, then, has been for specific political unities to devolve to their constituent parts, while larger unities have tended to form as the result of perceived or actual economic or security benefit. The idea of nation, then has tended to reflect a devolution, or largely a return to aspects of primordialism, rather than evolution, and as such reflect vertical rather than horizontal interests.

Assuming a common bonded political identity, that is, a nation, the focus on the welfare of the community supports the utilitarian proposition. However, the degree to which the community is bonded may not apply equally to all elements of the community. To ensure the good of the constituent community members must allow all individuals the opportunity to express their preferences (where there is no harm to others) and protect them from the potential imposition of a singular communitarian will. Figure 5.1 is intended to illustrate the elements of overlap of common interest which might lead to recognition of advantage in political bonding. Assuming, for example, that Interests A, B and C equate with specific language, economic and security concerns, these might collectively comprise sufficient common purpose to agree to the idea of a bonded political community (nation). This could be understood in particular in the case of a post-colonial state in which neither language, economy nor security are absolute unifiers in themselves, but which through sufficient proximity (perhaps borne out of colonial geo-spatial organization) identify enough in common to maintain the value of the point of overlap. This could be said to imply a tendency towards vertical social integration, with the areas where there is no overlap comprising assertions of local identity or, potentially, vertical disintegration.

Alternatively, assuming that these interests are all economic, for example around sectors of capital, technology and labor, but with a common language and security focus. There might be greater common ground to form a single community, creating the conditions for national identity, but a particular point where unity of purpose is contested by specific horizontal interests. The points at which these respective interest groups do not overlap suggest a probable desire to preserve or promote specific interests, and the capacity to be able to do so. Given the tendency of the center or middle ground to act as a median point of interest, utilitarianism would assume that the greatest number of people receive at least some benefit, while relatively few are disadvantaged. This implies mutual acceptance of legitimate plurality.

Assuming that each interest group will assert their primary interest, or at least assert a claim to what constitutes a fair balance of interests, the middle ground and definitions of "greatest good" become contested. Even where there is agreement about the greatest good, there may be instances where the greatest common good remains deleterious to constituent members. That is, it may be necessary to sacrifice the interests of a few for the greater good of many.

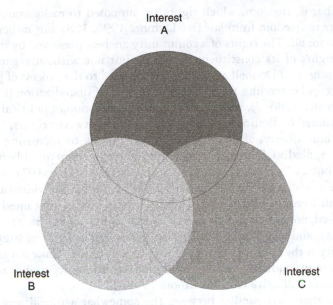

Figure 5.1 Overlap of common interest.

This then suggests an inconsistent application of agreed codes (law) or the expedient abrogation of the interests of some members of the community for the benefit of others. Due to either the inconsistency of this application, or the institutionalization of expediency, this is likely to lead to social discord, potentially at high and destabilizing levels. Ensuring that both judicial inconsistency or institutionalized expediency are constrained therefore requires the institutionalization of a counter-balance, that is, the rights of the constituent member to freedom from such impositions and the freedom to fully engage as an equal in the process of determination of the common good.

The contrary position to community rights and interests, then, is to assert the "right" of the social constituent – the individual – against the presupposed uniformity of interest, or the overarching welfare of the community. This then sets up a competition between community rights and individual rights. In putting forward a claim to individual freedom, Bentham (e.g. 1781: Chapter XVI) and Hobbes (1962: Chapter 21) argued that every law diminished freedom, even if the purpose of such law was to prevent a greater loss of freedom. Yet recognizing the practical value of majority claims, especially in a functioning democracy, the rights of an individual must on occasion be required to give way. Rejection of this compromise of absolute individual rights neglects the reality that individuals live within communities, and the rights of all cannot be compromised without exception by the rights on one.

This then posits liberalism (a preference for freedom) against libertarianism (an absolute freedom) particularly in the economic sphere, and recognizes that the rights of one are bounded by their capacity to negatively impact on others. That is, freedom, which rights are supposed to make available, does not equate to freedom from law (see Larmore 1996: 108), but rather freedom under law for all. The rights of a community are best preserved by guaranteeing the rights of its constituent members, but not without regard for the rights of others. O'Donnell and Schmitter referred to the process of positively redefining and extending rights as the substance of liberalization (O'Donnell and Schmitter 1986: 7), which is a step in the direction of political development. As noted by Berlin, in arguing for a balance betweens rights, "every law curtails some liberty, although it may be a means to increasing another" (1958: 123, nbxlix). Similarly, Rawls did not see freedom (or "liberty") as an absolute but as "a certain pattern of social forms" (Rawls 1971: 63), or as what might be described as the positive right of rational individual autonomy along with freedom from domination or unnecessary or unwanted interference. Indeed, not only is the idea of individual rights not contrary to a sense of community, and hence certain utilitarian values, but as Larmore suggests, the community is the safest place in which rights can reside. "Take our fate out of the hands of individuals," he said, "and give our immunity to interference an impersonal or collective basis" (Larmore 1996: 114).

In this, there is a parallel between the somewhat artificial separation of positive and negative rights and the distinction between the individual and the community. A community is nothing more than a collective of individuals, just as an individual is nothing more – or less – than a constituent of a community. A conceptual differentiation may be required of both for theoretical purposes, but in practise the community and individuals overlap and live within each other. As the individual goes forward, so too does the community; when the community regresses, so too do the individuals who comprise it. The political development of one implies the political development of the other.

Relativism and rights

The arguments in favor of the relativism of civil and political rights – the exceptionalism of particular cultures, nations, states or regimes – are generally put by two groups of people. The first group includes academics who have a particular focus on culture (largely but not exclusively anthropologists and other social theorists) who wish to defend the cultural particularities of their site of interest from a more generalized absorption into hegemonic or global culture. The second main group, who are sometimes uncomfortable bedfellows with the first, comprises political figures who use culturally relativist arguments about rights to sustain unequal power relationships or to excuse otherwise inexcusable abuses. Such individuals or groups may draw on pre-existing conceptions of power relations which may, in the absence of alternatives, be "naturalized" so as to preclude the conception that another possibility could exist (Lukes 1974).

Many critics of human rights, especially in developing countries, oppose universal conceptions of human rights as being specific rather than universal and as reflecting a type of cultural imperialism (for example, see World Conference on Human Rights 1993: 3; Suh 1997). These critics claim that rather than being universal, human rights generally and civil and political rights in particular are a reflection of particular cultural values and, as such, amount to the imposition of an alien culture. This argument is usually advanced in association with claims to other forms of imperialism or neo-imperialism, such as unbalanced economic or strategic relations. Notably, the issue of perceived or claimed imposition of an alien culture of human rights alone reflects cultural insensitivity, which calls forth rejection on such grounds alone. Arguments about the imposition of human rights, as with the imposition of democracy, contradict the underlying intentions of civil and political rights, so that such imposition becomes the enemy of the human rights it is trying to support. The claim to cultural relativism as a method of rejecting civil and political rights is, however, more difficult to sustain.

There is an inherent assertion of equality among those who attempt to legitimize claims against conceptions of universally valid human rights. That is, detractors of universal civil and political rights argue that their view is of equal validity to views expressed in support of such rights. Yet a relativized understanding should not logically accept such equality of the value of assertions. To accept such equality accepts the equal legitimacy of the right to express it as a freely held value. This in turn implicitly supports the case in favor of universal civil and political rights.

The only circumstances under which claims to relativization that propose an inequality of values can be sustained is where there is an ordering or hierarchy of value claims, for example that the individual is less important than the community, or that some individuals have less value than others. While hierarchical ordering has the potential to separate and privilege particular value claims, and thus avoid the egalitarian principles that underpin universal claims, there is nothing in this which presupposes that claims against universal civil and political rights would be sustained. Indeed, the argument in favor of the value of one set of cultural claims over another underpins the assumption of cultural superiority that helped to rationalize much of the European colonial expansion of the late eighteenth century. It has similarly helped to rationalize other acts of aggression, based on an interpretation of social Darwinism, perhaps the most extreme example of which was the Nazi occupation of Europe, in particular the Nazi plan to establish a *leibenstraum* in the western Soviet Union. The "Slavic" peoples were, according to this plan, to become slaves or otherwise dispossessed and forced to survive for themselves. This was the fate, under Nazi philosophy, of "culturally inferior" peoples. In this, the ordering of the value of cultures, and the consequent assumptions of superiority (or the dehumanization associated with "inferiority"), have been a key motivating factor in numerous conflicts, from Cambodia's attack against Vietnam in 1978 to the 1994 Rwanda genocide and the Islamist-inspired terrorism of the early twenty-first century. That is, cultural relativism opens the door not just to difference, but to persecution rationalized by such difference. The argument of a particular ordering of human value based on cultural specificity is logically weak. The underlying assumptions are too heavily interest driven and thus compromised and unsustainable on their own grounds. Conversely, if the argument for human rights according to cultural specificity is predicated not upon legitimacy, which assumes broad social acceptance, then it must be based on coercion or force, which implies the capacity to impose universal civil and political rights! However, as noted, the imposition of such rights remains contrary to their underlying principles and is likely to call forth rejection based on the fact of the imposition, rather than for the inherent quality of the rights in question.

Beyond this, if one wishes to assert the claims of relative values but by defending their legitimacy on the grounds of "difference," that legitimacy can only be sustained by the complete separation of values, in which values are not understood as actually relative to each other, but in which there is no dialogue between values. Not only does this contradict how the world actually works – that there has always been communicative permeability and that this is rapidly increasing – it also assumes there is or could be some intrinsic value in such splendid isolation. However, while this latter scenario makes little sense in theory and does not apply in practise, claims to the relativism of rights continue, if decreasingly at an official level. Like claims to democracy, the widespread acceptance of the terminology around civil and political rights has on the one hand tended to be devalued and on the other hand has been all too often observed in the breach. But despite such rhetorical if not actual acceptance of civil and political rights, there continue to be moments where, especially in specific cases, arguments are put to "explain" the special circumstances of particular cases. Atrocities against civilians in conflict zones are a principle example of "explaining" such "special circumstances."

Assuming the claim for the relativization of civil and political rights overcomes these hurdles, this claim then implicitly raises the question of different sets of rights for different people in different circumstances. That is, it assumes cultural or state specific rights, rather than rights predicated upon the universal quality of existing as a human being. Yet the universalist claim of civil and political rights pertains not to the specificity of one's circumstances but to the quality of being human, which is a commonality (*consensus gentium*) not defined by time, place or culture (for discussion on "generic humanity," see Geertz 1993: 43, 50, 60, 350–1; Geertz 1989: 15, 70; Todorov 1986: 374).

This then raises the issue of the moral basis of rights. Assuming that human rights are predicated upon certain moral principles, as asserted by Howard and Donnelly (1996),[2] there is equally a claim that different moral values will produce different understandings about rights. This then undermines the claim to the universality of human rights and indeed the status of rights altogether (see MacIntyre 1981). Apart from the theoretical arguments surrounding this issue, this claim to the validity of moral relativism is based on a weak practical argument. If morals are based on codes of behavior that reflect how individuals wish to be treated, there is a demonstrable commonality among humans to be treated with a degree of dignity and to be accorded the opportunity, where materially possible, to live without undue hardship or under oppressive or unnecessarily interfering rule.[3] No-one enjoys or accepts torture or arbitrary imprisonment, and around the world individuals and groups overwhelmingly choose, where they are given the opportunity, to contribute to decisions that directly affect their personal well-being and that of their loved ones and community. To this end, the moral basis of human rights reflects rational morality predicated upon the utilitarian value of protecting others as the best guarantee of protecting oneself, and the emotional good of doing so.

The issue of cultural relativism is difficult in relation to human rights generally and civil and political rights in particular. As discussed, claims to cultural relativism tend to argue that as human rights reflect a particular world view they are culturally specific and may not accord with other world views. The emphasis within human rights on claims to free expression and assembly are seen in some political environments as not just challenging the status quo but as creating an unstable political and economic environment and inciting already restive populations to illegal activity. In circumstances where the state is struggling to construct basic institutions, to provide services and to head down one consistent development path, such political distractions are often unwelcome and are arguably unhelpful. There are, however, futher internal contradictions within most culturally based objections to human rights.

A relative conception of rights assumes that what is understood by one might not (or cannot) be understood by another, and that neither understanding is privileged over the other. No particular meaning can assert its authority if meaning is constantly deferred via a chain reaction of questioning away from the source. Initially there is an internal contradiction of deconstructing relativism's own proposition and its implicit lack of engagement with demonstrable realities. Beyond this, where such relativism (or relativisms) acknowledges and respects difference, it could be understood as "positive relativism," and would be the type favored by most intellectual advocates of "difference," such as Foucault (1982), Derrida (1980, 1997) and Lyotard (1984), and linguists who broadly follow the Whorf–Sapir (Whorf 1956; Sapir 1955) incommensurability hypothesis of the ultimate inability to translate language. "Positive" relativism in this approach implies an affirming quality, in that such difference seeks liberation from imposition. Assuming that positive relativism involves acceptance of plurality (or pluralities) it positions individuals or groups in ways that cannot be regarded as the same. This then differentiates within groups, with the further assumption being that all individuals are both somewhat different but – if they are not to comprise a fundamentally differentiated and hence totally fragmented or atomized and internally alienated society – must be regarded as forming part of an overarching cohesive whole.

More disconcertingly, though, the deferrals of meaning implied in relativism can also be adopted to support "negative relativism." Negative relativism implies negation and, embracing nothingness, a nihilistic intellectual and human wasteland. As such, it positions people according to a subjective cultural or physiological scale, at the far end of which blurs the categories of value of existence ("there is no truth," "the other is subjectively imagined," etc.). Regarding all constituent citizens as of equal political and judicial value is the only alternative to employing a categorization of individual human worth. Without a consistent judicial process (that is, convicted criminals lose some equal value as citizens for the period of and sometimes after their sentence), individual measurement would be impossible to construct and thus administer. And, in both its theoretically questionable and practically unachievable modes, horrific in its application. Institutional racism (the hierarchical formalization of valuing ethnicity), of course, has done just this on the basis of group rather than individual identity. In this, racism assumes a profoundly subjective and hence inconsistent assessment of general human value and is, at best, an actor by actor and often victim by victim response. Such responses may be able to be applied in gross numbers as part of a specific program, the Holocaust and Apartheid being cases in point, but which beyond a rationalization for amoral power still suffers from arbitrary categories of victims which can, logically, change, including the program turning upon itself or elements of itself. Aspects of this latter phenomenon can be seen under Stalin's rule in the USSR, Mao's purges in the 1950s and again during the Cultural Revolution, in Nazi Germany and with Cambodia's Khmer Rouge. Despite targeting others as well as ultimately their own members, these events demonstrated more of an acute psychopathology rather than internally consistent political programs. That is to say, if relativism is consistent it must respect difference equally, or else devour itself.

Other objectors

Another rejection of human rights derives from a particular interpretation of leftist revolutionism, although this, too, suffers from internal contradictions. Communism tends to reject rights as a bourgeois sham within the context of an ideal (utopian) state. Other than using such rights as an anti-bourgeois ruse, it is regarded as an impediment to the dictatorship of the proletariat in the attainment of a utopian state in which rights are implicitly attained (for example, see Campbell 1983). This, broadly, equates to the "efficiency" argument for bureaucratic authoritarianism, in which the end justifies the means. Conversely, the radical left's claim to egalitarianism implies a right to material and political equality, in which attempts to disadvantage the "right to equality" of one must be resisted by all, which in turn implies the right to assemble, protest and free speech, and presumably the right to not be arrested, detained or tortured for engaging in such activity. Assuming the validity of these implicit rights, which any self-respecting revolutionary would assert in the face of oppression, it makes little sense to cast such rights away upon attainment of just the first step towards the socialist utopia. Indeed, apart from history's many specific object lessons, the principle of bottom-up solidarity would seem to require retention of that "reserve power" in case the road to "utopia" is paved with other than good intentions, for example, in Stalin's USSR.

In other potential or actual objections, egalitarianism tends to impose restrictions on individual accumulations of various kinds, thus restricting choice and capacity. Neither specifically left nor right, libertarianism proposes certain rights to, but does not protect others with rights from; there are no effective boundaries between "right to" and "right from," with all having the basic "right" to survive (or perish) as best they can. All of the political models noted above, then, suggest limitations to or restrictions on aspects of human rights, even if each potentially promotes a particular right or set of rights.[4] As Lukes (1993) proposed, each of these forms and their respective criteria can overlap on the grounds of respecting the claims of each other while acknowledging the legitimacy of (positive) difference. Lukes' suggestion, acknowledging the potential for disagreement, is to propose a "reasonably short and reasonably abstract" model of rights that emphasizes basic civil and political rights, rule of law, freedom of expression and association, equality of opportunity and the right to a basic level of material well-being. He constructs this model as an "egalitarian plateau," providing the field upon which contests of ideas, including about rights, can take place. It is, in a sense, a proposition about rules for civilized behavior in which competing ideas can be discussed and negotiated without resort to the barbarities that continue to plague many countries of the world, and which act as a barrier to – or destroyer of – political development.

Rights and political development

As noted at the outset of this chapter, the link between civil and political rights and political development is a basic one. One could even argue that they are but differing interpretations of or orientation of focus towards the same basic quality. That is, it is not so much that political development cannot be achieved without due regard for civil and political rights, but as a central component of political development, the presence of civil and political rights is a key marker of the extent to which political development exists.

There are various interpretations of what constitutes civil and political rights, but the UN Declaration of Human Rights is the most broadly supported and widely adopted version, with the International Covenant on Civil and Political Rights having been signed by most countries, if in many cases with specific qualifications that usually pertain to constitutional or legal issues (UNTC 2002). There are a total of 30 articles outlining people's human rights, but the central and arguably most important principles are the right to life, liberty, property and security of person(s), freedom from torture or cruel, inhumane treatment or punishment, freedom of thought, conscience and religion, and freedom of expression and opinion and assembly.

The rights to life, liberty, property and security of person are at the most basic end of the scale of rights and, at first glance, say little more than each person who is alive retains the right to stay that way and to own property. This then also goes to the issue of personal security. The question of property, however, becomes more problematic, not so much at the point where it refers to simple ownership of a home or the goods for a home, or tools or other means of making a living, but where the right to property for one impinges on the right to property of others. This potential caveat applies particularly to the individual or corporate accumulation of very large quantities of property. Hence, given the capacity for competing interests, the claim to property is left intentionally ambiguous.

The issue of freedom of thought, conscience and religion is closely associated with freedom of expression and opinion, in that the capacity to hold independent thought can only be manifested through expression. Conversely, if such thoughts are not expressed, they cannot in a practical or legal sense be held to exist. The capacity to think, and in a related manner to express oneself through language or other symbolic forms, is fundamental to the condition of being human.

The issue of religious freedom is closely linked to freedom of thought and expression in more overt political areas, with all world religions containing a normative world view expressed as a moral philosophy, and often a code of formal behavior up to and including rules for social organization.[5] For these reasons, religious belief is not only about how individuals relate to each other and to understanding their place in the universe and in relation to a meta-physical existence, but it is also about politics, including challenges to the political status quo. In China, for example, the Falun Gong organization is proscribed, while the theocratic Iranian state has persecuted followers of the Baha'i faith. This is not to mention the status of state religions prior to the separation of church and state and their frequent lack of tolerance of difference.

Beyond religion, at least as an exercise in metaphysics, assuming that a person has more material interests, which also appears to be a consequence of the condition of being human, that person will consciously consider those interests, and more than likely articulate them in support of their claims. It is at the point where the articulation of those interest claims clashes with the claims of another who is able to compel the circumstances to his favor that he may wish the former claimant to desist with his claims, and with expressions of his claims. This reflects the primacy of might over what could otherwise be a legitimate claim or a more equitable distribution satisfaction of interests.

In a more concrete example, a person or group of people who have an interest-bearing claim, say over a form of economic equity, will seek to discuss their claim among themselves by way of clarifying the legitimacy and practicalities of the claim and organizing to address it. The right to speak to this issue is fundamental to sharing such concerns or claims. The related right of assembly is also critical to such communication, especially in societies prior to access to mass communication but also as a physical expression of solidarity.

In contemporary societies in which mass communication has become the norm (in effect, this includes all but the most remote or underdeveloped societies), freedom of speech has evolved into the idea of a free media, media diversification and public access to that media. The idea of a free media is one that does not labor under censorship or restrictions on its ability to report, analyze and comment on public affairs – its "watchdog" role – and is generally accessible to most people most of the time. In developing countries, apart from government control or censorship, the principle restriction on public access to the media is cost, particularly in relation to print media and television, and literacy, in relation to print. Assuming literacy, most print media is too expensive for people living at or under the poverty line, although it does have the advantage of being able to be shared.

Television is even more expensive, not only in the purchase of the receiver but also in terms of production and broadcast. This is particularly so in relation to television news and information programming, which is most relevant to the dissemination of information that addresses interest claims. Production costs also affect the quality of information, with the tension between audience retention and information provision generally being weighted in favor of programming that has higher audience retention at lower cost, which tends to preclude or limit information programming (especially at the "quality" end of the information spectrum). Having noted these limitations, as developing countries climb the economic ladder, televisions are among the first consumer items to be purchased, and are very often shared by larger family or even community groups. Because of the lack of a literacy requirement, relatively low cost and ease of access, radio has been a popular form of communication generally and in developing countries in particular. It is inexpensive to operate, relatively inexpensive to own and often reaches over longer or more inhospitable distances than either print or television media.

Beyond such issues, limited sources of information – or restricted ownership of a number of media sources – has considerable potential to limit the range of information and ideas that might be made available to the public. Diversification of media ownership has become a critical issue in many societies with the potential for or actual concentration of media ownership. It was no accident that Italy's most dominant media owner, Silvio Berlusconi, was also Italy's longest-serving postwar prime minister, as well as being that country's richest citizen. More conventional, however, are alliances between media owners and politicians, in which there is both a cross-over of interest and influence, and it is common for particular media to openly campaign on behalf of particular politicians or parties. Indeed, the origins of the print press, in the seventeenth century, were as partisan publications.

The issue of media diversification has been one that has not only troubled states generally, but it has troubled developing countries in particular. There has long been a concern on the part of many developing countries that they have little control over what is said about them, or from within them, to wider global audiences, and this has often been to their detriment. It is a fair assessment to say that what constitutes news is generally negative – disasters of one type or another – and that developing countries are very often only heard about when they are experiencing a relatively serious disaster. This in turn creates a perception problem, which negatively influences economic matters such as loans, foreign investment and tourism. That global news media outlets are entirely owned by OECD countries, and largely located in the US, further concentrates both the ownership of the global news media and also its perspective. This in turn restricts the capacity for communication, which in turn limits the right to meaningful free speech.

Developing countries have at different times attempted to control this situation, most notoriously through so-called "development journalism," manifested in 1978 with UNESCO's introduction of the New World Information and Communications Order (NWICO). While its philosophical underpinning was generally sound, including the promotion of locally useful information and a balance of positive and negative information coming out of developing countries, the NWICO manifested as censorship and control. Despotic and authoritarian governments around the world leapt on the NWICO as an excuse to compel, or try to compel, the media to disseminate only positive information when there were genuine problems also to be reported, not least of which included human rights violations, corruption and generalized unaccountability. As a result, Western journalists and media outlets generally responded to the pressure with some hostility and refused on principle to modify their reporting. This was one clear case where what was taken as compulsion in favor of what was probably a good and perhaps even necessary idea resulted in that idea being wrecked and then abandoned. Attempting to regulate media responsibility was akin to abrogating human rights in order to ensure they were respected.

Beyond a diversity of preference – or strict neutrality – expressed by the media, access to the media has also been asserted as of importance to the promotion of civil and political rights, particularly in the case where certain relevant opinions are perceived to be marginalized or censored. However, opening the media to everyone with a desire to have their views expressed is a long way from practical and, as shown by "talk-back radio," web logging and internet chat groups, often results in some not especially enlightening commentary. The point of mediation of tensions between inclusion and "professionalism" is among the most contested sites of public life and a prime foci of communicative efforts by interest and pressure groups, not to mention politicians and parties.

Freedom of speech, then, has evolved from being a simple right to express a particular view in a public place, to a much more complex and nuanced debate about ownership, control and "gate-keeping" or censorship, technology, cost, quality and quantity of information and, perhaps most of all, access. Freedom of speech and its relationship with the mass media is widely recognized as being fundamental to contemporary politics and essential to an open political society, yet the balance within it remains contested and for many controversial. Given the centrality of this subject, the contest of ideas and interests over this subject is itself one of the points upon which contemporary politics turns. The way in which societies, and governments on their behalf, decide these questions speaks centrally to core issues of informed public participation, official transparency and accountability. How a society addresses elaborations of the first principle human right of free speech, then, is a central determinant of that society's political development.

Law

If the universal claims of human rights have a measurable basis, it is not so much in what people in common wish for, even though there is a high degree of commonality in basic aspirations. Rather, the most absolute point of consistency is in what people do not wish for, or, more to the point, wish to avoid at all cost. If there are quibbles about some universal claims, one that stands up irrespective of time, place, culture or other circumstances, is abhorrence of personal torture. That is, no-one likes it, no-one would willingly put up with it and everyone would wish that it did not exist should they be subject to it (see Singer 1979).

Similarly, being jailed is for most people a negative experience and few people would willingly surrender themselves to incarceration. This is particularly so if incarceration is outside of the due process of law and if it includes not the relative comforts and security of some of the more enlightened prison systems, but is constructed around the bare minimum to sustain life, and perhaps even then not for the long-term.

The question of normative forms of and respect for civil and political rights is best addressed by being directly tested against a specific universal set of criteria, and whether political rule meets the test of legitimacy (see Morris 1998: 24, 105–11). Broadly, "legitimacy," in the positive sense, complies with the exercise of power in accordance with a broadly accepted set of principles, procedures or method of conferral of authority. As this is generally codified in order to achieve some standardization of application, it implies the existence of law. Indeed, the word "legitimacy," like that of legal, derives from the Roman *lex* ("law"), and its original application did not distinguish between the legitimacy and legality of a regime; in order to be one it had to be the other, in contrast to arbitrary rule or tyranny. In later discussion, especially under the influence of Christian theology, the idea of legitimacy was linked to natural law, and through the Enlightenment gradually democratized. Weber's theory of legitimacy of rule canvassed different ideal models obtaining to different pre-conditions, but throughout asserted that legitimacy either arose through acceptance of a pre-condition, imitation, rational belief in its value, or its legality (Weber 1946: 130). Another set of criteria might construe legitimacy as being comprised either of a normative natural order that translates as political order. For example, such criteria can be found in traditional forms of rule and elements of "organic" political corporatism or in a liberal-minimalist model dependent upon a state's capacity to maintain peace under rule of law, characterized by the "small state" approach of neo-liberalism. They can also be located in a democratic-proceduralist model of agreement between free and equal citizens, based on individual self-determination (as the only rational basis for morality) as outlined by Kant and as social contract by Rousseau. It is also possible that claims to universalist legitimation may be abandoned in favor of relativism, as exemplified by the "deconstruction" of the universal to the particular of Derrida, the anti-"grand narrative" approach of Lyotard, and the micro-power structure focus of Foucault.

There is, of course, a claimed paradox between conceptions of freedom and law: to the extent that freedom is understood as the absence of domination, just laws form its pre-condition (Larmore in Weinstock and Nadeau 2004: 105). Yet this "sense of paradox is due to confusing the absence of domination with the absence of interference" (Larmore in Weinstock and Nadeau 2004: 106), which is most often associated with the utilitarianism of Bentham. Moreover, in ancient Greece, "Demokratia was committed to the rule of law because it recognized that the rule of law protected the interests of the poor as well as the rich" (Ober 2000). This is to say, while law imposes some limitations upon freedom, normatively it is only the freedom to restrict the freedom of others. In that law normatively guarantees protection from such arbitrary restrictions, it enhances real freedom.

Freedom from arbitrary arrest, detention and torture are among the first generation civil and political rights, as legal protection from authoritarian excesses intended to quell challenges to the authority of an oppressive state. These freedoms "from" are necessary rights alone, but are especially important as protective measures in concert with rights "to" freedom of speech and assembly, and so on. Freedom from arbitrary arrest, detention and torture also imply the existence of the rule of law, which is an essential component of the process of political development. Beyond that, strictures against the use of inhumane or degrading punishment, including torture, reflect the positive values of a society in relation to its own members, and imply a broadly benign approach and a degree of mutual respect as human beings, even for law breakers. Taken from a negative perspective, strictures on the use of torture or other cruel, degrading or inhumane forms of punishment also reflects an awareness that it is not entirely possible to separate one aspect of a society's behavior from others, and that what occurs in prisons, and the means by which citizens might get there, says much about how a society more generally treats itself, its capacity for empathy and its sensitivity or otherwise to human suffering.

If political development is held to be a normative good, then it implies the capacity and intention for the improvement of people's lives based on a wide-ranging sense of inclusion and participation through practical recognition of the validity and implementation of civil and political rights that are essential to such development. The key components of civil and political rights, as both rights "to" and rights "from," ensure the capacity for constituent members of a polity to communicate with each other without fear over matters of individual or mutual relevance and importance. The right to meet, to discuss, to express views and to disseminate those views among one's community is basic not just to political freedom, but to a full and fair manifestation of the human condition. The history of humankind has been one of gradual, non-linear improvement, with significant set-backs and developmental cul-de-sacs, but with an overall improvement in and increase of human awareness, under-standing, organization and implementation. The Enlightenment tradition might have corresponded to a particular historical era, but its antecedents date back to the earliest philosophers and the best aspects of religious trad-ition. Its legacy, meanwhile, continues to inform the spirit of inquiry, of tolerance and understanding, and of seeking ways forward based on rational decision making among human beings of intrinsic equal worth.

But even though humanity is now a very long way from where it has been, political development has been grossly uneven, and in some cases has not allowed even the beginning of the development of human potential. These basic abilities "to," enhanced by freedom "from," underpin any meaningful conception of political development, without which individuals could only be said to live in a state of political underdevelopment that is equivalent to economic underdevelopment for its poverty of freedom. To that end, we may have glimpses of what could constitute a free and fair society, but for many, and probably most people, that remains a distant dream. The full and equal implementation of civil and political rights, *primus inter pares*, recognizes their direct and central contribution to and underpinning of democratization in its most substantive sense. In this, there can be no political development without full recognition and implementation of civil and political rights, and such full implementation is itself the key criteria by which such political development must be measured.

6 Democracy

It is broadly held that the most desirable form of political organization is democracy. The normative use of the term across a wide variety of political systems appears to confirm the status of democracy, even if its content varies considerably in application. Like motherhood, almost no-one argues against the positive value of democracy, and those few who do invariably either do not enjoy popular support or, if they have political power, base it upon a capacity for patronage or imposition. Given a free choice, the individual members of a political society will invariably choose a political system in which their voice is heard as an equal participant in the political process. It would seem, then, that there is at least a nominal relationship between democracy and political development. The difficulty arises, however, in that the use and often abuse of the term "democracy" has meant that, for many purposes, it has been rendered almost meaningless. This chapter discusses the meaning of the term "democracy" and tries to locate it in a way that corresponds to the most consistent use of the term, thereby establishing an internal conceptual benchmark.

The first problem to afflict any discussion of "democracy" is semantic. The term "democracy" is used freely not only by regimes and states that are anything but democratic, but also by regimes and states that are conventionally considered as democratic but which, in formal terms, are not. The term "democracy" has been used in such a carefree and uncritical way as to assume its normative good without ever questioning what it is that inspires such uncritical acceptance. The singularity of "democracy" and the necessity of its establishment are not so much a given, but are an expression of an imposed singularity. The "idea" of democracy as an imposition implies a conceptual oxymoron; democracy is nothing if it is not voluntary and, as such, its voluntarism implies choice that may vary from circumstance to circumstance, at least around a core idea or set of ideas.

In this, it is useful to recall the point that the original definition of democracy was rule by the people, from the ancient Greek *demos* (people) and *kratia* (rule or system of government). In the ancient Greek sense, this literally meant direct rule or direct voting on all local decisions. Indeed, it has been suggested that the term *demokratia* from which democracy derives was coined as a pejorative term by ancient Athens' oligarchy (de Ste Croix 1987: 73). The contest for political control between elites and non-elites continues to this day, reflecting less traditional assumptions about the wisdom and necessity of elite rule as, more commonly, claims to utilitarian efficiency on the part of economic, technocratic and bureaucratic elites. In this, democracy as it might be commonly understood as "rule by the people" is therefore less a struggle over whether or not "the people" choose their government, but more over the choices that are made available to them, and the degree of control over processes employed by governments once such "choices" have been made.

Some scholars, such as Lev, have argued with considerable justification that what is now called democracy is not actually that. Democracy can, Lev notes, only be genuine if the community is small enough to personally engage in the decision-making process (personal communication 24.12.05–30.12.05). That what is often called democracy, which "serves a kind of conceit and makes people feel virtuous," has made the term "so problematic that it should probably be banned or a charge levied on its use by serious students of politics" (Lev 2005: 349). What is usually called "democracy," then, is elected representative government in which there is a degree of participation by the *demos* which implies a type of democratic engagement. But, as Lev notes, types of democratic engagement – of which there have been claimed to be some 550 sub-types (Collier and Levitsky 1997) – must be examined for accuracy as a descriptor. According to Lev:

> An election is "democratic" participation of a sort, but if we stop there it becomes a trope and cover-up, because the choice of who will run for office is obviously not made by the demos. My concern is simply that these limits, strictures, realities are constantly before us and not hidden from the demos. So, by all means we need elections, and we can call them whatever we wish – including "elections" – but we need to ask ourselves whether adding "democratic" helps us to understand what is actually happening.
>
> (Lev personal communication 30.12.2005)

Reflecting observations by Pareto (1984) on the formation of oligarchies, and Mosca (1939) and Michels (1959) on previous political study being largely recommendations on elite capture and control of political power, Lev noted that the choice of those who run for office is not made by the people, but rather constitutes part of the functioning of an oligarchy or political elite. In this, the question was not about the origins of elite members, who could be recruited from a range of backgrounds, or that such recruitment was sometimes based on merit and privilege. Rather, it was about the closed process of selection of elite members and the limited openness of elite formation to broad inclusion or public selection. Having accepted the basic democratic paradigm, elites then tended to assert economic or political power in disproportion to that available to the "common people." This conforms with the libertarian notion of "rights," in that all have equal right to participate to the fullest extent of which they are capable, but are equally entitled to be passive by exercising what has been referred to as "rational ignorance" (Downs 1957) or, in a more politically sinister turn, an equal "right" to become disempowered.

Lev was also skeptical about the value of democracy if it could exist, noting that genuine democracy could also degenerate into mob rule and that it was not, by definition, necessarily benign. "In sum, my point is simply that the safest state form now is the representative republic, more or less constitutionally driven, with dozens of controls on both leadership and society, and an emphasis on both political and social responsibility" (personal communication 30.12.05).

What Lev describes as a "virtuous conceit" – a sort of politics of self-congratulation – infers that "democracy" has come to mean an electoral representative system with a relatively high degree of actual or potential participation. In more complex political societies than ancient Athens or small political communities, such as those in which the number and geographic distribution of citizens means they do not know each other and cannot meaningfully gather, democracy can still exist in the form of referenda or, less commonly, deliberative democracy, in which citizens are polled for their views on political questions (see Fung and Wright 2000). Much more common is representative democracy, in which citizens vote for representatives to a higher political body in which political decisions are made on their behalf. Accepting this model, Schumpeter defines the method by which democracy functions as "that institutional arrangement for arriving at political decisions in which individuals acquire the power to decide by means of a competitive struggle for the people's vote" (1976: 269). In most instances, the representatives will outline their views or make promises on a range of issues so that voters will know prior to voting whether or not particular candidates for representative positions support their own views. Assuming a high degree of congruence between the wishes of the voter and the intentions of the representative, this general system can work as a satisfactory replacement for direct democracy, and is overwhelmingly the most common model among modern democratic states. But not all political systems that are called a "democracy" represent the term according to the above description, even though each might claim to do so.

From a less semantic and arguably less accurate perspective, Huntington described democracy as derived from and including social pluralism, class systems, civil society, the rule of law, representative bodies, separation of religious and civil authority and a commitment to furthering individualism (Huntington 2000: 5–6). This view, of course, reflects Huntington's own interpretation of a particular type of democracy that is practiced in the US (and in a more idealized sense, reflected Lev's responsible, controlled constitutional republicanism). Nevertheless, Huntington does broadly identify some, if not all, of the features that most analysts would include in a contemporary definition of representative "democracy."

Beyond these definitional qualities concerning the extent of direct or indirect popular rule, there is a clear distinction between what might be called "procedural democracy" (for example, see Schumpeter 1976; Burton *et al.* 1992: 1) and "substantive democracy," or a more expanded definition of the idea (see Grugel 2002: 6). Procedural democracy implies "free" and "fair" elections, low barriers to participation, genuine political competition and recognition of civil and political rights, all of which can promote political development. Substantive democracy, on the other hand, implies procedural values as well as a greater equality of opportunity (usually wealth distribution) and general social justice. There are arguments in favor of keeping economic claims analytically distinct from those of procedure, although this then opens a further debate (see Chapter 6).

A further definition of democracy derives from Schumpeter (1976), who elaborates on "institutional arrangements" by noting, like Lev, that democracy does not mean that "the people" actually rule, but rather that people have the opportunity to accept or reject those who do actually rule. Given that this could be decided in an undemocratic way, Schumpeter then defines democracy as comprising free competition among aspiring political leaders. That is, it is the role of the people to allocate legitimacy to one ruler or a group of rulers, rather than to actually make decisions about conditions under which they wish to live (1976: Chapter XXII). Such competition between aspiring political leaders, or political elites, was characterized by Dahl as a competitive oligarchy where there was public contestation (1971: 7), as well as a polyarchy where such public contestation was also inclusive (1971, 1989: 30). In this, Dahl declined to use the term "democracy," as "no large system in the world is fully democratized" (1971: 8).

While Schumpeter's definition of procedural democracy applies in some circumstances, and may be interpreted to apply more broadly in the post-cold war era and in the subsequent "third wave" of democratization, numerous states have embraced electoral politics and types of democracy which sometimes struggle to match even Schumpeter's limited definition. To illustrate, a state that has separate political parties in which candidates can contest more or less open elections may be considered a "democracy" if one does not consider other criteria. But the validity of that assertion is tested if, for example, parties are not defined by policies but by the populism of their leaders or if those leaders represent entrenched elite interests (for example, business, military, religion). This validity is also tested if the media and other forms of public communication are politically beholden rather than independent, or if there are other impediments to the free expression of political will.

An example of such a procedural democracy is Indonesia in the period after the fall of President Suharto, which corresponded to each of these restrictive criteria. It could be reasonably claimed that Indonesia was still in a state of transition from authoritarianism and that its evolution to consolidated democracy was not yet complete. However, eight years after Suharto's fall, parties were still based on personalities rather than policies (for example, in the 2004 elections, karaoke competitions were one of the most important methods of gaining voter support), elite self-interest was more rather than less entrenched, the media was largely captive to political interests, votes were (literally) bought, and political parties were stopped from participating if their previous vote was below a prescribed level, while in order to be eligible to participate, their organization required representation of branches in half of the districts in half of the provinces.[1] In this sense, Indonesia's elections only conformed to some democratic requirements, and were therefore largely procedural rather than substantive.

In another nearby state that claims, at least in a nominal sense, to be a "democracy," one might also consider Singapore in corresponding ways, in which parties do exist, but have been excluded from open political competition by a range of legalistic methods, including draconian "defamation" and public speech laws, a politically captive judiciary, and restrictive and quickly changing candidacy requirements. Malaysia has suffered similar limitations to procedural democracy, although more so from electoral boundary imbalances (gerrymandering) and ethnicity-based institutional control of parties. Cambodia, meanwhile, has had regular elections, but executive interference in the media and judiciary, the use of state funds to assist the party of government in electioneering, and violence against and intimidation of opposition figures. If these examples of limited forms of procedural democracy are specifically geographically located, similar forms of procedural democratic limitation – including limitations upon and threats or attacks against politicians – exist more widely, indeed globally.

Civic equality

Assuming that procedural democracy is at best partial, and that some examples of it do not have a legitimate claim to even its formally procedural definition, the most important aspect of democracy, whether that is understood in its pure "Levian" sense or as a representative process (assuming more than just restricted voting), is that it implies a nominal if not actual political equality. Such equality is realized through the status of citizenship, or by being recognized as a fully constituted member of political society. In this, one's contribution to decision making is neither more nor less than that of any other member. This intrinsic equality is supposed to be self-evident, and claimed as an ethical principle. As such, O'Donnell and Schmitter observed that democratic citizenship

> involves both the *right* to be treated by fellow human beings as equal with respect to the making of collective choices and the *obligation* of those implementing such choices to be equally accountable and accessible to all

members of the polity. Inversely, this principle imposes *obligations* on the ruled, that is, to respect the legitimacy of choices made by deliberation among equals, and *rights* on rulers, that is, to act with authority (and to apply coercion where necessary) to promote the effectiveness of such choices, and to protect the polity from threats to its persistence.

(O'Donnell and Schmitter 1986: 7–8)

The intention of this formulation is, then, to provide the individual with the greatest amount of freedom, to guarantee this freedom via civic equality, and to safeguard these arrangements through reciprocal obligations. This complies with Held's view that civic equality is both the practical and moral basis of liberty (1996), which in turn rests upon Aristotle's conception of democracy that regards liberty and equality as its fundamental elements (1997: 1317a, 40b, 16). In that democratic citizenship implies political equality, it can be extrapolated as a manifestation of civil and political rights in that it implies the presence of such rights as the means of guaranteeing democratic function and continuation. Without, for example, freedom of speech and assembly, or freedom from arbitrary arrest, detention and torture, democracy as it is understood would not have a functional capacity. That these rights do, or normatively should exist, in a mediated relationship between the individual and the state, implies the potential existence of the most politically favorable or socially desirable form of social contract. As noted, it is this mediated relationship that both guarantees and relies upon the prevalence of such key ("first generation") rights.

Basic elements of "democracy" could be generally said to include the capacity for political participation, representation and accountability. The extent to which these are available – and all are compromised in all systems to some degree – is a prime marker of the level of political development. How these forms manifest in practise may be far from ideal, with structural, institutional and cultural factors all playing a part in shaping how people variously choose, and compete to choose alternatives on offer. Hence the necessity of a "majority rule" model, which if not balanced with a duty of care for the political minority can turn into a majoritarian "dictatorship of 50 per cent plus one." As Spitz notes, a constitutional meaning of democracy implies a regime in which individuals enjoy some rights, even though these may be used to trump the collective will when this will is tainted with prejudices. In such cases, the capacity of individuals to be morally independent and equally respected may in turn be endangered. In contrast to majority rule, the majoritarian model proposes that individuals do not enjoy separate rights, since all rights are conferred by law which is enacted on behalf of the majority of people. In this situation, however, laws are increasingly compromised and no longer reflect a common interest, but rather the capacities of private lobbies to negotiate the distribution of advantages produced by social cooperation (Spitz in Weinstock and Nadeau 2004: 61). This explains why even if the core principles of "democracy" are relatively consistent, its application, appropriateness and social acceptance can be quite varied.

This recognition of the appropriateness or social acceptability of a particular form of rule raises the question of what constitutes legitimacy, or what the citizens regard as an acceptable legally binding authority. According to Diamond, legitimacy is an outcome of causal factors, including the trajectory of historical legacy, the comparative values of regime systems within that historical legacy, the experience of positive social and economic results from the regime in question, efficacy of the regime and the way in which the regime conforms to political aspirations (1999: 194–212). Diamond was referring to the legitimacy of democracy in this context, but claims for the legitimacy of democracy can be equally made to other regimes. It should be noted, however, that this assessment of (democratic) legitimacy is implicitly "rational-legal" in the Weberian sense of the term, and does not account for "traditional" political models or the compelling, if transient, legitimacy of charismatic leadership.

Criticisms of democracy

Even in its more complete forms, as many have noted, democracy is less than perfect and has been open to criticism. While such criticism has often been a blind for rationalizing authoritarian forms of government, many critiques of democracy can be substantiated in practise. Criticism of democracy has generally derived from one of two perspectives. The first perspective opposes democracy on the grounds that it is inefficient, encourages uninformed popular input in to complex policy matters, encourages factionalism or divisiveness, and that to overcome these problems it encourages descent to the lowest common denominator. The second main criticism of democracy is that it is a subterfuge for elite control (the oligarchic subterfuge), unless it is fully extended to include economic and political equality, access to means of communication (and hence persuasion), and equal access to the law and to legal representation (not just technical equality before the law). This second criticism is not of democracy as such, but of the incompleteness of what passes for democracy or varying degrees of access to democratic forms. A third criticism is that democracy constitutes a tyranny of the majority (the majoritarian model).

The first criticism, about democracy's lack of efficiency, that it is uninformed, encourages factionalism and descends to the lowest common denominator, is employed by the governments of countries such as Singapore and Indonesia under Suharto's New Order. There is little doubt that political systems that rely on regular elections of government rarely plan much beyond the existing election cycle. In a four-year political term, an elected government will implement policies, often with a degree of austerity for the first two years, and then become more generous in the third or fourth year as elections approach. It is not necessary that democratic governments respond in such a way, but such responses, which are common among Western democracies, are the logical outcome of governments' desires to retain office. In Japan, however, where there had been a long period of consistent government (primarily due to divided opposition), the government was able to engage in longer-term economic planning which in turn assisted Japan's economic growth from the 1960s through to the 1980s. This is perhaps one of the more valid criticisms of democracy, although a genuinely responsible democratic government could ignore the short-term electoral cycle and engage in longer-term planning, if at the expense of its short-term electoral popularity.

There is, also, little doubt that the complexity of most policy issues requires specialist analysis and responses, which ordinary citizens may be unable to grasp in their entirety or, in some cases, even on a singular basis. However, assuming that citizens are satisfied to leave day-to-day decision making to either representatives or bureaucrats whose job it is to consider such matters ("rational ignorance"), this is not necessarily a problem. Very few representative democrats would advocate referenda on all policy issues. However, there are some policy issues, such as the environment, the status of foreign relations and issues of social morality where citizens may feel their voice should be specifically heard. This has led to the formation of special interest or pressure groups and public protest. A more regularized method of channeling public expression would, though, produce a more democratic outcome on such public and often contentious issues.

The divisive aspect of democracy – that it allows and even encourages open debate – is a particularly sensitive issue in societies that continue to struggle with a sense of national or state cohesion. The problem here, however, is more with the inability of a political society to cohere around the state than about the principles of public debate and disagreement. If public debate does expose underlying social fractures, it may mean that the political society in question is largely an artificial creation, and that its consolidation as a polity is not yet established. This then raises the question as to whether at least some of the points for political discussion within such a polity would be around its legitimacy and continuation, or resolution of outstanding points in order to help create such legitimacy and hence continuation.

The issue of democracy's descent towards the lowest common political denominator harks back to the earliest criticism of democracy from ancient Athens: that this form of government constituted rule by the rabble, or rule by people's force or power (*kratos*, as opposed to *arche*, meaning to rule or lead), which implies rule by the mob. There is considerable legitimacy in the concern that should "the people" be allowed to dictate policy they will engage in direct short-term gratification and probably implement policies that are mutually contradictory (for example, lower taxes and higher government spending). There is also an elite view that the people will make otherwise unsophisticated decisions, responding quickly and emotionally to various incomplete external inputs. According to this logic, the people cannot be relied upon to make sound decisions (or even agree on decisions) in their own interests. The question that arises from this, however, is that even if such a claim can be substantiated, can non-accountable elites also be relied upon to make sound decisions in the best interests of the people? The answer would appear to be that where specialist knowledge and planning is required, the people can allocate such responsibility, but if they are to retain some control over the direction of events then only on the grounds that the executive actors remain accountable for their decisions.

There are also some practical considerations that affect the efficacy of democracy, such as economic and legal limitations on political participation (for example, lack of access to campaign funds or polling booths, or restrictions on party formation or voting franchise) and the removal from the public sphere of a host of decision-making processes (both executive and administrative) further reduce the meaning of democracy as rule by the people. This is not to deny the importance of timely and effective decision making which might only be able to be made by a highly trained and especially selected administration, but it does raise the concern that the argument in favor of speed and effectiveness can be used as a blind for a conscious transfer of effective power away from the people, and also, perhaps more commonly, as an only half conscious or unintended mechanism for disempowering the people. An oligarchic hegemony does not have to be spelled out (although it may be acknowledged in passing, such as in "old boys" networks) for it to function in practise.

The notion of hegemony can also be applied to criticisms of democracy as constituting a majoritarian "tyranny of the majority," or in which "fifty per cent plus one" have the capacity to lord it over the remaining 49 per cent. To put it another way, does democracy work in the context of two wolves and a sheep deciding on what is for dinner? There is no doubt that in a political system in which group decisions are intended to apply to the group as a whole, that a small majority may exercise undue influence over a large minority and that, unchecked, this would constitute a serious problem for democratic models. There are also the concerns of anarchists in the tradition of Proudhon, that democracy is the "most abominable tyranny of all, for it is not based on the authority of a religion, not upon the nobility of a race, not on the merits of talents and of riches. It merely rests upon numbers and hides behind the name of the people" (attrib.). Short of unassailable internal contradictions, democratic polities tend to default to cohesion and thus to moderation of views in order not to fundamentally alienate large majorities. However, while this is a common feature of working democracies, it is not a necessary feature of them, and thus methods of checks and balances also normatively applied to democratic models, which harks back to Lev's preferred political model.

Beyond this, democracy may be criticized for applying a representative model in areas that might otherwise be capable of direct democratic process, or for reducing all democratic processes to replicas of a single process designed to address the functional difficulties of a large and complex society. Rigid or uniform application of a particular democratic model may exclude the existence of other democratic forms in smaller or more localized political formats, including local councils, trade unions and other representative bodies. It may also exclude from consideration models of referenda or other deliberative mechanisms, which become increasingly viable as a consequence of technological advances. The problem may arise, however, in less technologically advanced societies, where access to, for example, on-line voting systems, is limited or non-existent. In such circumstances (and arguably in all others), there can instead be a devolution of decision making to that level where the decision is manifested. That is, assuming the pre-condition of equality of access to resources, which are rare in practise, a decision about, for example, village level health care or the provision of potable water could and probably should be made at the village level via a direct democratic process.

This more participatory approach to politics, and hence a more thorough form of democratization, but which is also rare in practise, is based on the premise that it is the people who are affected who should ultimately be responsible for (or at least meaningfully consulted on) decisions that directly concern them. Even assuming the practical difficulties in mass or decentralized participation in political decision-making processes, the tendency towards the centralizing decision making should, in a democratic society default to the local in the first instance and be balanced by a high level of accountability, so that decisions and their consequences are not significantly removed from the views of those people affected. As Sen (1999), for example, has argued, the best incentive for a government to alleviate poverty is direct accountability. A government may act in ways that are socially responsible, but unless there is a process of accountability there is little guarantee that it will consistently do so. In this sense, if democracy is necessary to help ensure public welfare, it is even more necessary in developing countries than in those that have already overcome most of their welfare problems (and which, more than coincidentally, are usually also democratic).

Perhaps the most common criticism of what can be generally called "democracy" revolves around the idea that while political choice is said to be available, actual choice is quite limited. In this discussion or debate about choice outside a commonly accepted framework may be discouraged in "democracies" through a range of obvious, subtle and sometimes hidden or unrecognized means. Lukes' seminal account of the subtlety of the exercise of power characterizes its range of manifestations as "dimensional" (Lukes 1974). The first dimension of power, as discussed by Dahl (1971), focuses on behavior in making decisions about issues in which there is an observable conflict of interests. This may be expressed as policy preferences and demonstrated through political participation (Lukes 1974: 15). What Lukes calls a "two-dimensional" view of power, as elaborated on by Bachrach and Baratz (1962: 947–52), incorporates not just active or overt uses of power, but passive or covert uses of power. This could be said to parallel Weber's "capacity" for the exercise of power. This is when a person or group creates or reinforces barriers to the public discussion of conflict, such as through media control, limits to free speech or other more subtle forms of control of communication. This raises concerns about exclusion, or what Lukes calls "non-decision making" (Lukes 1974: 18) and is probably the most common area of criticism of plural democratic processes, in that common or mainstream views achieve full representation, but do so to the almost complete exclusion of non-mainstream views, regardless of their validity. Debate over environmental issues is a case in point. Although the environmental debate is now increasingly on the mainstream political agenda in most developed countries, it has struggled to achieve this status because it was for decades not regarded as sufficiently observable or central to contemporary political dialogue. That is, according to Lukes, power is not just about acknowledging certain subjects as being legitimate for discussion, but about the delegitimization of certain subjects for discussion. This debate might revolve around the political role of the armed forces, or the removal of certain subjects from the public agenda such as the legitimacy of the king (implied *lese-majeste*). This "behavioralist" perspective is sometimes referred to as "culturalism" (for example, Pye 1985: 2).

Lukes sees this type of analysis of power as still relying too heavily on observable conflict. Yet power may be exercised by shaping the thoughts and desires of another, to have them act in a required manner that may not be in their interests. Such "thought control" may take "mundane forms," such as "through the control of information, through the mass media and through the processes of socialization" (1974: 24). Lukes suggests that because grievances about a power structure may not be aired or be able to be uncovered does not necessarily imply that the grievances do not exist. If a person or group does not have access to sets of ideas that inform political ideas they may still have a grievance, or continue to experience "an undirected complaint arising out of everyday experience, a vague feeling of unease or sense of deprivation" (1974: 24). Further, power may be exercised by shaping understanding in such a way as to legitimize respective roles in the existing order of things. This legitimization comes about because individuals cannot see or imagine an alternative, because it is seen as natural and unchangeable or because it is valued as "divinely ordained and beneficial." The absence of grievance does not, therefore, necessarily equal genuine consensus, as it may reflect the deletion of the possibility of false or manipulated consensus (Lukes 1974: 24). Lukes' definition of power, then, closely accords with the conception of "hegemony" as articulated by Gramsci. Hegemony in this sense implies the establishment and maintenance not only of political and economic control, but also agreement by a subordinate social group or class with a dominant group or class that a prevailing state of affairs is desirable (Gramsci 1971: xii–xiv). What are regarded as social and political norms, and the processes by which they are maintained, operate at both conscious and unconscious levels. Further, they are reinforced both overtly and covertly by existing power structures, which tend to primarily serve the interests of the power brokers who exercise such power structures. Some governments can therefore be seen to act primarily in their own interests, those of their close associates and of other elites. Lukes was also critical of the focus on a methodology in which power is about individuals realizing their wills (Lukes 1974: 21). He argued that the power to control the political agenda and exclude potential issues could not be adequately analyzed unless it is seen as a function of collective forces and social arrangements.

Types of democracy

As noted, the term "democracy" is has been appropriated and used in ways that have come to not just diminish but, in some contexts, have functionally eradicated its original and previously agreed meaning. Given that democracy is such a critical idea in political discussion, it appears necessary to briefly outline some of the ways in which the term has been used. There are a number of varieties of "democracy" (as well as non-democracy), which can be identified under several broad groupings, such as constitutional democracy, liberal democracy, social democracy, grass roots democracy, people's democracy, guided democracy, and so on. There is also the question of "pre-existing democracies," that is, polities that have participatory methods of government but which do not fall into the general category of "democracy" in the modernist and formally institutionalized sense of the term. Such polities may include smaller social groupings such as extended kinship units or tribes in which decisions are communally taken, or in which the leader or chief is directly accountable to his or her membership.

The term "liberal democracy" is almost oxymoronic, in that any political system that claims to be a democracy which is politically illiberal[2] would, at best, only constitute a qualified democracy, with the greater the restriction on liberalism equating a greater restriction on democratic freedom. That is, the basic qualities of political liberalism are fundamental to substantive democracy. The terms "liberal," "liberalism" and "liberalization" are often used freely in political discourse and, like "democracy," are frequently appropriated for purposes which contradict their meaning. Schmitter and Schneider say of political liberalization:

> At a minimum, this involves a passive and voluntary connection between individuals and groups who are permitted (but not compelled) by authorities to engage in certain forms of "free" behavior and a reliable and permanent commitment by authorities not to engage in forms of "coercive" behavior. The shorthand term for this in much of the literature is "exercising and respecting the rule of law" – even if this may imply a much wider range of connections and commitments.
>
> (Schmitter and Schneider 2003: 6)

The critical element of this definition is an institutional commitment to "freedom" and the minimization of official coercion.

Beyond this freedom, the particular quality of political liberalism that lends itself to substantive democracy is its moral neutrality. Moral neutrality might seem like an anathema to many liberals and supporters of democracy alike given their tendency to ascribe to democracy a significant normative quality. However, like the basic human right of freedom of speech, the principle of moral neutrality does not argue what should be said or done, but that there is a right of free expression of all ideas and a right to free action. This then raises that hoary old contradiction of the right of free speech to speak against free speech, or the similar liberal tolerance of illiberalism and the restriction of free action. Arguments against free speech or liberalism that are allowed by them do not negate such free speech or liberalism but by demonstration reaffirm their central philosophical position of plurality. If, however, arguments against free speech or liberalism result in the success of their imposition, they may be legitimately resisted on the grounds that they constitute an unreasonable limitation upon personal freedom. Following this, there is a point at which liberalism might countenance restrictions of free speech or, more probably, unrestricted action, where they directly impinge on the safety and physical security of others, which would be the point where law is transgressed. This protection of others' physical well-being, however, does not contradict liberalism as such, but rather offers the types of guarantees that could be expected in any society that has agreed rules of social behavior. In that this constitutes an impediment, it is in the way of liberalism's unrestrained sibling; libertarianism, rather than liberalism itself.[3]

For a "liberal democracy" to give meaning to the term, it must fulfill two broad sets of criteria. The first is that it must constitute substantive rather than procedural democracy. The second is that the substance it inscribes must accord with particular liberal values. According to Diamond, a liberal democracy should exhibit a range of mutually dependent and internally coherent features. Diamond appears to assume that liberal democracy and substantive democracy are the same, his dichotomy being liberal and electoral, rather than substantive and procedural (1999: 13). His version of liberal democracy includes control of the state lying with elected officials, that electoral outcomes are potentially or actually open and within the context of constitutional principles, and that there may be non-electoral opportunities for citizens to express concerns and values. In Diamond's liberal democracy, there may also be alternative sources of relevant and accessible information, some constraint on executive authority and institutional separation (especially of a competent judiciary), freedom of belief, opinion, discussion, publication, assembly, demonstration and petition, where citizens enjoy political equality under the law, and where basic human rights of protection from physical or political interference are guaranteed (Diamond 1999: 11–12). It is important to note, however, that Diamond argues that:

> Liberal democracy does not require the comprehensively exalted status of
> individual rights that obtains in Western Europe and especially the

United States. Thus one may accept many of the cultural objections of advocates of the "Asian values" perspective (that Western democracies have shifted the balance too much in favor of individual rights and social entitlements over the rights of the community and social obligations of the individual to the community) and still embrace the political and civic fundamentals of liberal democracy as articulated above.

(Diamond 1999: 15)

There appear to be a number of internal contradictions in Diamond's argument, perhaps because he does have a US-centric view of Western democracy. Diamond's claim that there are examples of excessive individualization is relatively correct, especially in the US (much less so in Europe, despite his claim). But what he does not note is that although such examples exist and there is a tendency towards a strong focus on individual rights, especially in the US, this remains the exception rather than the rule. Even in cases where "excessive individualism" does exist, socially determined laws tend to remain in operation and the state still functions on behalf of its citizens, if with varying degrees of efficacy. The question, then, is what constitutes "too much" in favor of individual rights. Diamond does not clarify this, but accepts the underlying premise of the Singaporean argument.

This then leads into the first fundamental flaw in Diamond's cultural qualification, which is that he cites as his prime example Singapore. Singapore is not a liberal or substantive democracy in any sense, and it would arguably be disqualified from consideration as a procedural or electoral democracy on the grounds that it functionally excludes viable opposition. Indeed, Diamond acknowledges just this where, recognizing its limitations, he cites Singapore under the category of "pseudodemocracy" or, citing Giovanni Sartori, a "hegemonic party system" (1999: 13). Parekh (1994) notes that a certain type of "liberalism" can be culturally restrictive through its lack of acknowledgement of difference under the banner of assimilated equality. However, as he further notes, the "central insights" of a liberal democracy can be "teased out, its weaknesses rejected, and the former are absorbed and preserved in a richer social framework" (1994: 218).

The second main problem with Diamond's analysis is that it accepts the claim that cultural differentiation implies political differentiation, which as manifested can only be substantiated on the basis of accepting an elite-driven politicized definition of culture. In other words, Diamond accepts a culturally specific application of political values which, on the face of it, tends to collapse into a disregard for the equal and non-racially determined application of common political principles. This also ignores that "cultural" claims are often invented (see Hobsbawm 1983) or reified (see Pemberton 1994), and most commonly used as a blind for the naked exercise of political power. It is not coincidental that such cultural claims primarily appear in authoritarian political environments where they cannot be tested (see Chee 1998). That is, "successful" authoritarian political systems do not allow plebiscites to test the validity of their own claims. Even allowing a cross-over between culture and politics, or the acculturation of political values, the underlying assumption is that such "culture" is static and not open to influence or change, and is overwhelmingly contradicted by the evidence presented by, for example, the cultural impact of industrialization and global communication. As Sen argues, the idea of democracy is not purely or exclusively Western, especially if it is understood as decision making through public reasoning, an idea that has a long tradition in many parts of the world. According to Sen: "The diversity of the human past and the freedoms of the contemporary world give us much more choice than cultural determinists acknowledge" (Sen 2006).

The third main problem with Diamond's claim is that it accepts a separation between the idea of liberal democracy and civil and political rights which, by definition, raises a contradiction between liberal democracy and the conditions required to sustain it. Democracy is predicated upon acknowledging and retaining a symbiotic relationship with civil and political rights, which even Diamond (1999: 11–13) appears to appreciate.

The underlying contradiction in Diamond's position that is the cause of this confusion is that it reflects the inherent tension within a common American political philosophy. That is, the political philosophy of the US is predicated upon a distinct version of liberalism segueing into libertarianism that tends to find expression in politically conservative values. In seeking an explanation for this tension, and perhaps internal contradiction, there are two causal factors, which in turn stem from an underlying pre-condition. The first factor is the claim of many of the founders of the US to religious freedom, which remains a continuing tradition, implying legitimacy of difference without state interference. The idea of separation of the church and state is here primarily a protection from the vagaries of official religion, as experienced in Europe, and to a lesser extent the protection of the state from religious edicts. However, religious belief tends to be, if it is consistent, morally and socially conservative and traditionalist in its outlook. Interestingly, religious belief is also a prime example of where the US is more rather than less socially focused, even if this does imply a cultural divide within the US between those who are a part of actively religious communities and those who are not.

The second causal factor is that the US places considerable emphasis on economic as opposed to social (or political) liberalism, with its implications for a default challenge to state authority, particularly around questions of taxation and social services. That is, economic liberalism finds itself in competition with social liberalism, which creates a philosophy of rights *vis-à-vis* the state while at the same time also creating polarized economic circumstances that, in their less privileged manifestation, fall back on the rhetoric of independence from state authority (for example, in the case of official threat, "I know my rights"). Economic liberalism is, at base, about the extension of economic opportunity, but also the protection from the state of the fruits of that opportunity. This then sets up a dichotomy between the claims of social liberalism, which would generally imply a degree of egalitarianism in terms of more equal civic participation through greater access to equal economic opportunity, and economic liberalism, or libertarianism, which denies such economic egalitarianism. This is the second and perhaps more important way in which the US is deeply imbued with socially conservative values. That is to say, if political societies are imbued with the genetic code of their creation, the US continues to play out the logical implications of an intellectual debate that flourished in the second half of the eighteenth century. Diamond has not escaped the political impasse that was at the center of this debate, just as perhaps my own position has not escaped from the Chartist claims that informed Australian reformist liberalism.

Some qualities of "representative" government

Representative political systems usually function on the basis of a simple majority, which ensures a basic utilitarian criterion for decision making. To overcome the problem of potential majoritarianism, especially in sensitive matters such as constitutional change, a majority of two-thirds or similar might be required (for example, in federated states a simple overall majority but also a majority of the federated states). In a country like Cambodia, which suffered the deprecations of misrule and failed state status, and in which politics was polarized to the point of civil war (implying the possibility of a dictatorship of the majority), even basic legislation requires a two-thirds majority. This meant that the government effectively had to enjoy a two-thirds majority, which in turn implied a coalition of parties. This arrangement was intended as a moderating influence on any potential dictatorship of "fifty per cent plus one." More positively, however, most democracies that give meaning to the term "representation" operate on the basis of the government being elected by a majority but governing on behalf of all, or the great majority of citizens. A further moderating influence on potential for "dictatorship of the majority" is, in most democracies, the existence of not just a legislature but an elected body of review, often referred to as a senate, or upper house. The "review," or moderating function, is particularly noticeable in cases where a majority of the review body derives from an opposing ideology (usually manifested as a minor political party or coalition of parties) to the majority of the legislature. In such cases, the moderation of legislation is usually required in order to pass the review process. Where a majority of the review body is aligned with the majority of the legislature, however, this review function may be compromised. There may also be constitutional constraints or other checks and balances on the operation of a simple majority or even in cases of individual exception to utilitarian preference.

In the early twenty-first century, democratically elected governments increasingly claimed to have a "mandate" to govern, or to implement a particular policy program, especially if their electoral victory was particularly convincing. Yet the term "mandate," as it has been come to be used, undersells the problem of the majoritarian model while at the same time exempting governments from accountability. By definition, a democratically elected government has the right and responsibility to govern. But for representative government to work well, it must also remain accountable for its actions, which implies the need for a high degree of transparency and cannot assume that a mandate to govern implies a mandate to disenfranchise the minority. The cost of doing so, of course, is civil discord which, increasingly, even the most "democratic" governments from time to time skirt dangerously close to doing. This has particularly been the case since the fundamental economic paradigm shift of the late twentieth century towards a more libertarian economic "user pays" model, especially for goods and services that for the previous half of the century had been widely considered as part of the role and function of government (for example, education, health care and basic levels of other social services).

The democratic model that most people are familiar with is that of representative democracy, which as its name implies allows decision-making by representatives who are in turn elected by citizens. The major distinction within the representative democratic model is between representatives who are elected on the basis of specific electorates and those who are elected as a proportion of the total electorate. The first system has the advantage of offering representation to a specific grouping of citizens, which in theory ensures greater representation of their specific concerns. More negatively, however, it means that only representatives who are able to claim a majority in each area can offer representation. This may mean that voters for minority candidates are left without representation, or that such representation can only exist outside of the ideology of the candidate (for example, a representative can represent a specific issue for a local citizens but not a policy position unless they are a majority voter). While this tends to balance between representatives of major ideologies, usually manifested as political parties, this has the further effect of marginalizing small but still significant political groupings. To illustrate, a political party that receives 20 per cent of the vote across all electorates will not win any of them, and hence 20 per cent of citizens will remain unrepresented. A system which elects representatives as a proportion of the total electorate is much more likely to redress this possible imbalance, so that there will be close enough to the same proportion of representatives as there are citizens' votes for them. This is more democratic in overall representative terms, but it has the effect of distancing representatives from specific voter bases, and thus decreases the opportunities for more direct representation. A balance between the two systems, with a bicameral legislature comprising a local representative model in the lower house, or house of government and a proportional representative system in the upper house or house of review (or checks against the potential excesses of the lower house), is close to the best possible balance in an overall representative democratic model.

There are two general representative political systems, each of which has advantages and drawbacks, and each of which can put a claim to greater or lesser degrees of political development. The models are republican and parliamentary. The parliamentary model differs from the republican model in that the chief executive is elected by the legislature (and often the elected review body/upper house/senate) by and from an elected majority which is usually the dominant party or coalition of parties. This means the executive necessarily represents a majority of the legislature, which means there is no separation between the executive and legislative processes. As such, there are consequently fewer opportunities for checks and balances, or more capacity for subverting the legislative process for executive reasons. The executive is also not directly chosen by a majority of the people, but is elected indirectly by already elected representatives, which acts as a layer of removal of direct choice by voters.

The republican democratic model proposes a formal separation of powers between the executive, the legislature and the judiciary (the so-called *trias politica*), with the chief executive (commonly a president) and usually a deputy (commonly a vice-president), as well as the legislature being popularly elected. The original intention of the separation of powers, based on Montesquieu's "improvement" of the British constitutional system, was to formally delineate the legislative powers of these three estates (as a limitation on the excesses of the French monarchy and oppression of the French judiciary), but that the actual separation in England and the US was based on separating the legislative function from other state functions. Those further functions were also divided between relevant institutions, thus ensuring a system of checks and balances (Huntington 1968: 110). One step further removed again is Neustadt, who suggests that the separation of powers is, in practise, the separation of institutions that share powers (Neustadt 1960: 33). The separation of powers has also been supplemented by a "fourth estate," which commonly refers to the "watchdog" function of an unfettered news media, but which can also apply to functionally independent government agencies or, indeed, to the role of an ombudsman as a source of appeal and adjudication on government actions.

The reality of the practise of the separation of powers has been, in functioning democracies, reflected in elements of overlap between the executive, the legislature and to a much lesser extent the judiciary, with the news media and ombudsmen normatively retaining distinct and separate roles, and with government agencies varying in their independent capacities. The executive can usually both propose and enact (or decline to enact) legislative provisions, while the legislature can support, modify or reject executive proposals. The judiciary is more limited, being employed to oversee the application of law, although it does have some discretionary power to apply legal sanctions according to circumstances and, to some extent, prevailing social expectations. Like other political models, the separation of powers exists in an idealized sense and works in a real, practical sense, with sometimes considerable degrees of success.

A further characteristic of republicanism, according to some theorists, is its constitutional orientation in contrast to the precedent of parliamentary democracy (even though most parliamentary democracies also enjoy constitutions). In this, parliamentary models are derived from the pre-republican French model in which parliament (derived from the French *parler*: "to talk") is the talking shop of vested interests (a continuing example of which in the UK system is the now reduced capacity of the House of Lords), and which tends to be based upon precedent. Republics, on the other hand, assume to devolve authority to the people via their representatives, but in any case under a more formal constitution. Conceptions of republicanism can and sometimes do also posit republicanism in contrast to liberalism, based on what is sometimes seen as an opposition between the state and the individual (for example, Hobbes as opposed to Locke), or the supposed opposition of the requirements of law and the claims of freedom (Larmore, in Weinstock and Nadeau 2004: 106–9; see also Petit 1999; Berlin 1969: 118–72). Digeser describes the former freedom of non-interference as based on Roman law, predicated on notions of justice, in particular natural justice (Digeser, in Weinstock and Nadeau 2004: 6, 10, 12). Republicanism does not require democracy to constitute itself, and indeed most non-democratic states are constituted as republics. However, the main claims to republicanism have been predicated upon assertions of civic freedom, and thus the possible dichotomy is a consequence of an imbalance in the application of law as opposed to individual liberty. Similarly, an absolute liberty without formal responsibility or socially agreed constraints can constitute a restriction on the freedom of others.

Romans generally, and Cicero in particular, defined republicanism according to the values and goals served by government, not according to its form or structure. Justice and common good were central to this (Digeser, in Weinstock and Nadeau 2004). However, this definition tends to confuse the political goals of republicanism with the method by which they are achieved. In this sense, republicanism is a goal rather than a method, which tends to undermine its later organizational meaning and quality that has been challenged by systems that place little emphasis on justice or common good in any meaningful sense.

Republican models of government can be found across a diverse range of states, ranging from the US and France at one end of the spectrum, which exemplify philosophically different approaches to the purpose of the republic (personal advance as opposed to social good), to China at the other end (which does not enjoy a functional separation of powers) and Indonesia (which in the early twenty-first century was still coming to terms with the idea of the separation of powers, see for example, Pompe 2005). The theoretical advantage of the republican system is that it ensures that each of the branches of government can operate independently within their own sphere of responsibility, and as a balance to the others. The legislature determines the laws of the state, executive authority determines the implementation of such laws and the general running of the state, and the judiciary is responsible for adjudicating on breaches of these laws, separate to the influence of either the legislature or the executive. Republics are also theoretically constituted to ensure the welfare of their citizens.

More negatively, however, the republican model is a somewhat under-developed version of constitutional elected monarchy, in which the chief executive functions as an elected monarch, usually with a high degree of independence once elected, which may have the capacity to destablize and/or delegitimize political processes (see Linz 1993). In this, the chief executive may act against the legislature or other bodies of review, or may act without prior approval or consultation, claiming as justification a "mandate." This especially tends to occur, for example, in cases where the chief executive has the authority to act unilaterally in times of emergency, such as war. Such unilateralism, however, may precipitate rather than respond to emergencies, or where after having made such a commitment there is a reduced functional opportunity for review. Once a war has been entered into, short of surrender and its consequent losses, there are few opportunities for deciding against it, to wit the Vietnam War post-Gulf of Tonkin incident, and the US-led war in Iraq. More generally, while republican models may reflect personalized authority, this does not necessarily imply either liberalism or democracy and is frequently a political vehicle for the centralization of power in the hands of a few, or one, and the consequent abrogation of the principle of separation of powers. In this, constitutions that give republics their legitimacy can be constructed or construed in anti-democratic and illiberal ways. For example, even in a democratic state, such as the US, the executive cabinet is appointed by the chief executive, and may receive portfolios on the basis of favor as well as competence, reflecting the patrimonialism of pre-modern or less developed political societies.

The most important aspect of the *trias politica*, however, is less in the separation of the executive and the legislature, which can have positive and negative consequences, but in the separation between the executive and the judiciary (and arguably the administrative bureaucracy), which gives sub-stance to laws passed by the legislature. Parliaments tend to operate either under a constitutional monarchy (for example, the UK, Australia, New Zealand and, less successfully, Thailand and Cambodia) or a limited or ceremonial presidency (such as India, South Africa, Ireland, East Timor), to provide a ceremonial head of state. The head of state may serve as a point of reference to determine matters concerning "reserve powers," such as the swearing in of ministers or, in extreme circumstances, the removal of minis-ters or, indeed, of a government. Some parliamentary systems also have a stronger or more active presidency, which reflects that they are also repub-lics (for example, France and Russia) although a stronger presidency in a parliamentary model can potentially create confusion and tension over the allocation of executive responsibility and accountability (for example, Laos, Vietnam and Sri Lanka).

Finally, the experience of most parliaments is that the chief executive, although chosen by the legislature, is invariably also the head of the majority party or coalition of parties, and hence arrives at leadership on the basis of already being leader in a pre-existing context. This and a common political tendency to centralize authority mean that the political leader is less a "first" minister among equals but rather a political leader to whom other ministers are subservient. Indeed, in most parliamentary systems, the prime minister has the authority to choose and dispose of his ministers in a manner not dissimilar to that of a republican president. Further, and increasingly, the media has tended to focus on individuals, and to some extent, the related "cult of personality." This has also meant that the political authority of prime ministers has increased, that their governments are identified with them as personalities (for example, the Thatcher government, Blair government). As such, the executives in parliamentary systems have tended to take on a more personalized form of rule in a manner again approaching that of a republican chief executive (president).

In both parliamentary and republican democratic systems, there are two broad sets of qualifications which temper the potential excesses of individuals or political groups that could be considered as principle markers of political development. The first is the constitutional constraints that can apply to democratic rule, including reference to the separation of powers, the role of a house of review, and other possible limitations such as reference to affected parties (especially in federated states). Further to constitutional constraints are political conventions, or the articulated but not codified rules that apply to the conduct of political life, such as general respect for civil and political rights and freedom of speech in societies that do not have legislated rights, or the legislative passage of "supply." In a parliamentary system, such conventions may also include legislation to enable government financing by a house of review, recognizing the legitimacy of the government deriving from the legislature. The second qualification is the legislated right of the people to vote at regular intervals for and against individuals or parties of their choice, in which the adequate representation of interests is rewarded, and inadequate or counter-representation is punished. This then raises debate about the adequacy of representation of interests, the influence over or control of such interests, and the subtlety as well as bluntness of the exercise of power.

Some other "democracies"

The term "people's democracy" has come to describe those political systems which claim that by ending the economic dominance of capitalism and the consequent imbalance in, access to, or influence upon political power, such a system represents "true" rule by the people. The assumption is that if the people have an opportunity to choose a government outside of the constraints of bourgeois (that is, capitalist economic) control, they will rationally choose a form of socialism that leads to communism (or economic egalitarianism leading to material freedom).

While there are debates for and against the claim that economic power equates with, determines or leads to political power, the problem with this "people's democratic" system as it has been applied is that it has almost always arrived as a consequence of either violent revolution or external intervention. That is, "people's democracy" has been almost invariably achieved by imposition, and, once established, it has tended to constrain the choices for voting to those political parties and organizations that promote the anti-capitalist premise. The rationalization of such parties is that, already representing the people in a claimed absolute democratic sense, the idea of democracy is already fulfilled by the fact of their existence. This assumes an absolute communitarian approach to democracy. In practise, this means that the prevailing political organization – usually a party that claims socialist or Marxist inspiration[4] – tends to dominate the political landscape. It may do this by only allowing marginally different or closely affiliated parties to exist, vetoing candidates for ideological "taints" (for example, the Communist Party of Vietnam also allows approved non-Party candidates, who in 1992 took 8 per cent of the vote), and otherwise ensuring through a series of bureaucratic and quasi-legal processes that only the party of government can win any "elections." Thus communitarianism tends to assume a bureaucratic or technocratic style which, according to its own internal logic, diminishes alternatives and tends to replicate itself. This necessarily becomes authoritarian and, in its more absolute manifestation, totalitarian (see Weber 1948; also Liebman 1975: 290 on concerns by the USSR's Democratic Centralists over the tendency towards "bureaucratic centralism" and "authoritarian centralism" soon after the Russian Revolution).

If one agrees with the internal logic of the "people's" system, it does indeed produce a "people's democracy." As Desai noted, the Soviet Union conducted five yearly elections of candidates chosen by constituent groupings – professionals, factory workers, farmers and women – while allowing three-week election campaigns that included rallies, canvassing and active discussion of local and national issues. Non-compulsory voter turnout was also relatively high, at above 70 per cent. On the face of it, this would appear to represent a democratic system of at least the procedural variety. However, while in the post-Stalin era there was a greater representation of constituent groups and candidates for election were locally selected, what was also noted was that "the party dominates the choice of candidates put on the slate for approval," meaning that "parallels with pluralistic democracy are . . . superficial" (1989: 125). If one assumes that democracy connotes a plurality of choices and the consequent freedom of expression to comment in favor of such choices, then this system fell far short of democracy in any meaningful sense of the term. The imposition of a political and bureaucratic elite via a pre-ordained choice of candidates that is not meaningfully subject to external change in fact implies a form of dictatorship rather than democracy. This tendency towards a totalizing control of the political environment is usually referred to as "totalitarianism."

Another form of "democracy" existed in Zimbabwe, where there were regular elections and parties receiving state funding. President Robert Mugabe's attempts to create a one-party state were even defeated in 1990 by his own party, the Zimbabwe African National Union-Patriotic Front (ZANU-PF). However, ZANU-PF had won every election in Zimbabwe since 1980, opposition parties and their rallies were infiltrated and disrupted by ZANU-PF agents and their candidates were harassed, threatened and attacked. The media was also tightly controlled, the electoral commission was deeply compromised and the president could appoint 30 members to parliament which, along with a number of opposition candidates boycotting the elections in 1995, gave ZUNA-PF an absolute majority even before it went to the polls (Dashwood 2000: 109–10). It therefore did not conform to a standardized definition of democracy in any meaningful sense.

If there is a further category of democracy that is predicated upon the logical extension of the idea of citizenship and the common human basis of civil and political rights, that is the rather grandly or impossibly idealistically named "world democracy." The idea of "world democracy" does not and can not practically exist, in a contemporary sense in which each "world citizen" would vote for a world government or on global referenda. In the first instance, there would be required a functionally similar or same democratic system at work in each constituent country (and there are currently a number of countries that are not in the least democratic), along with external monitoring of such voting conditions.

Each of the world's states could potentially function under a global coordinating body, such as the UN, as a type of global parliament, or via other global bodies. The key argument against the UN is that, under the "realist" international relations theory that the internal composition of states is irrelevant to their external relations, it allocates equal representation to each of the world's states regardless of their population size. This means that states such as Tuvalu (population 11,809 as of mid-2006) have the same voting rights as China (population 1,314,093,060 as of mid-2006).[5] Other problems include some of the permanent structures of the UN, such as the Security Council, which allocates permanent seats to five members (China, France, the Russian Federation, the UK and the US), and ten rotating members, which functionally gives some countries greater capacity to influence global events without recourse to popular or rotating ballot. Beyond this, the UN's other agencies have been claimed to be unrepresentative, as have other global bodies such as the WTO and the World Bank. At the same time, many policy issues are increasingly global in nature, such as global warming, other major environmental issues (such as the extinction of species), the extent of nuclear weapons, and the global reliance on oil and other non-renewable energy sources (see, for example, Holden 2000). Answers to these policy problems increasingly appear to be found in shared or global agreement, which implies at least a global consensus, and sometimes a global decision by vote.

The idea of global democracy might be a distant or unrealistic goal for most people, or indeed a distant nightmare for those who believe that government is inherently untrustworthy and that the larger its scope the greater its capacity for insensitive interference. However, the ideas that inform global democracy do find a foundation in what might be called a "global civil society," or civic cosmopolitanism. Assuming that the idea of civil society is a necessary component of substantive democracy, and that processes of democratization only arise in response to civil movements and are sustained by civic values, then civic cosmopolitanism is at least a substantial step towards a global democracy (see Archibugi and Held 1995: 121–62 regarding the UN and global democracy). The critical links between civic cosmopolitanism and global democracy are predicated upon three interlinked criteria: civil and political rights, global communication, and conceptions of global citizenship.

In the first instance, as noted above, conceptions of civil and political rights are both necessary for substantive democracy and are implicit in it. As such rights are basic human rights, they apply to the quality of being human, rather than belonging to a specific cultural group or polity. In turn, this quality of being human is manifested uniformly among all people, regardless of location, and thus constitutes a legitimate basis for global citizenship. Assuming that attached to the idea of citizenship is active participation in the affairs of the polity, and certain reciprocal obligations via the idea of citizen's consent (see Rousseau 1973), it is possible to extrapolate from civil and political rights a claim to representation. The biggest stumbling block to this, however, is that civil and political rights are often recognized in the breech, and hence the practical reality that claims to those rights are in such cases built upon an idea and not a substantive base.

The second link between civic cosmopolitanism and global democracy derives from the first generation civil right of freedom of expression and its confluence with enhanced global communications (Beetham 1999: Chapter 7). The idea of freedom of expression is not just a constituent civil and political right and, hence, part of a reciprocal political claim, but it is the primary method by which such claims are made. The simple fact is that the vast increase in global communications since the early 1990s has meant while one should not overstate the effect of global communications (many less literate, illiterate or technologically or economically disadvantaged people still have little or no access to such communications) it is now possible to transmit and receive information and ideas to and from otherwise largely inaccessible areas, and between communities that might have previously had quite limited outside communication. As such, individuals and groups around the world can now talk with and debate each other almost synchronically, as well as politically organize. The global anti-WTO movement and various global solidarity movements are cases in point, as well as the provision of information about specific situations that call forth an international response. It has been said that America's Vietnam War was the first war to be televised, and that this had a major impact upon its outcome. If this is true, then the explosion of global communications since the early 1990s has meant that no major event can go entirely unnoticed, and that all are open to scrutiny, if also media management, and, at different levels, intervention.

This then raises the idea not just of passive global citizenship implied in civil and political rights, but of active global citizenship in which "world citizens" seize opportunities for global engagement and democratic participation. Within this is the idea of citizens asserting their claims to civil and political rights, not as official representatives of a particular state or institution, but as free thinking individuals and constituent members of freely constituted groups and organizations (for example, Global Trade Watch, Third World Network, Greenpeace, East Timor Action Network, and so on). It may be that global democracy is a distant idea, but the reality of global citizenship has arrived and is increasingly available to those with the requisite literacy, technological access, and political will.

While the term "democracy" can be argued to have a particular etymological meaning, even its theoretical meanings are numerous and varied. The use of "democracy" in practise, then, is even more inconsistent and, at times, contradictory. Perhaps when talking about political models that most closely equate with or support the idea of political development, it is more useful to describe their particular qualities, and to include in such description a series of checks and balances that require a type of moderation. Many might argue that the requirement of moderation is not itself democratic, and that it could be a limitation upon democratic will. This is correct but, as Lev notes, if democracy equates with unrestrained mob rule, then perhaps this is not really the political system that most people have in mind when they consider the term. That is to say, the greatest degree of political participation and, in a representative system, accountability, must be balanced against rule of law (see, for example, Walker 1988), which constructs the framework within which sets of decisions may be taken. Within this, the minority must be protected from the possible depredations of the majority, lest the political community divide and devour itself.

Assuming, then, that some sort of political system that encourages a high degree of participation, representation and accountability based of regular free and fair elections, and assuming it is called democracy, it remains possible to criticize it in both theory and practise from a range of perspectives. Each one of these perspectives will have a greater or lesser degree of legitimacy attached to them. In practise, it appears that what we call democracy (or even a Levian elected oligarchy) will remain fraught with structural problems, and that addressing each of these will only produce new problems. Democracy is, therefore, beset with weaknesses and flaws, some of which might or might not be seen to be critical. Yet it is difficult to conceive of a political system that is inherently fairer, more equal or more open in both theory and in practise. It therefore might be that, as Churchill once famously noted, "democracy is the worst form of government . . . except all those other forms" (1947).

7   Democratization

Assuming that a political system that is agreed to be "democracy" exists or can exist, it does not just manifest as an expression of normative but otherwise unstructured political desires. At the very least, democracy arrives via a process of transition from non-democracy, almost always with some disagreement as to its desirability, frequently in tandem with at least some conflict and almost always incompletely, at least for the initial period. Moreover, once democracy has been established, it invariably remains vulnerable to diminution, often by those people and institutions that are its putative principle guardians and beneficiaries (that is, elected politicians) (see O'Donnell *et al*. 1988). Indeed the most self-satisfied democratic state can see its democratic credentials diminish as sacrifices are made to various forms of political expediency. If not quite the political dance implied by "one step forward, two steps back" (see Lenin 1961, Vol. 7),[1] the path towards democracy is usually indirect, its outcome is often far from inevitable, and such democratic outcomes are almost certainly never permanent. More to the point, there is no final point at which democracy can be said to have completely arrived, as even the most inclusive and democratic states are able to improve upon their own political systems.

Beyond democracy's uncertainty, while there is an assumption that democratization will produce liberalization, and it can be argued political liberalization is a necessary component of democracy, liberalization and democratization are not synonymous. Indeed, it is possible, if not especially common, to have liberal regimes that are not democratic (such as benign monarchy). Without the guarantees of individual and group freedoms implied in liberalization, democratization risks at best not moving beyond a basic proceduralism, and at worst degenerating into a mere shell of the term "democracy," in which the substance completely subverts the intentions of its title (O'Donnell and Schmitter 1986: 9). This does not imply that both democratization and liberalization should or can be introduced completely at one time. It is likely that a radical shift from non-democracy to liberal democracy will produce not just a political shock, but will destabilize existing institutions in ways that could decrease their efficacy and thus undermine the potential material benefit of such changes. This situation would be likely to engender a greater backlash from political and economic forces that are most likely to see their interests diminished by such a change.

To that end, and because of the practical difficulties of implementing major change across a whole political, social and economic spectrum, a formally structured approach to the introduction of democratization and liberalization is desirable. To confound a precise analytic approach, however, there is a great deal of difficulty in accurately measuring gradations of democratization (Elklit 1994: 104–9), or perhaps even measuring it at all (O'Donnell and Schmitter 1986: 9), other than as tactical gains in a strategic political environment. Having noted that, Schmitter and Schneider (2003: 15) have been able to present a time series approach to the liberalization and consolidation of democratizing countries, in which they identified what they considered to be key criteria. These include significant public concessions on human rights, none or almost no political prisoners, increased tolerance for dissidence, more than one independent political party, at least one legal opposition party in the legislature, free trade unions or professional associations, and an independent press and access to alternative means of information.

The criteria outlined by Schmitter and Schneider correspond closely to those outlined by Dahl as necessary for a functioning democracy. But while these do constitute identifiable measures, there remains ambiguity around the function of each criterion, deferring to the earlier concerns over the consistency of democratic measurement. Having noted that, the logic of tactical victories is that each one makes a strategic victory seem that much closer and possible, if not inevitable. Moreover, sometimes if winning partially is by definition incomplete, it produces a better real-world outcome that attempting to win completely but ending up losing everything. If democracy is seen as a process rather than an outcome, then there is no final destination and, as such, there is continual engagement with and reflexivity towards the idea, and the guardians of democracy will be more likely comprised of the wider citizenry, thus increasing its prospects for protection and subsequent extension.

Within the various categories of "democracy," there is the question of method of obtaining such a political system or how such a political system arises. Various methods for political evolution can include revolution, devolution from another political structure or external introduction or imposition. This then raises the questions of political acculturation (habituation) and the material conditions necessary to maintain social cohesion to allow democratic forms. There are also a range of other political systems or political outcomes, as well as "blended" political systems, that contain some elements of democracy and other political systems, which may even call themselves wholly "democratic" or be so called by those whose structural or institutional interests benefit from the acceptance of such a rhetorical device. It is in such blended political environments that freedom of expression and other basic human rights remain inherently uncertain.

The political contexts within which the processes of democratization occur usually fall into one of two categories. In the first context, the undemocratic government of the day recognizes that democratic change is inevitable and voluntarily accedes to the introduction of a democratizing process. The second, most common context is when an undemocratic government is forced to change and inevitably is pushed from office. Continuing on from this forced process, there may be a coup or revolution against a non-democratic government which then introduces a democratizing process. It is worth noting, however, that forced change can and often does produce an unstable political environment. Such regime change is often not accompanied by democratization, but by an initially more benign form of authoritarianism or a relatively liberal version of "non-democracy." The extent to which such an alternative regime remains benign or liberal is open to a range of variables, but it is important to note that governments that do not come to power by democratic means are not often interested in voluntarily, or at least immediately, continuing the process of political transformation to democracy.

Any discussion of "democracy" in its more or less complete form will necessarily have to address its constituents; that is, the people who comprise this political manifestation and their respective forms of individual and social organization. Key within this framework is the idea of "civil society," which assumes a capacity for individuals and constituent groups to act politically across a range of issues or areas, both directly in relationship to government, and also in non-government or even anti-government ways. Professional associations, unions, student groups, interest groups, the media, NGOs and active individuals all comprise civil society. The political and social health of such groups and individuals are usually markers of the political health of the society they help constitute. Similarly, the capacities of groups and individuals to act in various ways, the extent to which they can draw on public goodwill or government attention and the relationships between them ultimately define the balance between people and political institutions, and the responsiveness of those institutions. That is, civil society is "deemed to be a "realm of freedom" – by comparison to the state, which is a "realm of coercion" – but it is also seen to reflect the principle of balance or equilibrium" (Heywood 2003: 48).

Assuming a "naturalized" view of a political model that corresponds to at least some of the more apparent, and perhaps superficial, aspects of "democracy," and which happens to work well (or is broadly perceived as working well) for and within a particular hegemonic framework, it is possible to convince oneself that this represents the highest manifestation of political existence. In such situations, humanity could, at least in part, be conceived of as reaching "the end of history" (Fukuyama 1992). The idea of the "end of history" does not assume that historical events will cease to continue, but that, following Hegel's view, key historical development has an end. For Hegel, history "ended" with the battle of Jena in 1806, in which Napoleon's army defeated Prussian and Saxon forces, ending what was left of the Holy Roman

Empire and allowing the wider introduction of the Napoleonic Code, which is widely regarded as the first successful civil legal code in Europe. Hegel thought that as a consequence of this effective foundation of rule of law, the era of modernity had arrived, through which human society had reached the highest possible point of its development towards the goal of freedom. Fukuyama followed Hegel in this belief in a highest point towards the goal of freedom, arguing that the era of liberal democracy (and accompanying neo-liberal economics) had achieved this end. Following Hegel, if from an oppositional perspective, Marx saw communism and its attendant resolution of socio-economic contradiction as the "end of history." In this respect, the "end of history" is supposed to reflect the demonstrator effect of a claimed final point in the practical aspirations of political life.

As discussed elsewhere, however, this "end of history" thesis implies the totalizing belief that one world view – in this case about what constitutes the greatest realization of freedom – can account for all world views. It also implies that the world view in question is actually what it is presented to be; in these cases, that political modernity was made available by the imposition of the Napoleonic Code throughout much of Europe or, according to Fukuyama, that the US had led the world to an otherwise mythical political golden age. In this more contemporary sense, Fukuyama presented liberal democracy and "liberal" (or neo-liberal) capitalism as an "ideal" model, assuming a correspondence between the rhetoric of liberalism and its reality that even many in the host country (US) do not agree to be substantiated. That is, liberal democracy as such does not work as it is ideally supposed to,[2] and (neo-)liberal capitalism is far from a universally accepted good. Nor can the latter be said to promote freedom, except for those less than universal recipients who are fortunate enough to be liberated by its bounty.

More disconcertingly, there is a strong argument to suggest that as states increasingly lose control of their economies to the globalized movement of capital, they compete in an also globalized wage market in which, in a cost-cutting race to the bottom, the lowest wage for common skills becomes the common denominator. Advanced industrialized countries have not yet entirely succumbed to this pressure, continuing as they do to profit from their technological and educational advantages. However, as many states climb the technological and educational ladder – China and India being notable examples – the increasing competition for the provision of goods and services provided by the OECD countries forces them to compete on more even terms. Somewhat paradoxically, at a time that would infer greater mobility in (cheap) labor, governments have increasingly restricted access to their own countries via stricter border controls, immigration provisions and rejection of or serious limitations upon refugees. Not entirely coincidentally, at the same time, such governments are moving towards introducing tighter security legislation, greatly improving their capacity for intelligence gathering and surveillance and, in some cases, introducing "racial profiling" of people suspected of presenting an actual or potential threat. From the perspective of a middle class OECD citizen, such security restrictions would seem not to apply. Yet this raises two further issues, the first being that this narrowly defined sense of personal security is *prima facie* morally devoid, with all the implications this has for logical permutations. The second is that often what end up as horrific governments begin their slide away from inclusive democratic principles and towards a widespread abrogation of civil and political rights by initially applying such abrogation selectively, especially to people who have been demonized by group identification such as racial profiling.

It could be argued that Hegel's "end of history" was simply a victory for a section of Europe's bourgeoisie, although another interpretation might suggest it was a victory for the modern state. Marx followed Hegel by arguing there could (and inevitably would) be an "end of history" of an idealized type, but for Marx this would arrive once the contradictions inherent in a class-based society were resolved; freedom would arrive with both political and economic equality in a utopian communitarian society. Marx envisaged a voluntary society comprised of free people not alienated from either the product of their labor or each other, who divided their time between necessary labor, creative and intellectual labor and social pursuits, and who shared their economic benefits on the basis of capacity to provide for individual needs. The term "communism" in this sense functionally means free communitarianism, but interpreted as a dictatorship of the proletariat, and through its practical application, it came to take on a more authoritarian meaning.

Based on the failure of communism as it has been commonly understood, and the relative success (not to mention triumphalism) of liberal democracy and capitalism,[3] Fukuyama claimed that liberal democracy was indeed the "end of history" and that Hegel, not Marx, had been essentially correct (Fukuyama 1992: Chapter 5). While it is possible to put forward a strong claim to fundamental universals – including for a political system that could be accurately described as liberal democracy – the charge of ethnocentrism is in part validated. The key problem is not that there cannot be a universal assumption about the desirability of "freedom" and its practical application through liberal democracy. The problem is that what is defined as "liberal democracy" may not actually be very liberal or democratic, and may reflect a peculiarly American world view, or indeed a particular view within a broader American cultural framework. This applies in particular to Fukuyama's assumption that (neo-)liberal economic policies are necessarily compatible with liberal politics.

> For labor markets to function efficiently, labor has to become increasingly mobile: workers cannot remain permanently tied to a particular job, locale, or set of social relationships, but must become free to move about, learn new tasks and technologies, and sell their labor to the highest bidder. This has a powerful effect in undermining traditional social groups like tribes, clans, extended families, religious sects, and so

> on. The latter may in certain respects be more humanly satisfying to live
> in, but since they are not organized according to the rational principles of
> economic efficiency, they tend to lose out to those that are.
>
> (Fukuyama 1992: 77)

It is correct to note that the US labor market has become increasingly
deregulated, that there is a relatively high degree of mobility in its workforce,
and that advanced technological societies are increasingly moving towards
"multi-skilling," or mid-life retraining. However, to assume that these qualities apply elsewhere requires not only a particularly blinkered view of the
world, but that this model is somehow desirable or necessary. The process of
economic modernization and attendant urbanization has, in those societies
where it has been successful, created new sets of social relationships (and
problems) that are far removed from village life. This does not then imply
that urban workers should be the rootless cogs in an economically efficient
machine as Fukuyama suggests. Apart from the value of stability and security
to both employer and employee, one might be left wondering what is the
purpose of this type of economic development if it produces an efficient
economic machine but makes living in it, without social depth, stability
or economic security, less than worthwhile. If alienation is the outcome of
"efficiency" – and in this one might wonder about the contextual efficiency
of Britain's nineteenth century labor mills which gave rise to the original
version of communism – the problem would appear to be less about the
manifestation of alienation – and its potential consequences – and more with
its "efficient" cause. In an ideal "efficient" economy, both nuclear and extended
families that are increasingly dependent on dual incomes or dual sites of labor
(for example, the field and the mine, or offices in separate cities) would be
torn by the requirement of individual mobility, with the final "rational" unit
of economic production being the lone, rootless, alienated individual. This
equates to the compulsion of a state of "individuality," or more accurately
atomized isolation, rather than the dignified autonomy of the individual as an
equal and respected member of a plural democratic community.

It is such cultural assumptions, in this case based on the privilege of
control over mobility and retraining (and Fukuyama himself has had a
comfortable career in policy development), that in many cases masquerade on
behalf of structural economic requirements. These sorts of assumptions, have
for instance, led the US into war in Iraq. The structural requirements behind
the Iraq war were, essentially, to put in place a "friendly" government in a
state that holds the world's third largest oil reserves and huge natural gas
reserves.[4] At the time of writing, the war itself appears to be un-winnable
because, assuming a democratic united state as the criterion for a successful
outcome, Iraq's internal structural circumstances that shape the competing
visions of the final polity, even with agency, do not support the external
model. Former parties (for example, Ba'ath Party, Kurdistan Democratic
Party) retain vested interests in maintaining or regaining power, while

institutions such as the National Assembly and government, are neither embedded in the total national structure nor the "culture" they claim to represent. Similarly, these institutions are disinclined to account for an authentic expression of local agency. More widely, significant sections of the global Islamic population, itself around 20 per cent of the world's population, prefer a completely different model of social organization based to a greater or lesser degree on *syariah* (Islamic law), while others live in pre-modern patrimonial societies.

The American model of liberal democracy itself comprises vast inequalities of political capacity and opportunity, with status at birth and financial capacity being key markers of political opportunity, as well as low levels of political participation. Only 58 per cent of all eligible US citizens voted in the 2004 presidential elections, with far smaller numbers in other elections. African-Americans and Hispanics proportionately vote in even smaller numbers. These low levels of participation cannot stand as desirable qualities for peoples who genuinely aspire to freedom via a political process. Fukuyama has described the shortcomings of the US political system, and others like it, not as a failure of liberal democracy but as a failure of the full implementation of "the twin principles of liberty and equality" (1992: xi). One might counter that the full implementation of liberty and equality, and hence liberal democracy, in such societies is structurally constrained by pronounced economic inequality. Beyond the US's and other countries' inconsistency in supporting these principles abroad, liberal democracy can in practise be beset with a range of similar problems based on illiteracy, tribalism, physical access, patrimonialism and institutional violence, as well as simple misunderstandings over form and content. For example, the common assumptions that the Philippines' "people power" revolution of 1986 was both driven by the "common people" and resulted in liberal democratic change, are incorrect. As Fukuyama points out, the practical problems of liberal democracy do not deny the basic legitimacy of its claim. But a more realistic understanding of the application of liberal democracy, its compromises and the often contradictory requirements of liberal economics, would qualify the hubris associated with "end of history" claims. As such, satisfaction with a liberal-democratic model may obscure inherent practical flaws which could compromise and may fatally weaken it.

Democratic failure

This view on the incomplete application or misunderstood meaning of democracy errs towards the pessimistic, and is unfortunately too often confirmed, especially when goals are not understood in terms of how they are achieved. That is, the end of democratization is often portrayed as more important than the means by which it is supposed to be achieved, even though the means tend to determine the end result. There are two paths to democratic failure arising from this perspective. The first is, broadly, that democracy is construed as a singular entity, that it is a given or only viable option, and that governments based on other political systems will ultimately lose legitimacy and default to the popular desirability of democratization. The second is that the means of achieving or sustaining democracy may in themselves undermine basic democratic principles.

Fukuyama and others argue that there is only one form of democracy, and that any variation on its theme reflects a failure of its complete implementation. This implies either a grand, singular vision, or a circumscribed or minimalist understanding of the full meaning of the term. Assuming the grand, singular democratic model, there is no effective room for debate or alternative, as this visionary model casts itself as an absolute, which is in turn reflected in dogma. It is reasonable to argue that there are conditions that do not comply with any internally consistent meaning of democracy (for example, absolute monarchy or totalitarian dictatorship), and the rejection of these models or substantive elements of them can be claimed on behalf of democratic meaning. But the logic does not necessarily follow that democracy can be defined by the absence of such systems; democracy is not the sum of the parts of what it is not, but the sum of the parts of what it is. What it is, however, creates a democratic tension.

Democracy can be understood as system that constantly gravitates to and defers away from the center of its ideals, allowing scope for interpretation, variation and plurality, but at the same time confirming and reconfirming the common principles that bind it together. It is, in effect, a continuing agreement on the value of allowing disagreement, or of disagreement existing within the framework of an agreement about the value of its existence (echoing Voltaire's ascribed saying that "I may not agree with what you say, but I shall defend to the death your right to say it"). From this, the singularity of democracy is its pluralism.

In some circumstances democracy may not be available as a consequence of non-democratic oppression, leading to the reasonable conclusion that the best means of achieving democracy is by removing any anti-democratic apparatus. Given the predictable resistance that such a non-democratic apparatus is likely to exhibit, however, the means of obtaining its removal are likely to require the application, imposition and maintenance of force, which may then lead to the institutionalization of structures that differ from their predecessors in type but conform with or even exceed them in critical aspects of their character (the English, French and Russian revolutions being cases in point). The passive acceptance of claimed political necessity in this way leads to the inadequate implementation and ultimately failure of the democratic project.

The second, more passive manner in which democratic fatalism manifests itself is where democracy is established but is allowed to slip, usually through appeals to immediate contingency and the assurance that democracy's diminution does not affect its day-to-day functioning. This can be seen most clearly in appeals to "security" or less urgently in bureaucratic efficiency, but can also be detected in a widening income gap in most democracies, which *prima facie* is not in the interests of the majority whose incomes are declining, thus reflecting acceptance of a non-democratic hegemony, and in declining levels of political participation in parties (Keane 2006) and other interest groups such as trade unions. Instead political decision making may increasingly be allocated to "experts," bureaucrats and other elite actors.

In this respect, history is not circular, but equally it is not a clear, unbroken line, from "then" until "now." Rather it is a process of movement forward, regression, internal loops, the occasional social, cultural and political *cul de sac*, periods of cyclical repetition, and cathartic events that can usher in a new phase. The existence of liberal democracy in this is not guaranteed and its position, content and meaning, if achieved, is not necessarily permanent.

Regime change

The issue of regime change is critical in the process of political development and often at the point at which options for democratic openings occur. At the point of regime change, there may be a fatalistic belief that political change necessarily produces normatively positive outcomes. The period of regime change is the point at which there is greatest political flux and hence both opportunity and threat. Where there is opportunity, it is often understood in terms of the resolution of a negative (usually associated with the end of an authoritarian government or dictatorship) through the positive introduction of a democratic government. In fact, while new forms of government may have the external characteristics of democracy (such as in the Philippines in 1986, or Indonesia in 1998), there may be partially or completely hidden components that fundamentally compromise the capacity of the general population to meaningfully participate in political affairs or to be genuinely represented (see O'Donnell 1996 for discussion on this broader topic). That is, regime change towards democracy is often procedural rather than substantive or, as the US Central Intelligence Agency hopefully put it, such states reflect "emerging democracy" (CIA 2006), that is, states in the act of becoming democracies.

Beyond this, regime change is not by definition towards a normatively more desirable or participatory outcome. Although the tendency towards the end of the twentieth and early twenty-first centuries has been for regime change to move away from authoritarian models, it can also impose non-democratic or authoritarian rule. More recent examples of this latter form of regime change include Pakistan in 1999, the Central African Republic in 2002, Sao Tome and Principe in 2003, Guinea-Bissau in 2003, Haiti in 2004, Mauritania in 2005, Nepal in 2005 and Thailand in 2006, along with attempted coups in numerous other countries. The tendency for the direction of regime change from approximately 1947 until 1977 was also against democracy, as a result of the rise of communism in Europe and Asia, one party or military dominated states in Africa, the Middle-East and Asia, and one-party or military governments in Latin America.

By regime change, what is meant is a fundamental shift of political values, and is more commonly not via an orderly handing over of government within an established and agreed political framework, although there have been exceptions to this general trend in the post-1989 era, for example in some formerly communist east European states. The literature on regime change suggests that it usually follows a period of rising political tension and that its common feature is political instability in the period leading up to, surrounding and following it. As a consequence, regime change can be accompanied by political violence, especially between groups representing the status quo and aspirants for change.

The causes of regime change are various, but change that is internally driven tends to reflect a failure of the existing system to either fulfill the basic requirements of a key social sector or sectors, such as rural or urban workers, the middle class, business owners, traditional oligarchs, or the military. This failure to fulfill sectoral interests may reflect a basic ideological position which predisposes the government to ignore or oppose particular interests. It may also reflect a government's incapacity to function in favor of its preferred interest sector, such as where the government becomes excessively corrupt, factionalized or otherwise unable to exercise authority, or where its key institutions cease to meaningfully function. In this respect, regime change is most commonly a consequence of horizontal political change. A government either tends to represent one horizontal group by replacing another, or a horizontal group or coalition of groups replace their own, failed government. Regime change is rarely vertical because vertical divisions that are so strong as to successfully challenge a government tend to want to establish a separate state. Absolutely successful vertical challenges are rare (the USSR, Yugoslavia, Bangladesh, Eritrea and East Timor being notable exceptions), while partial successes such as greater regional autonomy are more likely (for example, Spanish regional autonomy, Finland's Aland island, Indonesia's Aceh, and so on). Vertical regime change may also occur in a tribalized society, such as Afghanistan or Rwanda, where the government tended to reflect the assertion of specific tribal interests within the state.

Political models

As discussed, regime change can be from or to any other particular regime type, the criteria for which can be assessed by the extent of their democratization and liberalization, or lack thereof. Regime change therefore marks a distinct shift in political organization. O'Donnell and Schmitter identify eight basic political model types, each characterizing degrees of democracy and liberalism, although interestingly, in contrast to other interpretations of economic liberalism which usually imply laissez-faire capitalism and equate political liberalism more or less to economic equality. Assuming, however, that liberalism implies the greatest economic freedom for the greatest number (a variation on the utilitarian theme) rather than the greatest economic freedom for whoever is able to exercise it if at the expense of others, O'Donnell and Schmitter's interpretation can be accepted as liberalism, though of a more political than purely economic type.

At the most authoritarian end of their scale, O'Donnell and Schmitter identify autocracy, or "dictadura," as constituting low democratic capacity and low levels of liberalization, moving to or from a plebiscitary autocracy usually via a coup, or revolution. Moving towards a medium level of liberalization while retaining low levels of democratization is characterized as liberalized autocracy, or "dictablanda," which might characterize a number of authoritarian but not dictatorial regimes (such as Singapore). Instituting limited political democracy with medium liberalization, or "democradura," opens the next political category, characterizing less authoritarian but still restrictive regimes, such as in Malaysia and perhaps the democratizing states of sub-Saharan Africa states moving towards popular democracy, representing high democratization with low liberalization might be characterized by India or Sri Lanka before the effective limitation of the latter's political space.

O'Donnell and Schmitter's next category of political democracy, reflecting higher democratization and greater liberalization, appears to correspond to a number of Western or OECD states, such as the US. Their use of the term polyarchy to describe this category is further developed by Dahl's seven attributes: elected officials, free and fair elections, inclusive suffrage, the right to run for office, freedom of expression, alternative information and associational autonomy (Dahl 1989: 221). Related to the form of polyarchy that is reflected in the political status of many OECD countries is the category of social democracy, implying higher democratization and high liberalization.

Assuming that authoritarianism and its variants have a negative normative value, this implies that the opposite has a positive normative value. Although perhaps reflecting the era in which it was written, O'Donnell and Schmitter's assessment of the positive is in contrast to even then more economic libertarian views. In this respect, they equate higher democratization and highest liberalization to welfare democracy (presumably of the type then found in Scandinavia and to a lesser extent Australia and New Zealand), and to socialist democracy (O'Donnell and Schmitter 1986: 13), although it is unclear where such a socialist democracy actually exists, or has existed, other than in theory.

The evolution of political forms from absolute autocratic rule towards civil government that encourage political participation, representation and accountability, require a type of social contract between citizens and its government. Under absolute rule, a sovereign monarch or tyrant is not party to any contract but rules with unlimited authority. This is not a form of civil government because there is no neutral authority to decide disputes between the ruler and the citizen. Under the "social contract" model, however, the government accedes authority to the population, mediated by an independent authority (for example, an independent judiciary) in return for right to rule. This occurs on a sliding scale of a balance of authority until it is agreed that authority is ultimately vested in the citizens, is only held by the political leader or government on behalf of the citizens, and is able to be rescinded by the citizens in an agreed and orderly manner (that is, through regular elections).

Assuming that much regime change will be opposed, and that transitions especially from authoritarian to democratic models require a shift in allegiance of the military, the military itself will often be politicized and divided between those who support regime change and those who oppose it. O'Donnell and Schmitter (1986: 15–17) characterize such military factions as "hardliners" and "softliners." As these terms imply, hardliners oppose change, while softliners facilitate change, usually cautiously. Examples of successfully facilitated change by military softliners who have taken advantage of "the military moment" (1986: 39) include Portugal and Greece in 1974, the Philippines in 1986, and Indonesia in 1998, although there are also numerous examples in Latin America. Moreover, limited liberalization away from a direct military rule while retaining a capacity for existing elite control or liberalization without introducing democracy may also be facilitated by such a softline military approach (for example, the removal of direct military rule in Indonesia 1986–8, and relative liberalization without democratization in 1991). Softliners, however, sometimes over estimate their popular support, and may engender a backlash which sets back movement towards liberalization (O'Donnell and Schmitter 1986: 58). For example, in Indonesia, President Habibie's decision to allow East Timor to vote on independence in 1999 resulted in his own political denouement just weeks later, and his liberal successor being ousted half way through his presidential term. Softliners also encountered a backlash in the initial military-led steps of Portugal's "Carnation Revolution" in 1974, and during Turkey's return to electoral politics in 1983.

Following the collapse of the Soviet Union and the end of the cold war, there has been a claim to a global democratic transition which, assuming a relatively generous interpretation of the term "democracy," appears to be supported by the general tendency. Huntington identified and characterized this tendency as the "third wave" of democratization (1991), starting in 1974[5] with Portugal's shift from authoritarianism, but accelerating in the 1980s to include more than 60 countries. A democratic "wave," according to Huntington, was when the shift from non-democratic to democratic forms of rule outweighed the opposite tendency. The first two "waves" grouped global shifts towards democratic rule into broad periods from 1828 until 1926, which corresponded with a move towards European democratization and nation-state formation (with a reversal from 1922 until 1942), and from 1961 until 1975, corresponding broadly with the decolonization process, even though the post-Second World War period saw a significant rise in the number of authoritarian states, in part due to the relative prevalence of "communist" states and a number of post-colonial states abandoning their more immediate embrace of democracy in favor of less contested visions of development options within an economically constrained environment.

Since around 1990, Europe's former "communist" states all moved towards more open electoral political systems, as have some of the Soviet Union's Asian states, while some authoritarian states formerly supported by the US, such as the Philippines under Marcos and Indonesia under Suharto, have also moved to establish procedural democratic systems. In the case of both the Philippines and Indonesia, elite rivalry contributed towards the opening of political space, initially exploited by "oblique commentators" (artists, religious figures, etc.) who could manifest public concern without as a high risk as more conventional political activists (O'Donnell and Schmitter 1986: 49). Pro-democratic forces were able to capitalize on, and mobilize within this political space, even if they could not completely capture it. Similarly, a number of Sub-Saharan African states have also chosen governments by relatively open elections and can be characterized as procedural democracies. In each case, however, the success of the "democratic transition" has varied according to a range of local and sometimes global circumstances.

The collapse of the Soviet Union not only resulted in regime change in most of its former constituent states, but also the formation of governments that contained greater and lesser degrees of democratization and authoritarianism. It also resulted in the assertion of new nationalisms, and, like a Russian wooden doll in which each doll contains another, further deconstructed nationalisms and sub-nationalisms (Taras in Bremmer and Taras 1997: 683, 706–7). Regime change in Chechnya, between Armenia and Azerbaijan, and in Georgia have led to bloody conflict, while the Siberian peoples continue to chafe under ethnic Russian domination. Russian minorities throughout former Soviet Central Asia have also complicated other nationalist assertions. The assertion of a specific national identity, then, does not necessarily imply a democratic outcome, much less peace. The issue of transition from a non-democratic to a democratic model of state rule then begs the question of what conditions are necessary to allow or ensure a democratic transition and the sustained progression of such a transition.

As Dahl noted, a state is unlikely to quickly develop a democratic political system if it has had little or no experience of public contestation and competition, and lacks a tradition of tolerance towards political opposition (Dahl 1971: 208). That is, regime change in such a state is at least as likely to default to an alternative authoritarian government, or to partially do so. Similarly, although cautioning against political expectations arising out of such structural pre-conditions, Di Palma noted that economic instability, a hegemonic nationalist culture and the absence of a strong, independent middle class all impede transition from an authoritarian political model towards one that is more democratic (Di Palma 1991: 3).

In considering transitions from authoritarian to democratic models, there are a range of conditions that might be claimed to be essential for successful regime change. As noted by Dahl, these include control of the military and police by elected civilian officials; democratic beliefs and culture (which might translate as politically enlightened understanding) (Dahl 1989: 111) and no strong interference by foreign powers that are hostile to democracy (for example, the USSR in Eastern Bloc countries). Further, Dahl identified conditions that were not absolutely necessary, but which were favorable for the establishment of democracy, including a modern market economy and society, and weak sub-cultural pluralism (or lack of opportunity for inter-ethnic conflict) (Dahl 2000: 147; see also Dahl 1989: Chapter 8).

The incompletion of regime change can be demonstrated in the Philippines where, in 1986, the dictator Ferdinand Marcos lost the support of his US backers and, eventually, the country's oligarchic elite and sections of the military. In this respect, there appeared to have been an elite pact for careful change in the Philippines (O'Donnell and Schmitter 1986: 40–5). Capitalizing on the "political moment," elites, with the support of mass mobilization, developed or reasserted political parties and organized political constituencies under a "grand coalition." In Indonesia in 1998, this also occurred, although rather than reflecting a more gradual economic decline and a sudden political incident, there was a more gradual political decline and a sudden economic incident, or "economic moment" (O'Donnell and Schmitter 1986: 45–7), followed by a sudden "political moment." In the case of a sudden economic crisis, such as the 1997–8 financial collapse in Indonesia, there is an implied socio-economic pact between those who are most disaffected or economically disadvantaged and those appear to be able to assume responsibility for alleviating the crisis (whether they are able to do so or not). In what Dahl has referred to "the democratic bargain" of trust, fairness and compromise (1970), this pact normatively corresponds to a type of social contract. In this, it is important that elites who intend to continue or expand their political rule are able to satisfy, or be seen to address, most outstanding demands while at the same time avoiding the strongest dissatisfactions from manifesting into collective action. As O'Donnell and Schmitter note, and which appears to be borne out by experience, transitional regimes from authoritarianism tend to be smoother and more successful if they promote essentially conservative or right-wing political outcomes, as this is seen as less threatening to out-going authoritarian elites. Democratic recalcitrants, usually on the left and center-left, are only given the opportunity to engage in transitional processes if elite survivors from the previous regime are willing to negotiate a mutually satisfactory set of rules of the new game (O'Donnell and Schmitter 1986: 70). Where such negotiations fails, more active, usually leftist, political actors may be rapidly marginalized, as occurred in post-1986 Philippines and in post-1998 Indonesia. In the latter case, those demanding *reformasi total* (total reform) of the political system were quickly marginalized, resulting in the fragmentation of the reform movement (comprising in particular students, civil society and humanitarian NGOs and coalitions). The consequence of this leftist marginalization and fragmentation was that the political agenda quickly reverted to control by conservative elites, while the election as president of the reformist cleric Abdurrahman Wahid by an oppos- itional if conservative coalition resulted in his own ouster by those same elites less than two years later.

In the case of the Philippines, public protest against then President Marcos and the blatant falsification of election results, backed by sections of the military, led to his ouster and replacement by his electoral opponent, Corazon Aquino, the widow of Marcos's murdered former opponent, Senator Benigno Aquino. While Corazon Aquino came to power on the back of a popular protest movement (known unreflectively as "people power"), she in fact ushered in elite rule mirroring that of the oligarchic pre-dictatorship era. Under Aquino, the Philippines' elite structurally excluded genuine open participation in politics, despite it formally being an open electoral contest, and returned to squabbling over the spoils of state between them (see Belo *et al*. 2005; Hutchcroft 1991). In Indonesia, by comparison, the resignation of Suharto in 1998 and the weakening of the highly centralized state apparatus he and the military had constructed, led to a rash of genuine political reforms under his immediate successor, Habibie. A reconsolidating status quo elite and partly intentional destabilization of the state under the reformist presidency of Abdurrahman Wahid contributed towards his ouster and replacement by pro-status quo elite/pro-military Megawati Sukarnoputri in mid-2001. Of particular transitional note, however, was the role played by military "softliner," Susilo Bambang Yudhoyono, first as the leader of the reform faction of the Indonesian military in the early 1990s, following on from dissent towards then President Suharto in 1986–1988) and then as a political actor and finally as president (Kingsbury 2005: Chapters 12–14). Shifts from authoritarianism or totalitarianism towards democracy occurred in the period immediately following the Second World War, in which (part of) Nazi Germany, Fascist Italy and imperial Japan were reintroduced to the idea of democracy, while states that had been under Nazi or Fascist occu- pation were also re-democratized. One might also see the eventual re- democratization of Spain and Portugal in the 1970s as a conclusion to 1930s Europe's experiment with varieties of extreme right-wing authoritarianism.

In the post-Second World War period, a significant problem lay with a vacuum of democratic beliefs and culture (democratic habituation), particu- larly in the then divided Germany, Italy, Spain and Portugal, and to a slightly lesser extent, Austria and the occupied European countries. In Germany, the process was one not just of building up a new political culture, but comprehensively destroying the old, under the "four Ds program" of "denazification, demilitarization, decentralization and decartelization" (Herz 1982: 17–18). This program attacked, dismembered, dismantled and des- troyed the previous ideology, its political organization and centralized govern- ment structure, the bureaucracy and much of the economic foundation linked to the previous political system. Like Japan, however, in which a similar pattern was followed, the West German economy rebounded in the

1950s and 1960s with renewed energy based on the foundations of its previous industrial experience, and tapped into a rapidly expanding demand-led economic boom. But, in large part, the destruction of the previous political order was completed by military occupation and the construction of a new, pro-democratic political elite modeled more or less on the US political system. Previous tendencies and tensions remained as the legacy of authoritarianism among at least some of the new (or not so new) political actors. But the imposed occupation model of punishment and reward, along with the real social, political and economic benefits of democratization, eventually took hold, melding those holding on to less acceptable political belief systems to modify them in ways that became more acceptable in public fora.

In Italy, the process of democratization was more mixed, as internal Italian political movements ousted the fascist government to forestall further engagement in the European war. These movements coalesced with external forces (the Allies) and even some Fascist administrators in establishing a re-introduced electoral framework which, in its tolerance, allowed the re-establishment of a new Fascist party, Movimento Sociale Italiano (Di Palma 1982: 110–28) and later the neo-Fascist Avanguardia Nazionale, Ordine Nuovo and Movimento Fascismo e Libertà. These "evolved" Fascist movements such as the Alleanza Nazionale displayed elements of traditional fascism. Varieties of fascism have also recurred in Spain (Malefakis 1982; Herz 1982: 275–6), Portugal (Maxwell 1982), Greece (Psomiades 1982) and throughout Latin America, while fascist and Nazi revivalism in organizations such as the various versions of the neo-Nazi National Front/Action and different chapters of Blood and Honor organization/movement enjoy limited support in many otherwise democratic countries.

While free-market capitalism has more or less prevailed in these states (assuming that varying degrees of state support or intervention, such as in Japan, are not seen as incompatible with private profit-making), Dahl's observation that democracies require a modern market economy appears to equate to the truism that there have been no modern democratic states that have not also been capitalist (although there have been democracies in mixed state-capitalist economies, or so-called social democracies). Herz agrees with this assertion, citing capitalist free enterprise as "instrumental in the demise of authoritarian political structures" (Herz 1982: 276), while Bernholz claims that a free market economy is a necessary (if not sufficient) condition for democracy (1997: 89–90). However, beyond Beetham's notation of an ambiguous self-serving relationship between capitalism and democracy (1999: Chapter 3), there is another truism that there have indeed been capitalist societies without democracy. The alliance between corporate interest and authoritarian rule, as demonstrated by the *junkers* (industrial elite) and Nazism, *zaibatsu* (industrial conglomerates) and imperial Japan, *chaibol* (industrial conglomerates) in pre-democratic South Korea and landed and industrial elites and Latin American oligarchies, are prime cases in point.

One interesting aspect of regime transitions is the role played by external events. Although there are numerous exceptions, it appears that critical political shifts most often occur at times of pronounced social, economic and/or political dislocation. A range of pre-existing tensions or pressures must already exist in order to capitalize on the subsequent rupture, but the rupture itself appears to act as a catalyst for regime change. By way of illustration, the Russian Revolution took place after its disastrous involvement in the First World War, and regime change arrived in Germany-Austria, Italy, France and Japan at the conclusion of the Second World War. China's nationalist revolution was precipitated by colonial domination and its communist revolution came in response to Japanese occupation, while Portugal sloughed off dictatorship in the wake of economic collapse and failed colonialism. Similarly, Nicaragua deposed its dictatorship after a destructive earthquake, the Philippines and Indonesia removed dictators following economic crises, Greece after the Turkish invasion of Cyprus and Argentina removed its military junta following its defeat in the Falklands War. In the two latter cases, democracy was achieved by stalemate and lack of consensus rather than by prior unity and consensus (see O'Donnell and Schmitter 1986: 72). Indeed, virtually the whole post-Second World War decolonization period could be attributed, to a greater or lesser extent, to the direct and indirect economic, military and political effects of the war.

Foreign powers can play a role in regime change by supporting various parties which might, at any given time, be in external exile or which may be underground within the country in question. It has been common practise for groups attempting to overthrow a particular regime to receive external assistance, by way of receiving sanctuary, training, logistical support and representation in international fora.

Transitions born of crisis are, of course, not consistent in their outcomes, illustrated by the shifting contest between democracy and authoritarianism throughout Latin America and in countries such as Thailand and in much of Sub-Saharan Africa. There are even cases of voluntary political redundancy, such as in Spain after Franco's death, although this too might be seen as a political "shock." In some cases, the "shock" itself, though, is little more than an excuse to exercise an overdue necessity, where an ossified regime is aware of its redundancy, yet still requires an excuse to dignify and hence ease its departure.

Change towards authoritarianism

As noted, not all regime changes are towards democracy. Some changes may be partial (for example, Philippines post-1986, Indonesia post-1998) or lead to conflict (such as Cambodia 1975–98). Others simply revert from one type of authoritarianism to another, such as Portugal, where a military dictatorship founded in 1926 gave way to a fascist dictatorship in 1933. Still others change from democratic models to authoritarian ones, examples of which were littered throughout the 1920s and 1930s in Europe and elsewhere in the 1940s to 1970s. These different experiences of regime change invariably reflect competing views of what constitutes political progress; what is fairness to some is interference to others; what is freedom to some is disorder to others depending, as discussed earlier, on how one views the basic concepts of freedom and equality.

One of the two principle forms of regime change is where a democratic and/or liberal government is replaced by an authoritarian, usually single party, regime, the other being where authoritarianism is replaced by liberal pluralism. Change towards authoritarian status mostly occurs in the case of a *coup d'etat*, and is principally undertaken by the military or with military support. The rationale for such action is usually that the existing government does not adequately function to protect and develop the interests of the state. This may be a consequence of excessive corruption, a claimed anti-developmentalist ideology (for example, socialism or, more rarely, crony capitalism), or other failure of leadership and authority, for example in Thailand in 2006. Such rationalizations are often employed to conceal other, less supportable reasons, such as promoting a particular economic or political interest or securing an external ideological alliance.

Locating authoritarianism

"Authoritarianism" can and does have a range of meanings, most of which are arguably antithetical to political development, but which may be argued to be a necessary stepping stone in such a process (as per aspects of the "Asian values" debate). In this respect, political development is like (and indeed must reflect) justice, in that if it is deferred, it is in effect denied for the period that it is deferred. It is consequently affected by this deferral when it is finally employed. An authoritarian political model, which assumes a relatively non-consultative political process and which applies its decisions either by force or with the threat of force, must by definition be considered a limited or negative form of political development. As a further or more radical development of authoritarianism, absolutism must be defined as diametrically opposite of political development.

The following diagrammatic model (Fig. 7.1) provides a method of locating political positions relative to two fundamental political criteria: the binary oppositions of authoritarianism and liberalism (or libertarianism) and between economic redistribution and accumulation. The assumption with the economic scale is that there is a natural tendency for capitalism to accumulate wealth either for the purposes of reinvestment or as a reward in its own right, and that economic accumulation most accurately describes capitalism. Conversely, the polar opposite to capitalism is absolute economic redistribution, in which there is no greater capital accumulation available to any part of society. This can be described as "communism," although in its most developed form it matches communism in theory only. In a practical

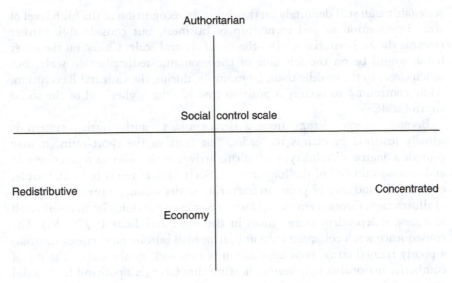

Figure 7.1 Political location relative to the extent of authority and economic
distribution.

sense, the greatest point of redistribution has been under socialist governments, including high levels of state ownership on behalf of its citizens.
Anarchism, in its formal political sense, also implies complete economic
redistribution, although this is fundamentally linked to the abolition of
power structures that maintain privilege, including those of the state.

Figure 7.1 does not posit absolute locations as equivalent to political
position; for example, it does not suggest that, on a ten point scale, a social
welfare state should be located three points left of center along the scale of
economic redistribution. However, the position of social welfarism relative to
the center would be somewhere in this area. The purpose of the diagram, in
this sense, is not to show where specific positions are, but to indicate the
tendency of influences, such as having a greater or lesser preference for capital
accumulation of redistribution, or a greater or lesser preference for social
control or liberty. That is, a system that is moderately liberal socialist (such
as the social democratic parties of Scandinavia) might find itself located
somewhere in the middle of the bottom left quadrant (though in the early
twenty-first century having moved closer to the center of the economic scale),
while a more authoritarian socialist system might find itself located somewhere towards the furthest point of the upper left quadrant. So too for liberal
and authoritarian capitalist systems. For example, Fukuyama's liberal capitalist model of the "end of history" would be located somewhere towards the
further bottom right corner of the bottom right quadrant (although not at its
farthest edge – Fukuyama is not that radical). The American state, however,
would probably be closer towards the middle point on the social control scale.
Singapore, on the other hand, would be closer to the middle of the economic

scale (although still definitely on the right), in recognition of the high level of state intervention in and ownership of business, but considerably further towards the authoritarian end of the social control scale. China, on the other hand, would be on the left side of the economic redistribution scale, but much closer to the middle than, for example, during the Cultural Revolution, while continuing to occupy a position towards the higher end of the social control scale.

Because regime change from a democratic to authoritarian system is usually justified by claims to "order,"[6] at least in the short-term, it may provide a degree of stability, even if this arrives at the price of repressive rule and is unsustainable in the longer-term. Such "order" tends to be inflexible, even brittle, and may be prone to fracturing under sustained pressure. By way of illustration, Georgia employed former Soviet methodologies to assert itself as a new, independent state (Jones in Bremmer and Taras 1997: 515). The consequence was a collapsed economy, atrophied bureaucracy, rise of militias, a poorly trained army, poor application of law, and, symbolically, the use of combative nationalist language indicating that Georgia's political leaders did not appreciate the idea of a legitimate loyal opposition. The political chaos and slide towards authoritarianism of Georgia in the 1990s was in part due to historical, structural and psychological factors but, as Jones notes, it was not inevitable (Jones in Bremmer and Taras 1997: 529). Similarly, Belarus transited from the Soviet to post-Soviet era without liberalization or democratization, and its president has even acknowledged that he employs authoritarian methods (BBC 2006). By contrast, regime change away from authoritarian government does not bring with it an imposed order, and is thus vulnerable to a variety of pressures and influences, all of which can add instability to the process of political change.

Democratic transitions

In his 2002 analysis of transitions to democracy, Carothers identified five fundamental flaws in the assumptions that constitute the "transition to democracy paradigm." The first of these, which includes the other flaws, is that states moving away from dictatorial rule are necessarily moving towards democracy. While many states change their regimes, Carothers noted, the forms they end up with are very often much less than democratic, despite them being cast in such terms. Echoing O'Donnell and Schmitter, second, Carothers noted that democratization does not unfold in a consistent pattern or set series of stages, and that there is no universally applicable path towards democratic outcomes. The third flawed assumption is that elections constitute democracy as such. While elections are important in democratic outcomes, their capacity for manipulation means that electoral processes do not necessarily lead to more representative or accountable governments. Given such potential for limited transitions, Carothers recognized that agency could produce democratic outcomes despite limiting structural circumstances.

However, he noted that structural limitations created more challenges for incipient democratic governments, and that structural pre-conditions did contribute to shaping political outcomes. Finally, Carothers noted that Huntington's "third wave" of democratization thesis assumed the pre-existence of "coherent, functional states," in which democratization only required a modification of existing political forms. While there were pre-existing established, functional states in Latin America and southern Europe, this assumption did not universally apply, and the subsequent process of democratization often paralleled state and state institution building as a critical part of the transition process (Carothers 2002). As Carothers noted, all of these factors contributed not towards an eventual, much less inevitable, substantive democratic outcome, but one which often ended up somewhere along the unstable scale between substance and the shallowest of procedural forms.

Regime change is most likely to be successful, or not experience debilitating challenges, where the state is otherwise cohesive. Successful regime change is most likely to occur in states that have a strong sense of national identity, institutions that otherwise function well and can maintain continuity across the period of change, and a widespread commitment or at least little serious opposition to such change. In instances of voluntary regime change, from an authoritarian to an open model, an authoritarian state that has succeeded in imposing a successful developmentalist economy, such as in South Korea or Taiwan, could voluntarily liberalize, overseeing a graduated shift towards a participatory political process. The issues of economic prosperity, institutional functionalism and national identity already having been resolved (in both cases along with radical land reform programs that would have been difficult to institute under an elected government), the otherwise successful state is handed over (if not entirely without hesitation) to civilian rule. Not having to contend with major, potentially fractious issues, regime change in these instances is successful.

Once regime change has completed its first phase, of replacing one form of government with another, it has two subsequent tasks. The first task is to consolidate such change, and the second is to build a hegemonic framework in support of such change, in order that it becomes self-sustaining and not merely a form of rule by (temporary) imposition. One view of democratic consolidation is that it comprises support for and compliance with democratic institutions and rules. The marker of consolidation is where democratic regimes can remain stable in the face of serious challenges such as major economic or international crises or outbreaks of violence. O'Donnell and Schmitter are, however, critical of this approach. They claim this approach fails to distinguish between stability as a definitional component of sufficient consolidation and consolidation that results from the attitudinal and behavioral acceptance of the regime. This emphasis on stability also fails to distinguish between democratic consolidation as a process and as an existing regime attribute (O'Donnell and Schmitter 1986: 389). Schmitter and Schneider (2003) go one step further by identifying the extent of liberalization as the key marker of consolidation in regime transitions from authoritarianism towards democratic rule.

Regime consolidation also requires a clear program and attendant ideology, procedural and institutional capacity and broad social acceptance, resulting from state legitimacy and, if necessary, the capacity for coercion. Schmitter and Schneider refer to consolidation as the process of transforming "accidental arrangements" into consistent institutions (2003: 9–13). That is to say, regime consolidation implies the successful establishment of hegemony (see Gramsci 1971), with all that implies for the creation of a sense of legitimacy, that stems, at least in part, from a widespread perception of reciprocal relations, backed by the capacity for coercion, and decorated with the symbolic attributes that are often expected of such authority. With the establishment of such accepted hegemony, regime change can be regarded as successful. That regime change should open up a process of democratization, hegemony will be normatively confirmed by a regime's capacity for establishing legitimacy on the basis of a social contract involving citizens' participation and state accountability. In this sense, regime change towards democracy is likely to be more successful if it is able to promote its legitimacy through a sense of public inclusion, that is by being more openly democratic.

8   Institution building

In the study of politics, a focus on institutions has come and gone according to prevailing analytical fashion, and, to some extent, the perspective of the observer. Those closer to institutional failure and its consequences have tended to accord it somewhat higher value than those for whom institutions are but a functioning reflection of other sets of circumstances. As a consequence of analytical fashion or the necessity of focus shifts, considering the behavior and function of institutions tends to receive sometimes more and sometimes less attention. A focus on institutions was popular in the 1950s and 1960s, and was again finding favor by the early twenty-first century (for example, Fukuyama 2004; Jutting 2003; Steinmo 2001; Weingast 1996; Rothstein 1992). In particular, following the apparent failure of Marxism, the rise and fall of more relativized (culturalist) analyzes in the 1980s and 1990s, there was a continuing and pressing need to address institutional, and hence, state weakness and failure.

As an explanatory method in understanding the behavior of political societies, the term "institutionalism" has been used to counter both the economic reductionism of structural Marxism in which social and political actions are only explicable by focusing on economic interest, and culturalist responses which see social and political behavior as determined by pre-existing socio-psychological perspectives. In contrast to these economic and cultural approaches, an institutionalist analysis proposes an understanding of society and politics predicated primarily upon the roles and functions of state institutions, essentially government departments and agencies or, more broadly, political and social conventions.

It appears to be correct that an economic explanation alone for political and social organization is inadequate, although any analysis that does not include material constraints and interests will be incomplete. Similarly, cultural influences or the capacities of individuals are important, although these are rarely uniform and are not immune to change. An institutional analysis, by contrast, considers the role of dominant state actors or forms of capacity, such as electoral processes, the behavior of governments, the efficacy of departments, and the role of custodians of state violence,[1] the police and the military. From a behavioralist perspective, in which analysis is predicated upon what can be observed, the role of institutions can appear dominant (for example, see North 1990).

This chapter supports the general contention that institutions are central to achieving or maintaining the success of the development project, not just in developing countries but also in developed countries, noting that the "development project" as has been commonly understood largely focuses around conceptions of enhanced material well being. It could be suggested that developed (OECD) countries are less troubled by the function or capacity of their institutions, which is reflected in their relative development status. This is generally correct, but it would be an error for developed countries to become complacent, and hence potentially decline; some institutions may have a self-perpetuating tendency, but this tendency itself has a capacity to turn malignant if left unaccountable. Similarly, arguments against certain existing institutions, usually around the rubric of "smaller government" cannot assume that because an existing state of affairs has been achieved through the use of differentiated institutions that are no longer necessary for the maintenance or improvement of that state of affairs.

Conventional criteria

A common understanding of the term "institution" will usually reflect not just a definition of formal institutions, but also include bureaucratic institutions or institutions of authority, not least because these forms are most visible to people living in a complex society. Any complex social organization that is positioned within a functioning economy and polity will have institutions, manifesting the regularity or consistency of its system of operation. Institutions, therefore, are a necessary quality of any functioning state. It has been argued that the presence and efficacy of institutions is not just a defining quality of statehood but is a necessary condition for states to be able to successfully function (Huntington 1968; Jaguaribe 1968; Fukuyama 2004).

In a conventional sense, institutions are generally understood to be those formalized bodies that have a regular and definable quality and which in most cases have some sort of official status or recognition. Huntington (1968) focused on political parties as the most important and necessary institutions in the early post-colonial period of new states, during which he identified a common disjuncture between political mobilization and political organization leading to state disorder. Jaguaribe (1968), on the other hand, also identified this disjuncture between political mobilization and political organization, but saw parties alone as inadequate. Borrowing from Marxism, Jaguaribe considered the balance between economics and politics, and the planning component that existed between them, as necessary to ensure their mutual survival and development. After a long lapse in focus on what was termed by these authors as "political development," or the establishment of political institutions, Fukuyama (2004) later saw state institutions as being a necessary condition for successful state function. The World Bank's view on the other hand turned slowly back from state-led investment, and then forms of economic structural adjustment, towards notions of "governance" as being critical to the development project. The meaning of "governance" has increasingly broadened from rules of oversight of financial matters to incorporating systems of checks and balances, in particular in the economic sphere, but more broadly across all elements of economic and political organization.

Each of these approaches ascribe different core characteristics to the role, or function, of institutions. Huntington assumed that institutions were necessary to bring political order, which in turn created the conditions for economic development. Jaguaribe believed that the capacity of institutions was a condition of material circumstances, while Fukuyama saw state institutions as being the prime manifestation of state capacity, which in turn led to conditions for economic development. The World Bank, by comparison, viewed the rules of economic behavior as central to ensuring appropriate economic responses (see also Jutting 2003). Each of these sources, however, focused on economic development and the conditions that made it possible as their ultimate, if not sole, concern. All regarded political development, in so far as they considered it, as being a means to an economic end; none saw political development and the social conditions it created (and protected) as an end in itself.

In conventional thinking, there are broadly four complexes of institutions. The first are political institutions to regulate the competition for political power, that is, political parties and systems of government. The second are economic institutions that are concerned with the (public and private) production and distribution of goods and services (for example, corporations, corporate collectives and state services). The third are cultural institutions that refer to social organization around beliefs, values, interests and (creative) expression, such as organized religion, interest groups and social and cultural associations. Finally, there are kinship institutions that refer to the status of marriage, children and familial bonded social organizations (extended families and close social associations). All of these institutions relate to Weber's "ideal" types of legitimacy, in that none can exist in a pristine or isolated condition, and that elements of one are often found in aspects of another. As the formal social regulatory method of participation, representation, organization, delineation of authority and compliance, however, the institutional complex that is of primary concern here is that of politics, although each of these forms of institutions could be seen as reflecting hierarchies or associations of authority, and are hence all "political" in the broadest sense of the term.

More specifically, "institutions" as they are discussed here, and their corollary of institutionalization, are not just understood in terms of Huntington's parties and order, Jaguaribe's conditions for planning, Fukuyama's state bodies or the World Bank's measurements of "governance." Rather, a functioning, coherent, cohesive and mutually advantageous society is assisted by promoting a wider scope of definition and recognition for what can be said to constitute institutions. Progress in political development is thus achieved by formalizing a broader recognition of institutions, increasing the opportunity for the introduction of new "institutional" actors, and promoting the political participation of a wider range of institutional and political actors in ideological and policy debate and decision making.

Civil society and the state

If there is a differentiation between early and more recent approaches in thinking about institutions, it is in understanding institutions as not being just organizations of people with particular roles, but sets of rules or codes of behavior that can include, for example, respect for the rule of law, notions of equality, and tolerance of or respect for alternative views. The key distinctions here are between formal and informal rules or codes of behavior, with greater emphasis being placed on important informal rules that nonetheless effectively play a formal role in political society. An example of an informal rule that might be considered critical is the opportunity for the creation and maintenance of civil society organizations, which appear to have a central role in the functioning of a healthy political society. The "rules" by which such groups organize themselves are one way in which they constitute institutions, but the fact of their existence and their shifting social and political roles have also become institutionalized. That is, there is an expectation that such organizations will exist, will be acknowledged as existing and will from time to time contribute to public debate and decision making.

Understanding development in its conventional, "modernization," sense, Stepan noted the putative if changing focus of the state from economic to political development:

> The assumptions of modernization theory that liberal democratic regimes would be inexorably produced by the process of industrialization was replaced by a new preoccupation with the ways in which the state apparatus might become a central instrument for both the repression of subordinate classes and the reorientation of the process of industrial development.
>
> (Stepan 1985: 317)

The development of what have been called "Bureaucratic Authoritarian (BA) regimes" that are associated with, if not necessarily responsible for, economic development (seen as industrialization) has also fragmented and inhibited potential political opposition. The rise in relative authority of formal or recognized state institutions, and the non-negotiable imposition of their development programs, has diminished other political institutions, including both the formal pluralist institution of "Opposition" and the capacity of civil society (Stepan 1985: 317). That is to say, there can be and often is competition between formal institutions, as well as between formal institutions and those institutions that are regarded as less formal. This in turn comes back to attempts to delegitimize political alternatives, and in particular, those that are necessary for a successful plural polity but which have an imposed reduced capacity which in turn delegitimizes them.

The relationship between civil society and government has been proposed as an indicator of the democratic health of the state, with the varying capacities of each institution being a key determinant. Stepan posits four sets of relationships between the state and civil society, which are characterized as the following:

1. Growth of state power and diminution of civil society power
2. Decline of state power and growth of civil society power
3. Growth of both state and civil society
4. Decline of both state and civil society (but with option of civil society growth outside the state).

(Stepan 1985: 318)

Stepan was primarily concerned with the growth of state power at the expense of civil society, or the imposition of bureaucratic authoritarianism with a parallel reduction in the capacity of non-state actors to compete with state power. This situation could characterize "strong states" such as China, Vietnam or Syria in which an independent civil society is relatively weak. In the transitional phase away from bureaucratic authoritarianism, state power declines and civil society strengthens as a consequence of the opening of greater political space (for example, as military domination declined in Thailand). Civil society may also increase in its own right and therefore act as a contributor to declining state power (for example, Poland). Growth of both state and civil society power can be seen either in competition or as providing a balance for each other. With the former, the instability that derives from competition is unable to be sustained, and tends to either degenerate into internal conflict or the state or civil society fails to sustain its position and hence declines in power relative to the other. More positively, however, state power can be defined not only as bureaucratic authoritarianism (negative state power) but also as benign state capacity (positive power). In such cases, where there is strong civil society and strong positive state power, the two are likely to interact together to increase their respective capacities. Perhaps the best examples of this can be seen in the Scandinavian states, and to a lesser extent in other plural democracies.

In cases where both state and civil society power decline, however, there is the possibility of state failure or reversion to pre-modern methods of state organization (ASC *et al.* 2003: 4), as neither institutional segment is available to compensate for the weakness of the other. Such a power vacuum often draws external actors into the collapsed political space. This could be seen in the case of Iraq during the insurgency against US intervention from 2003, where US intervention created the power vacuum and then led to the necessity of its continuing, if increasingly troubled, presence. Similarly, the political space collapsed in Afghanistan prior to the rise of the Taliban, and in East Timor from late April 2006 (see also FfP 2006). In studying the reduced autonomy of the Brazilian state in the early 1980s, Stepan noted the view of executive branch leaders that only the reduction of state autonomy relative to civil society through a process of liberalization could reign in the state's security apparatus. That is, if the state was weaker relative to civil society, then its institutional components would also be relatively weaker, including those that political leaders viewed as rather more malignant (The Editors 1985: 355).

While no OECD countries can be considered as failed states, many of them did begin to show signs of institutional weakness in both government and civil society as a consequence of restructuring of the public sphere along "user pays" lines. This public sphere restructuring occurred as a consequence of the imposition of a neo-liberal economic paradigm, or what Stepan more accurately calls "economic libertarianism" that is identified with, for example, Friedrich Hayek (for example, 1960, 1976, 1988), James Buchanan and Gordon Tullock (Stepan 1985: 322). This "marketization of the state" effectively turned the state into a "company" and atomized civil society into an apolitical market (Stepan 1985: 322–3). Stepan characterized this situation as the Bonapartist exchange of the "right to rule" for "the right to make money," or the diminution of the state in order to facilitate narrow economic benefit, which in turn had the effect of advancing the material freedom of a few while limiting the material freedom of many.

Similar to Stepan, although from a different ideological perspective, Fukuyama identified the "dimensions of stateness" according to strength of the state and scope of its functions (2004: 7–30). Fukuyama's concerns were with economic development rather than political development, though he did not consider the function of civil society relative to that of the state, and his views were underpinned by an assumption that economic development could best be realized by the application of neo-liberal economic policy prescriptions of the type noted above. Typically, in this approach there is an implicit assumption that overall growth is the sole concern of economic development and that the corporate sector is best equipped to provide such growth, with little or no concern for issues such as sustainability, distribution of wealth in the form of a social contract, or the positive economic effects of more rather than less widespread discretionary spending.

Following this, Fukuyama identified what he saw as "the optimal reform path" as maintaining or increasing state strength, but in some particular cases reducing its functions (Fukuyama 2004: 20–1) and only in one increasing its strength while maintaining existing functions. There is no capacity within this "reform" model for actually increasing the scope of state functions, even though certain state functions could be demonstrably insufficient (for example, provision of basic education, health care and infrastructure). Fukuyama was concerned about the possibility of a decrease in state strength, and hence state capacity in those reduced areas where it continued to operate. At the same time, in line with the neo-liberal economic paradigm, he regarded the scope of state functions as an area worthy of reduction. This is a view of "liberalization" peculiar to "neo-liberal" economists which privileges economic freedoms above political freedoms, and generally militates against the maintenance, much less expansion, of institutions in the state-defined sense.

Confirming his preference for "strength" over "scope," Fukuyama favorably quoted the leading neo-liberal economist Milton Friedman as observing that "the rule of law is probably more important than privatization" but that the basic purpose of this allocation of priorities is economic efficiency (2004: 25). Yet Fukuyama later noted that "some of the most important variables affecting development weren't economic at all but were concerned with institutions and politics" (2004: 29). Unsurprisingly, he still identified "development" with economic growth (see also 2004: 30), and further qualified the role of institutions and politics as "The New Conventional Wisdom" (2004: 28), all forms of which "should make us cautious" (2004: 29). In that Fukuyama allowed that the "supply" of institutions was necessary (for economic development), he maintained that there could be "no optimal set of institutions" as each would "tend to favor one set of goods over another."

Offering a very different perspective to Fukuyama specifically, and the Haykeian neo-liberal economic school in general, Weinstock proposed an understanding of liberalism in relation to institutions that was rooted in politics and not economics. This understanding drew from an internally consistent (Lockeian) philosophical perspective rather than from the "freedom from law"[2] or "neo-liberalism" of the economic libertarians. For Weinstock: "The primary goal of institutions in the liberal view is to provide citizens with the freedoms they require in order to lead their lives according to their own conceptions of the good" (Weinstock in Weinstock and Nadeau 2004: 2) This, then, would appear to conform with the idea that while institutions have a positive political and economic function, which may or may not reflect the greatest economic efficiencies, but which are able to offer a wider rather than narrower social purpose.

Ideas of political participation, representation, transparency and accountability – what might be considered as foundation blocks of what is understood as democracy – also constitute institutions in themselves. Indeed, it would be impossible to have any sort of political organization without institutions, and it would be impossible for such political organization to be successful without those institutions having a continuing function and being embedded, that is, being "institutionalized." Within a democratic framework, there are (or should be) a range of institutions, including the offices of elected officials, free, fair and frequent elections, freedom of expression, alternative sources of information, autonomy of association and inclusive citizenship (Dahl 2000: 85). Inclusive citizenship as an institution highlights an ambiguous and quasi-formal critical aspect of both democracy and political development. If the citizen is the key component of the state, upon which state legitimate authority and capacity are built, then the active engagement of the citizen is a necessary condition for the success of the state. In this, citizens must not just have the freedom to engage with the state and its institutions, they must be welcomed into such engagement. One might then understand the process of such "welcoming" as the institutionalization of arrangements by which citizens may actively contribute to the wider political society.

In reality, citizens rarely actively participate in the life of the state, or do so only on an irregular and conditional basis. This might be said to reflect the institutionalization of specific interests, or of voting. It might also be said to reflect the competition for authority between institutions, and the prevalence of formal or more highly structured institutions over less formal institutions, and the advantage of organizational coherence over social atomization. Another way of looking at this is that observable consistent behavior is more likely to be acknowledged as having a legitimate social and political function, while that which is actively excluded or not even recognized in debate plays a denied or non-existent role (see Lukes 1974). Thus, not only is observable behavior institutionalized, but so too are limitations on behavior. To follow the logic of "non-behavior," not only can limitations upon behavior be seen as institutional, the non-availability of certain ways of thinking itself can be said to constitute the institutionalization of non-awareness, with the consequence on non-action. That is, the greatest institution is not the organization of social thinking into formal and informal patterns of inclusion and exclusion, but the institutionalization of "non-thinking" as a form of hegemony.

Mill was attuned to the possibilities of hegemony, which drew from the earlier, overtly formal institutionalist work of Hobbes (1962) in offering:

> As between one form of popular government and another, the advantage in this respect lies with that which most widely diffuses the exercise of public functions; on the one hand, by excluding fewest from the suffrage; on the other, by opening to all classes of private citizens . . . the widest participation in the details of judicial and administrative business; as by jury trial, admission to municipal offices, and above all by the utmost possible publicity and liberty of discussion, whereby not merely a few individuals in succession, but the whole public, are made, to a certain extent, participant in the government.
>
> (Mill 1910: 243)

In this idea is a form of popular democracy, as well as the particular idea of political participation, which militates against hegemony. The question, however, is not one of support of or opposition to institutions, but the nature and quality of those institutions.

Institutions and development

Institutions, as they have been traditionally or narrowly understood (for example, Fukuyama 2004) tend to develop a quasi-independent capacity and sense of self. That is, in the search for meaning by the individuals who comprise such institutions, there is a tendency towards a higher level of self-regard which derives from a sense of institutional relevance and capacity. This sense of self-regard in turn derives from the necessity of institutional function, the usually internally defined level of quality that should be achieved, and the resources that are necessary in order to do that. As a consequence, the self-maintenance (and expansion) of institutions may take precedence over the function they were initially designed to undertake. This is particularly the case concerning most classic institutions, especially the bureaucracy (see Weber 1948: 338–41). The key criterion for bureaucratic performance is performance assessment criteria set against "stakeholder" interest.[3] But in spite of stakeholder assessment, institutional self-affirmation continues to be a powerful source of policy inertia.

While institutional self-affirmation can account for bloated and slow moving bureaucracies, it can also account for the political role of organizations such as the military, police or intelligence agencies. Having established themselves as relatively organizationally efficient, with the sole legal capacity to employ state violence (naked power), often economically self-benefiting and not infrequently having an over-developed self-regard, institutions also come to develop a "culture" or world view which explains and rationalizes not just their continuing role but the orientation of such a role (for example, as reflected in the myth of the post-revolutionary "people's army," public order, etc.). Given the economic benefit (employment and promotion, quasi-official business, corruption) that can accrue to institutions, they may be reluctant to adapt relative to changing circumstances, and can consequently be a considerable force for reaction.

The role of institutions has been identified by the World Bank, among others, as being central to the success or failure of development projects, particularly in their larger and more bureaucratic sense. That is, the capacity of states to make use of aid and to deliver its benefits and indeed to sustain the process of development generally is seen by the World Bank, and many others, to be vested in the institutions of the state. This thesis was first developed by Huntington (1968) and later addressed by Fukuyama (2004).

After his earlier foray into determinist normative claims of the inevitability of democracy and free market capitalism, Fukuyama appeared to recognize that a liberal democratic capitalist outcome was not necessarily a given. Responding to his country's assertion of military power (itself a reflection of an isolationist-interventionist policy dichotomy), Fukuyama recognized two sets of closely related problems. The first was that the US had intervened in the affairs of other states (most notably, Panama, Lebanon, Somalia, Afghanistan and Iraq) with the explicit intention of ending non-democratic regimes, and in most cases, at least rhetorically, ending support for terrorist organizations and those countries' related military capacities (for example, "weapons of mass destruction"). Such intervention was justified on the positive grounds that it was intended to bring democracy to these countries. However, local populations did not automatically see the benefits of a "democratic" system of government when it was imposed and appeared to represent an alien ideology. More to the point, it was difficult to establish a democratic framework in states that did not enjoy the range of institutions that allowed democracy to exist, much less flourish. It was the lack of such institutions that was in most cases responsible for allowing particular states to degenerate to the point where they were unable to prevent or allowed the existence of organizations, such as Al Qaeda, which were claimed to present an external threat.

Similarly, it was a failure of state institutions more generally that provided fertile ground for the establishment of organizations that were regarded as an anathema to the US, and which might more generally be seen as antithetical to political development. Beyond this, the lack of capacity or performance of state institutions was widely and increasingly seen as a key reason why such states remained mired in underdevelopment. This shift to an institution-focus began in organizations such as the World Bank following the collapse of the Soviet Union, and the shift from communitarian-bureaucratic systems of government (that is, communism) in a number of eastern European states towards a more free-market liberal democracy. The initial impediment in these regime transitions was a lack of institutional capacity. This was mirrored in the parallel transitions from authoritarian forms of government towards more open and generally increasingly democratic forms in developing countries such as the Philippines, Thailand, Indonesia, Argentina, Nicaragua and Chile.

Institutional capacity and its role in wider development is generally regarded as being sustained through the intention and capacity of states to satisfy the needs and wants of their citizens, and to ensure the consistency of government service. In this capacity, it must be embedded in the institutions of state, which must be autonomous of private or sectional interests, including having an ability to resist corruption (see Evans 1995). However, this assumption is limited in that this intention and capacity can be too easily understood in purely bureaucratic or instrumentalist terms. Not only does this assumption focus on formal and usually hierarchical (and therefore not always responsive) structures, which are too often self-referential, but it ignores informal and non-codified social structures that also have an important institutional quality. Informal social institutions may include, for instance, an assertion of egalitarianism (for example through the institutionalization of social contract provisions) or of certain fundamental rights which implicitly underpin the way in which a state operates. That is, institutions are necessary for political development, but when defined in a narrow bureaucratic sense they are not sufficient. This requires the scope of institutional recognition to expand to include non-bureaucratic and in some cases non-state institutions.

Having proclaimed an Hegelian "end of history" (Fukuyama 1992), Fukuyama belatedly recognized that not only were many states a very long way from the "end of history" but, even assuming the appropriateness or inevitability of this model, many states were simply not heading in that direction (2004: i–xii).[4] In order to bolster the opportunity for an "end of history," Fukuyama focused on what was restraining states from achieving this "final" outcome. In this, Fukuyama's thesis reflected a slightly more nuanced political version of the "modernization" theory of the 1950s and early 1960s (see, for example, Rostow 1960, 1971), which assumed that all states, including those that had recently achieved independence, could move along an approximately linear path towards a political and economic model that replicated that of developed (often formerly colonizing) states.

The key difference between Fukuyama and earlier modernization theorists was that, following Huntington (1968), Fukuyama's reiteration of the importance of state building placed institutional development ahead of economic and social development as the key criterion for the creation of stable states. Both Huntington and Fukuyama disagreed with Rostow's assertion that "development" first required an economy to progress through stages before reaching a point at which it would "take off." According to Rostow, this economic "take off," this would then create further economic conditions for social development, which would in turn provide a foundation for political development. This assertion that "development" was a structural process, in which some parts generally preceded others, was contrary to Huntington and Fukayama's more agency driven approach. Huntington's approach did not so much reflect the pro-individualist political values of the US at the time, but more those values that came out of the post-Great Depression/post-Second World War era, in which there was greater emphasis on planning and large-scale political and economic guidance. For example, the creation of the UN, the World Bank, the IMF, and until the late 1970s the general acceptance among developed countries of a Keynesian model of economic intervention, in turn implied economic planning in which governments played a leading role. A similar although not identical focus on economic institutions was illustrated by the Canadian born US economist John Kenneth Galbraith (1967), who was probably the last of a tradition of influential "economic institutionalists."

In his major, albeit compromised view of political development, Huntington proposed that the character of the political system was less important than its legitimacy and efficacy. In this, he was concerned with the establishment of political order, which in turn required a constructive relationship between developing political institutions and the mobilization of new social forces into politics. This followed Huntington's concern that in new or post-colonial states, political mobilization could exceed the establishment of institutions (primarily political parties), and that this would lead to continuing institutional weakness. Barongo viewed this situation as the failure to replace dismantled traditional institutions with modern (or modernizing) institutions that were "capable of constraining political behavior and structuring political relations" (Barongo 1984: 139). Not surprisingly, Huntington was unenthusiastic about non-party political mobilization, in particular popular protest movements and what has since come to be termed "civil society." In that Huntington laid a claim to the idea of "political development," he did so by promoting a parallel concern with economic development that posited a political outcome that was the "opposite of backwardness and stagnation" (1968: vii). But Huntington's focus on "political order," beyond considering the types of systems in which such order was created, or what order might mean in practise, places his work in a different order of political consideration to that which is understood here as "political development." In simple terms, Huntington appeared to be more concerned with ends rather than with means and in this he appears to bend the suitability of ends to suit his proposed method (for example, the legitimacy of the Soviet system as an outcome of institutional order).

The distinction between Huntington and with the position offered here is that while this position agrees that political development is a necessary precondition for other forms of development, and that political institutionalization is the clearest form of such development, it disagrees in that institutions are not by definition legitimate, and legitimacy can lie outside formal institutions. In this respect, legitimacy can and often does exist within a framework that does not comply with narrower or more traditional definitions of institutions. The issue, then, is less around questions of institutions and more around whether or not they can establish a claim to be legitimate. That is, "development" is viewed here as holistic and inclusive. It is necessary to institutionalize certain elements, such as transparency and accountability, in order to ensure other forms of development. It is also possible to institute elements of political development in otherwise weak development environments, for example, democratic processes in one of the world's poorest, smallest and most fragile countries, East Timor. But it is clear that where there is inconsistent economic or other forms of development, political development will have to contend with the extra tensions that will inevitably create, and that a fragile political environment could collapse under such tensions (as East Timor almost did in 2006). Further, a wider understanding of institutions has a greater capacity for inclusion and participation, satisfying primary political claims and thus helping to ensure a more grounded political stability, or "order" by consent rather than by compulsion.

Political control

As noted in the previous chapter, the institutionalized role of political elites is, from a democratic perspective, contentious, as the notion of elites and elitism implies a functional political inequality. By definition, elites are not of "the people," even though they might arise from those people and even be chosen by the people via an electoral process. Indeed, the word "elite" derives from the French word for "elect." However, the common contemporary usage of the term "elite" implies social stratification, which has the effect of segmenting society on the basis of a range of criteria which, in a political sense, might reflect other areas of elite formation, such as the contributing elements of socio-economic class, education, language or religion.

While the idea of elites is problematic from an egalitarian perspective, even societies that claim to be explicitly egalitarian (such as communist societies) also have elites. In such societies, elites are, at least, "first among equals" (see Orwell 1946). However, as Mosca (1939), Michels (1959) and Pareto (1984) note, a default to elite rule, or oligarchy, is inherent in complex social structures. This is reflected in organizational capacity, as argued by Mosca and Michels, or in psychological capacity and self-interest, as argued by Pareto. Mills (1956) meanwhile acknowledged that in industrial societies, in which state power and authority tended to be divided between marginally accountable political, economic and military elites, elite rule existed in a particular self-interested and mutually reinforcing form.

The hierarchical ordering of complex societies and the rationalizing and routine of decision-making processes (see Weber 1968), particularly around the allocation of tasks, implicitly leads to the development of elites. However, whether or not there is an "iron law" of oligarchies, as argued by Michels, is debatable. While there is almost certainly a tendency towards oligarchy that can at times be overwhelming, the process and orientation of this tendency can shift dramatically in different circumstances, not least with changes in technology and education. Such changes suggest, if not guarantee, potential for an open and deliberative political society. Further, having started from an anarcho-syndicalist perspective, Michels' own acceptance of such an "iron law" led him to believe in the inevitability of oligarchy and hence endorse it in its most extreme and opposite form (in Italy's case, Fascism).

While the notion of oligarchies can be challenged, it would be naïve to conclude that the tendency towards oligarchies is other than a default position in social organization. In an earlier, somewhat more nuanced and less "scientific" approach, Mosca noted that while elites exist, they are obliged to draw on the support of sub-elites (Mosca 1939: 410; see also Pareto 1984; Mills 1951), which in turn presents the option of elite replacement through renewal, and further, the interaction between elites (decision makers), sub-elites (opinion leaders) and the *hoi polloi* (the many). This interaction contains within it the seeds of the egalitarian principle of participation and a rudimentary social contract which, in a practical if more limited form, can act as a brake on the extent to which elites can operate unaccountably.

In terms of the institutionalization of economic distribution and social control, political orientation can be identified as a circle, in which the bottom position indicates a balance between private and public ownership and distribution and the greatest amount of social freedom. To the left, the greater tendency towards economic distribution also complies with greater social control to the point where, after a particular threshold has been crossed, (half way for the purposes of Figure 8.1), the tendency towards social control exceeds the claimed value of economic redistribution. Similarly, to the right, the greater tendency towards economic accumulation is matched to the degree of social control required to maintain capacity for accumulation, to the point where the extent of social control exceeds the claimed value of accumulation. This model does not necessarily argue for or against economic redistribution or accumulation. However, where either is out of balance with a capacity to allow or encourage the least social control, arguments in favor of each appear to be compromised by the social price that is paid for whatever material benefits these positions might be able to offer.

It can be assumed that the greatest amount of social control implies the greatest negativity in terms of political development. Actual political systems that have diverged to the greatest extent from a centralist position, such as Stalinist communism and fascism, appear to meet at the point where their capacity (and desire) for social control is at its greatest. This conforms to the view that what totalitarian systems share in common as their most important feature is social control. It can be reasonably argued that there was a relatively high level of state intervention in Germany's economy and that, in this sense, it did not qualify as a purely right-wing party in economic terms. However, this

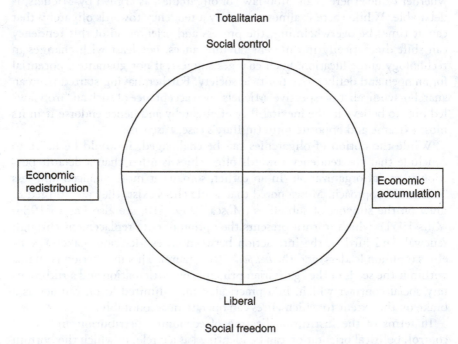

Figure 8.1 This diagram is intended to indicate the extent to which the greater the divergence in ideological positions, the greater the tendency towards authoritarian positions until such time that authoritarianism predominates as a political factor, to the point where it becomes the major or sole identifying feature.

overlooks the decline in social economic independence relative to state power as the latter increases, which is illustrated by this model. Similarly, while the Stalinist communist model and its derivatives can be claimed as exhibiting the greatest degree of economic redistribution. In fact, there were high levels of accumulation by the state at the expense of redistribution, as well as personal privilege and enrichment by elite members of such political systems.

The argument, then, that the greatest extent of social control reflects least political development in turn compromises the capacity and claimed benefits of the furtherest reaches of economic distribution or accumulation. From this argument, it logically follows that the greatest degree of social freedom also implies the greatest balance between economic distribution and accumulation. This allows considerable scope for accumulation and investment but also sufficient distribution to ensure that social freedom is not undermined by economic distribution and a consequent inability to provide an economic basis for full social participation. This economic balance at the point of greatest freedom approximates what Rousseau and others have referred to as the "social contract," in which elements of society enter into an agreement to sacrifice some benefits to themselves and to enhance the benefits of others on the understanding that they will retain sufficient benefits to be able to meaningfully pursue their own interests. Underscoring this position is the idea that both state and society will achieve sufficient social cohesion in order for this "contact" to occur.

Taking Hegel's "proposed end of history" in 1806, it has become clear that since that time there have been significant moves towards both greater authoritarianism and greater liberalism, in ways that Hegel would not have been likely to be able to predict. The rise of European nationalism and the advent of colonialism in the second half of the nineteenth century were both forces for and against more liberal approaches to politics.[5] Similarly, the post-First World War period saw the rise of both liberalism and totalitarianism, as well as the widespread continuation and application of other authoritarian political models (for example, populism and military-oligarchic rule in Latin America).

Fukuyama's argument is that the political trajectory of most of the twentieth century was an aberration and that the tendency, since the 1970s, has been towards democratic liberalism (1992: 262–4). It is accurate to note that more states are nominally or actually democratic in the early twenty-first century than they have been at any previous time. In part this reflects the increase in the absolute number of states. According to the politically conservative think-tank Freedom House,[6] democratic states increased from just 14.3 per cent of the total number of states in 1950 to 62.5 per cent in 2000. However, according to this assessment, there were no democratic states at all in 1900, on the basis of universal suffrage (principally including the vote for women), which contradicts other conceptions of democratic process (for example, universal male suffrage).[7] The Freedom House survey also shows that there was a decline in the relative proportion of totalitarian states between 1950 and 2000, from 7.8 per cent to 2.6 per cent and the decline of restricted democratic states from 13.6 per cent to 8.3 per cent. However, contrary to Fukuyama's assertion of the victory of democratic liberalism, the proportion of authoritarian states rose sharply between 1950 and 2000 from 6.5 per cent to 20.3 per cent (Freedom House 1999). In one sense, the extent to which one can view the world as slightly, significantly or no more democratic in part depends on the criteria for assessment, and the limited or more complex categorization of forms of government.

Beyond this, even liberal democracies have shown that they are not immune to authoritarian tendencies, or the imposition of some formal institutional requirements at the expense of others, as well as of less formal institutions. The US, since the 1950s has frequently supported authoritarian regimes and has imposed totalitarian-type restrictions on people alleged to be involved with the terrorist organization Al Qaeda. Prisoners taken at a number of sites, but primarily in Afghanistan, have been held without charge or trial, and in most cases incommunicado (at the time of writing), and have been facing the prospect of a closed military court since 2002 at the US military base at the Guantanamo Bay enclave in Cuba. The choice of Guantanamo Bay employed the rationale that as this was not US territory it did not have to comply with US law. This was overturned by a US Supreme Court ruling in July 2004 on the grounds of *habeus corpus*, or the necessity of producing a prisoner in court, and in turn overturned by a new Military Commissions Act, which was in turn being challenged as unconstitutional (de Young 2006). In Australia, in 2005, "anti-terrorism" legislation legalized the arrest and detention without charge of people suspected of being involved with terrorist organizations, and the administrative imposition of "control orders" limiting the actions of individuals deemed to be a "terrorist" threat. Similar laws have been common in many less liberal or democratic countries (e.g. the Internal Security Act of Singapore and Malaysia) and, indeed, have been one of the characteristics of such countries and their governments.

Political parties

As Huntington noted, the institutionalization of political parties is a necessary requirement for political development, even given his more limited understanding of the term. Huntington also noted that against parties was the claim that they promoted divisiveness, instability, corruption and susceptibility to external influences (1968: 405). But as he argued, these were characteristics of weak parties, not strong ones, and were principally found in political societies in transition from pre-modern political forms to modern political forms, or from authoritarian to liberal forms of government.

The benefit of parties, according to Huntington, and others, is twofold. In the first instance, parties promote the organization of political ideas within an institutionalized framework that reaches across communities within a state and hence promotes a national consciousness and cohesion. Second, the social divisions that then exist stem from "horizontal" rather than "vertical" (or regionally or communally based) cleavages, which may have the capacity to divide the state along regional or communal lines. Thus political parties are seen to have a bonding effect on the state.

This view of the "horizontalizing" value of parties assumes the primacy of the state and the logic of its connection with the nation. That is, the value of parties as reflecting horizontal values *prima facie* assumes state unity or, where it does not, assumes the capacity of horizontal institutional association to create such unity. The internal tension in this view of parties may be that in the case of regionally or communally fragmented societies within relatively arbitrarily constructed states, such as Indonesia, Burma or Iraq, the tendency has been to impose horizontal representation and to institute impediments to vertical representation. The practise in such states has been that the greater the potential disunity, the more the nominal or actual vertical influences have been tightly bound to the state. Each of the three above-mentioned examples was constructed as a unitary state in order to overcome the development of vertical tendencies.[8] Moreover, in each case the state was dominated for the greater part of its existence by a strong, highly authoritarian government that was in turn based on a strong state party (Golkar in Indonesia between 1966 and 1998, various iterations of military government in Burma from 1962 to the present, and the Ba'ath Socialist Party in Iraq from 1948 until 2003). The problem in each case, however, was that minorities (or in the case of Iraq, a majority) believed they were inadequately represented by the unitary model and its imposition had the counter effect not of creating stronger horizontal links, but of strengthening vertical sentiment.

Huntington would have argued that this counter-horizontal tendency was a consequence of the weakness of the party system. Yet another view, expressed in Iraq and parts of Indonesia in the early twenty-first century, has been that if the state as constructed does have a future, it must be accompanied by the institutionalized devolution of state authority. Indonesia moved to institutionalize this devolution of political, economic and administrative authority in 2001 in the form of "regional autonomy," while the citizens of Iraq voted in favor of a new effectively federalist constitution in 2005. Indonesia rejected "federalism" as contrary to the spirit of the Unitary State of the Republic of Indonesia (Negara Kesatuan Republik Indonesia – NKRI). The adoption of "regional autonomy" signaled that strong national parties in a unitary state could not adequately meet the concerns of specific geographically located interest groups. The problem was not that the party or parties were not strong enough, but rather that they were too strong and allowed little or no specific alternative. Similarly in Iraq, having established their own political parties, Kurds and Shia Muslims voted overwhelmingly in favor of a functional federalism as a means of redressing the inequities of a centrally controlled state in which a single "vision" was intended, but failed, to account for all political possibilities.

The argument, therefore, in favor of the institutionalization of parties is not that parties should not exist and be strong, or, perhaps more appropriately, be deeply embedded in the political life of the citizens and the state. Rather, it is that there be a multiplicity of parties that reflect the plural quality of any polity. Taken to its furthest extreme, the potential devolution to the smallest common political denominator of a single person restricts the size of parties and thus limits the capacity to challenge political control. Geographic uniformity, however, does reflect established or potential horizontal participation but may also deny local specificity that might have a horizontal logic (for example, a political party based on factory workers in a specifically industrialized area), as well as the legitimate claims to protection of local cultural particularities or the retention of community unity and identity.

There is, in the final analysis, no perfectly integrated horizontal society, even in the most developed countries (for example, the UK,[9] Italy,[10] Belgium, Spain, Canada and the US).[11] Assuming, however, a sufficient political commonality to allow the formation of a party, the question arises as to the nature of political parties, what types of parties can and do exist and their respective costs and benefits. In the first instance, any grouping with a common political goal could identify itself as a political party. This minimalist definition would also encompass single issue pressure groups, trade unions and a range of other politicized social movements. More loosely conceived parties (such as parties constructed as "umbrella" organizations), on the other hand, might not adhere around a common political goal but reflect agreement around differentiated sets of goals within an overarching framework, or indeed simple opposition to an external proposition without necessarily specifying alternatives. More confusingly, different parties may agree on a common goal but disagree (and in some cases only slightly) on how that is to be achieved. Still more confusingly, if one is to believe the rhetoric, political goals can be done away with and material conditions of living can be achieved in a "depoliticized" environment administered by a "non-party," as has been the claim of numerous developing country coups which have opposed parties on the grounds they promote division and discord.

According to Jupp, there are eight categories of party systems that can be broadly divided into two groups. Jupp's first grouping includes parties within competitive political systems, and the second is within non-competitive systems. The former grouping includes an indistinct bi-partisan system, including a loose party structure, often notable-led and where policy differences are less substantial (for example, the US, Russia, Indonesia, Philippines and with an increasing tendency in most western European states and Australia). The second category within the first grouping comprises a distinct bi-partisan system in which there is a greater degree of party hierarchy and policy differentiation (such as Venezuala, East Timor and most eastern European states). The third category includes multi-party systems where governments are comprised of coalitions (for example, Italy, Israel, Germany in 2005). Fourth, there are dominant party systems, in which one party dominates through elections (Cambodia, Malaysia, Singapore, South Africa, Zimbabwe). Jupp's second grouping of non-competitive political systems includes broad single party systems, which have elections and may allow factions within the single party (for example, Egypt),[12] and narrow one party systems, that are lacking in genuine political contests in which there is relatively little, or no factionalism (for example, Syria, Eritrea, Vietnam and Laos). The third category within this second grouping comprises totalitarian systems, which are similar to narrow one party systems but have a rigid hierarchy, detailed ideology and effective control over all agencies of force, government and communication (Burma, Turkmenistan, China, Cuba, North Korea). Finally, "non-party systems" occur where parties have been abolished (such as Brunei, Nepal between early 2005 and April 2006 and Saudi Arabia) (also see Jupp 1968: 111–12 for an earlier set of examples).

If it is possible to classify these examples on a scale of an institutional version of political development, those parties that offer a distinct dual party (or stable coalition) system would rank highest, although there would be considerable variation among them based on the extent of practical openness, capacity for participation and guarantees of human rights. Totalitarian systems would tend to be at the lowest end of this scale, although non-party systems could potentially vie for that status. The final quality of both totalitarian and non-party systems depend on whether they are open to advice and persuasion (limited participation), and whether they tend to be more or less benign or malignant. These qualifications raise the further issue of non-competitive party political systems, which to a great extent comply with Huntington's requirement for a formal political party but, by the definition offered here, reflect low levels of political development.

Though political parties are normatively participatory institutions, they can potentially both represent and exclude wider social participation. At one level, political parties represent aggregates of social interests (for example, economic, security, ethnicity/culture/religion or patronage), but at another level can succumb to their institutional structure, by default conforming to unreflective or elite-led or populist policy positions and limiting the capacity for participation. As such, political parties do not conform to a uniform type. Nor, as suggested by Huntington, do they necessarily imply "order" or promote political development. A political party may be little more than a loose structure around which poorly articulated preferences or concerns gather. Conversely, it may represent a value system that is contrary to the existing "order" and thus be a force for radical change, which implies at least short- to medium-term instability and possible longer-term repression in order to limit public expressions of dissent (for example, in the former Soviet Union and allied states, and in Nazi Germany, and in fascist Italy, Spain and Portugal). However, most parties do not propose radical or revolutionary agendas, and many (perhaps most) tend to sit within the relatively conventional political parameters implied by state maintenance.

In their more positive sense, political parties can and often do represent and articulate the views of their constituent members, who in turn are more politically engaged members of particular social groups. Parties also often order and temper competing social and economic claims, which both channel and regulate political tensions and the capacity for such tension to be manifested as violence. Within the context of a competitive, party-based political system, political parties generally "play by the rules" which in turn ensures a higher degree of stability through consistency and regularization of political application.

Despite the positive outcomes of the existence of political parties, their creation alone, even with the establishment of "order," is not a sufficient condition for other forms of development, and underestimates the importance of full political development as a good in itself. To illustrate this point, the Communist Party of the Soviet Union was, by any measure of "order," a successful political party, which Huntington acknowledged, dominating the state for most of the twentieth century. Yet one of the Soviet Union's founders, Leon Trotsky, viewed the emerging Soviet state as having been captured by the bureaucratization of the party and the wider institutionalization of state bureaucracy, which he saw as betraying the emancipatory principles of the revolution (Trotsky 1937: Chapter 9). More to the point, however, the logic of bureaucratic institutionalism removed the party from the will of the people. The large size of many communist parties relative to the population of the state could be argued to be a mechanism for inclusion and hence, in theory, emancipation. It is clear from the experience of Vietnam that party membership does facilitate specific member benefits, even if this does betray the claimed representative quality of the party. Bureaucratized and regularized, such parties tend to be run on a top-down basis, reflecting Lenin's principle of the "vanguard of the proletariat." As such, they are effectively doctrinaire in their self-replication, allowing little or no room for alternative views, much less dissent.

Like the Communist Party of the Soviet Union, Germany's Nazi Party was remarkably successful in capturing power and establishing "order," and in this respect it admirably fulfilled Huntington's principle concern with "order." Yet its claim to being representative was undercut by its political strategy of political destabilization and eventually capture, initially from a minority position, as well as its use of exemplary violence and terror to persuade its opponents or those undecided on its merits. The primary downfall of the Nazi Party was its goal of dominating Europe, which, to the future of the party in Germany, was not necessary to its immediate survival. In so far as it reflected the will of the people, the Nazi Party was fuelled by a romantic fantasy about its relative worth, and hence, manifest destiny.[13] The accusation of being removed from the will of the people can also be leveled at Italy's Fascists, Spain's Falangists,[14] and so on, even where a degree of popular support did appear and constructed a hegemonic acceptance. These parties all imposed an extraordinarily high degree of "order" in their respective societies, strengthened the capacity of the state immeasurably and were, outside military ventures, relatively economically successful. But the human cost of this "order" was such that only an extremist would argue that the ends justified the means. A similarly high degree of "order" has been delivered by Burma's State Peace and Development Council (previously the State Law and Order Restoration Council), but which has only delivered gross underdevelopment in tandem with institutionalized conflict. Indonesia's New Order, Taiwan's Guomindang (until political liberalization), military regimes in Latin America and Africa and all "communist" states have also imposed a high degree of internal "order." In each case, the capacity of the dominant state party as an institution has not been matched by, or has intentionally diminished, the capacity of the people and hence "order," not balanced by freedom, is the opposite of political development.

This particular issue of top-down party organization raises the further issue of party structure, and the varying capacities for participation within different types of political parties. As discussed, parties can either be categorized as hierarchical, bureaucratic or personalized, or as more participatory decision-making structures that reflect a greater level of accuracy of representation in policy outcomes. As institutions, most political parties have a relatively clearly defined hierarchical structure. Through a process of elections (or sometimes acclaim or patrimonial "ownership"), parties have leaders who are the senior party representatives and who allocate decision-making responsibility. Leaders comprise the party's elite who usually have decision-making power (or influence) outside of their formal executive capacities and enjoy influence over policy making disproportionate to their party membership (even in formally full and equal processes of participation). Through either patronage or bureaucratic self-replication, party elites tend to encourage or select members for promotion within the party system who conform to their pre-existing preferences and prejudices. As such, the question of political development, as defined by completeness of participation and accuracy of representation, is often limited in parties across the entire political spectrum, from the Labour Party of the UK and the Australian Labor Party, to more extreme examples of the Communist Party of Vietnam and the Lao People's Revolutionary Party.

An alternative party structure, and one upon which most parties at least initially base their appeal, is that which is relatively level, strongly participatory and more closely representative. Short of force or the use of terror, parties can only succeed in establishing their ideological preferences and achieving policy goals by appealing to a majority of the population, based on a coterie of active and committed party members. These members often voluntarily undertake the manual or lower level administrative work that is required to disseminate information and to promote party policies and candidates.

It may be that party members have near to complete faith in the wisdom and benign intentions of their party's leadership, and sometimes this faith can even be rewarded. However, it is much more common for party leaders to not have a monopoly on wisdom, nor to display intentions that are entirely in the selfless interests of the party membership and their greater constituency.

Indeed, even where it can be claimed that party (or other political) leadership is both benign and relatively wise, it cannot be assumed it will always be so, or that its inevitable successors will display the same characteristics. The allocation of power, and the responsibility it carries, must always be transparent and fully accountable if it is to remain immune from personalized decision making or other potential evils of political temptation.

As a consequence, a high proportion of party participation by rank and file members in deciding the party's policy platform, and in the highest practical level of direct election for choosing representative candidates for government office, equates with greater political development. At the local level, to conform to the highest level of political development, the selection of candidates for office should be based on direct, secret elections and followed by a process of direct accountability thereafter. In electorates that cover a dispersed geographic area, the practical value of an electoral model can be best gauged by the extent to which it is closer to or removed from direct elections. As a default position, the devolution of political power ensures the greatest participation and most accurate representation of interests and values. The tension within political structures is therefore principally between the defense of direct, personal interest and its surrender.

In both hierarchical and more participatory systems of party organization, the party's ideology and policy platform should and in most cases will reflect an internal coherence and consistency in application. This consistency itself constitutes the institutionalization of political values, and becomes the defining characteristic of the party, manifested as ideology. While there may be variations of opinion on particular policy issues, but within an overarching conceptual framework – that is, difference over degree rather than principle – there is ideally the further capacity for the organization and institutionalization of such differing interpretations. When organized along internally coherent lines in the form of a first principle being reflected in policy areas such as health, education and other public amenities, the institutionalization of these ideas begs consistency of support or rejection. It is upon such commonalities that allegiances are built. In a political party that has a relatively higher degree of top down organization, this may take the form of formalized factionalism, or the formation of sub-parties within the overarching party framework. In parties that have either a more level structure or which operate under a patrimonial system, there is likely to be less propensity towards factionalism, with policy decisions being taken on a more direct basis and settled either through acceptance of majority decision[15] or consensus without the institutionalization of formal distinction. In more patrimonial systems, however, Solomon-like wisdom over policy distinctions is exceptionally rare and tend to be over-ridden through application of personal authority, which militates against participation.

In theory, political parties have been seen in three broad ways. The first, echoing Huntington, is that parties represent aggregate interests that are reflected in both ideology and policy. Short of complete political breakdown, parties allow political conflict to be played out according to agreed rules. This does not allow much scope for party capture by limited interest groups or repression, or the possibility of party interests being served by open conflict. A second view is that certain types of parties necessarily serve confrontational-ist aggregate interests, such as Marx's proletariat being best served by a revolutionary socialist or communist party. Both of these approaches can suffer from a crude determinism. In the first instance, certain types of parties or party systems will inevitably arise in particular social and economic set-tings. Second, group interests can only be rationally represented by parties to which they are economically aligned. These latter approaches can find some validity in political representation, but say little about economic or social aspirations as political determinants, competing theories about maxi-mizing total social well-being, or the personal and social complexities of ideological allegiance which may produce a third, quite different approach to understanding party formation (see Jupp 1968: 22–5).

Beyond this, the creation of parties and "order" says nothing about the tendency towards corruption by a single or dominant party, the necessity of transparency and accountability, or the organizational and intellectual scler-osis that affects political institutions when they are not subject to reasonably regular change. Indeed, it is quite possible to have parties that employ a narrow political base, especially if there is little or no political opposition, and this can and often does lead to numerous forms of patrimonialism or "state capture" by unrepresentative interests. It may also remove power brokers from popular will and increase tensions between power holders and non-power holders, which in turn usually requires a large and expensive state repression apparatus. This situation assumes that the primary focus of economic invest-ment is not to serve social needs and interests, but to retain a repressive and brittle grip on state power.

Huntington's model theoretically accepted the political system of the USSR because of what he saw as its legitimacy and efficiency (both of which could then be, and were later shown to be unsubstantiated). His theory of "order," however, was largely an endorsement of US client states that employed strong government and established state institutions but in most cases, ignored claims of political difference. That is, Huntington's theory of order could rationalize military-backed governments which suppressed alternative opinions. While Huntington's theory could be argued to have its own internal coherence, it was similarly argued to be intellectually misguided[16] and served as a rationalization for what were then US foreign policy interests, such as America's support for the South Vietnam government (Republic of Vietnam), Suharto's military takeover in Indonesia in 1965–6, and a series of other military or military-backed governments in Latin America, Africa and Asia.

Taking a different political economy perspective, Jaguaribe (1968) argued that parties could not be effective without supporting economic and social development. Without accountability, Jaguaribe argued that a government becomes "irresponsible." "Once the elections are over," he said, "the political parties, which are little more than self-serving machines for conquering power, practically disappear, to hibernate until the next elections come around. Other forms of political irresponsibility also occur when parties fail to fulfill expectations vested in them . . ." (Jaguaribe 1968: 55). Where Jaguaribe might be closer to Huntington, however, is in the latter's assertion that for "order" to be achieved, which might be equated with Jaguaribe's capacity for planning, political participation should be balanced with political institutionalization. Further, the establishment of other types of institutions, such as bureaucracies, leads to a higher level of formalistic interpretation of substantive rationality (Weber 1948: 340). As institutions develop, their rational function is increasingly expressed as "formalistic impersonality" (Weber 1948: 340), not just in terms of internal workplace relations, but in terms of the external function for which they were established. Such formalism and impersonality may lead to a disassociative attitude expressed as: "I don't make the rules; I am just doing my job" (Parkinson 1957).

Related to the institutionalization of this formalized impersonality is an implicit belief that bureaucracies are not driven by particular sets of values, other than those which derive from government policy. However, this belief ignores the fact that bureaucracies may comprise long-term specialists in specific fields, and are hence in a strong position to provide advice to governments and their ministers. This claim to formalized impersonality also precludes open acknowledgement of institutional biases and the capacity for self-replication. Bureaucracies that claim such a formalistic impersonality implies a procedural objectivity and do not encourage views that run contrary to their self-perception or self-interest. However, bureaucracies do tend to retain institutionalized values, derived in the first instance from the twin influences of original or long-term senior appointments and self-preservation, which inform their inclination or otherwise to respond appropriately to government directives.

One serious outcome of this formalized impersonality is that bureaucracies are most inclined to appoint or promote staff who reconfirm the prevailing bureaucratic perspective. No self-respecting senior bureaucrat would appoint or promote a more junior member whose first task would be to question that bureaucrat's decision making. As a consequence, bureaucracies tend to employ or promote staff who reconfirm existing values and prejudices, be they about questions of managing health care, transport or foreign policy. Particularly in areas outside direct public awareness, such as foreign policy, bureaucracies may become self-replicating fiefdoms that can not only ignore alternative perspectives but may actively dismiss or repress them. This may occur in areas in which policy is seen as "too important to be left to the general public," hence precluding meaningful public participation or representation in policy debate.

Where there are low levels of participation and institutionalization, the state has a tendency to fragment. According to Huntington, however, higher levels of participation without commensurate institutionalization also tends to produce demand without capacity and hence, state instability (1968: Chapter 7). By contrast, strong institutionalization with high participation would provide an effective channel for participation and therefore limit its negative tendencies.

While high levels of political participation and institutional capacity are both necessary for political development, a high level of institutional capacity with a low level of political participation produces bureaucratic authoritarianism. This can be expressed through the bureaucracy of the political party, the formalistic impersonality which tends to preclude wider participation, or through the state bureaucracy, which excludes participation and reduces representation to the most indirect level. Assuming a technical proficiency of the bureaucracy, its capacity to diffuse accountability "upwards," and its formalistic impersonality towards its "client" base, meaningful accountability is precluded. Mosca saw the threat of the bureaucracy as comprising a new, small ruling class of technocrats and administrators (Mosca 1939), while Mill saw the bureaucracy as a threat to representative government. "A bureaucracy always tends to become a pendantocracy," argued Mill. As Mill noted, "When the bureaucracy is the real government, the spirit of the corps (as with the

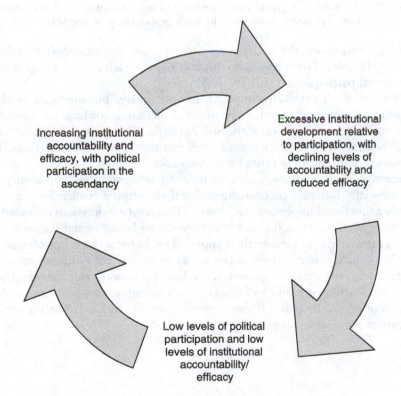

Increasing institutional accountability and efficacy, with political participation in the ascendancy

Excessive institutional development relative to participation, with declining levels of accountability and reduced efficacy

Low levels of political participation and low levels of institutional accountability/efficacy

Figure 8.2 Political institutions: institutionalism and accountability.

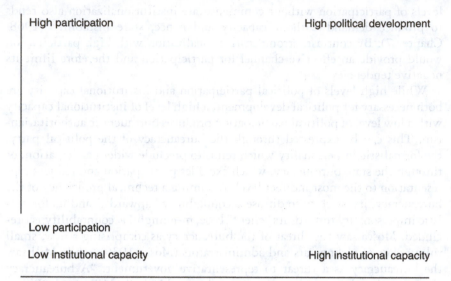

Figure 8.3 A model of political participation and accountability, evolving through linked phases in a manner which suggests a cyclicial potential.

Jesuits) bears down the individuality of its more distinguished members" (Mill 1910: 246). The exception to this is a "popular element," or a higher level of external participation (Mill 1910: 246).

If there is no externally imposed accountability, bureaucracies tend to become self-referential and increasingly function according to internally determined ("bureaucratically rational") criteria. This in turn increases technical separation up and functional impersonality down. In such cases, the bureaucracy increasingly exists for its own sake.

Exemplified as the state, which has no or little "upward" accountability, its "functionally rational" centralizing and self-reaffirming tendencies similarly imply a functional impersonality "down." This is where decisions are taken by the state administrators (elected or otherwise) on behalf of state constituents (citizens) without recourse to their approval or, in some cases, knowledge.

This is to say, institutions in the wider as well as conventional sense are necessary to political development, if for different reasons. But the capacity to question institutions, and to keep them accountable, is what ensures their contribution to the political development project, and is it itself a critical feature of political development.

9   State and regime failure

State failure is a relatively recent idea, reflecting global acceptance of a standardized norm for the definitive characteristics of states. Regime failure relates to state failure in that regime failure can lead to state failure, and state failure implies that an existing regime is also no longer capable of fulfilling its principle functions.

According to the World Bank, there were 26 states at risk of collapse in 2006, or more than 10 per cent of the total number, showing the alarming extent of potential or actual state failure (World Bank 2006). Prior to the end of the colonial era, this situation did not, and could not, exist, and prior to colonialism there was no single model for the state, but rather a variety of polities that succeeded, expanded, merged, contracted or disappeared according to the prevailing strategic environment. But along with the idea of state inviolability, as defined by the UN, there is now a more or less set model for what should constitute the state. Variations away from this model, particularly towards disorganization and malfunction, internal incoherence and a lack of organizational centrality over a state's claimed territory are generally deemed to constitute state failure, especially where such attributes once existed but have since collapsed or disappeared.

Regime failure, on the other hand, may at its most simple mean the collapse of a particular political order. At its most positive, regime failure can mark the point of transition to another regime type. However, regime failure can also create a political vacuum, which in turn reduces the capacity of state institutions and therefore threatens the viability of the state.

State failure may reflect a range of political circumstances. The most basic is where the state simply ceases to function, where there is no centralized or relatively consistent rule of law and where state sovereignty ceases to exist or is widely unable to be enforced. State failure might also imply the collapse of state institutions, in particular the bureaucracy, but also the security forces or other institutions that result in the consequent ending of state function. Further, state failure might imply factionalized state capture, in which a state's territory or institutions are divided between competing groups that deny access to state territory or institutions to each other. Finally, state failure can occur as a consequence of natural calamity in which the state is unable to respond to radically changed circumstances, such as earthquake (Niacaragua 1978) or drought (Ethiopia 1970–85), or especially in the case of invasion and occupation, in which the state functionally ceases to exist as an independent political entity.

According to the *Foreign Policy* failed state index, state failure can be measured by consideration of extreme demographic pressures, refugees and displaced persons, group grievances, human flight, uneven development, dramatic economic decline, delegitimization of the state, limited public service capacity, gross abrogation of human rights, an unaccountable security apparatus, seriously factionalized elites, or external intervention (FP 2005). These criteria can measure aspects of state failure, but may not necessarily determine whether a state has failed. By way of illustration, demographic pressure may impact on OECD countries where the trend is towards an ageing population and an imbalance of state functions, yet no OECD countries register on the *Foreign Policy* failed state index. Similarly, population growth alone is not an indicator of state failure if there is capacity to support it; for example, in China the institutional and economic success of the state is growing rather than declining. Similarly, factionalized elites occur in most states and could be considered part of a plural political process, while external intervention may reflect less the failure of the state itself and more the capacity for an external party to intervene, for example Europe at the beginning of the Second World War. In this case, many of Europe's states were successful by conventional criteria, but were relatively vulnerable to attack by a more powerful and belligerent neighbor. This reflected on a quality of the neighbor, not on their own relative success or failure. These criteria are thus an incomplete measure of state failure. According to this index, the top 9, and 14 of the top 20 failed states are in Sub-Saharan Africa. At number 13, North Korea registers highly in terms of "delegitimization of the state" (9.8 on a scale of 10), which may be correct but, given that it is unmeasurable and in this case unknown, could also reflect a subjective external perspective.

Where a state fails to act in a manner that represents the interests of its citizens, and where its institutions have little capacity or are severely compromised by sectional interests, corruption or external attack, state failure, or aspects of it could be said to exist. When the failure of aspects of state function or institutions reaches a certain critical point, it has the effect of damaging other aspects of the state, thereby weakening the whole. An example of this could be the failure of an independent judiciary, which in turn subverts the rule of law and accountability of state institutions, and has the capacity to develop a culture of impunity. In such circumstances, various state agencies and state and non-state actors have increased license to engage in corruption or other forms of subversion of state function and sovereignty. When the primary failed functions or institutions are beyond repair, and have a knock-on or multiplier effect, the state then becomes vulnerable to overarching failure. That is, the key elements that define a state, such as full application of law up to the sovereign limits of the state, cease to functionally exist. In the case of state failure due to external attack (or internal rebellion), the existing state may be replaced with another state (through revolution) or states (via devolution).

A final form of state failure is where the individuals or institutions that comprise the state "feed off" the state and its citizens in what has been described as a "predatory" manner (Evans 1995). Predatory states are characterized not by their capacity to meet the needs or aspirations of their citizens, but by exploiting their citizens for the benefit of a small minority, usually with the application of actual or implied violence.

> . . . some politicians may not be inclined to follow them (political rules) because what is at stake – the power to control the use of scarce resources – means a great deal to either of the competing parties and which must therefore be acquired or retained by any means not particularly consonant with the limits of the general standards of morality.
>
> (Barongo 1984: 147)

Regime failure

From the perspective of political development, state failure represents the denouement of the political development project, assuming that one is not aspiring to non-state organization models. What might be termed "democratic fatalism," then, appears to be the most unnecessary and avoidable form of regime and sometimes state failure, and hence, the failure of political development.

Democratic fatalism is the assumption that "democracy," defined idealistically but shaped in practise by particular structural, institutional and cultural paradigms, will either arrive as a matter of historical logic or will be the common aspiration and hence logically manifest destiny. This assumes that democracy is "fated" to exist, and requires little more than passive acceptance of it to ensure such existence. It also implies satisfaction with a particular version of a democratic model, which might belie internal weaknesses or fundamental flaws which may allow such democracy to retain external appearances but hollow out its practical meaning, leaving it as an empty shell or vulnerable to collapse. As O'Donnell and Schmitter note, democracy "usually emerges from a nonlinear, highly uncertain, and imminently reversible process involving the cautious definition of certain spaces and moves on a multilayered board. . . . As to the case with liberalization, there does not seem to be any logical sequence to these processes . . . Nor is democratization irreversible . . ." (O'Donnell and Schmitter 1986: 8; see also Carothers 2002).

Fukuyama claimed that the US political system, which he held up as a model for the truth of the universal applicability of liberal democracy, was not discredited as a consequence of the impact of the Great Depression (1992: 29). In putting this proposition, Fukuyama ignored four fundamental features that give lie to his claim. First, that the legitimate protest movements of that period were only repressed with the use of extensive violence by capital in close cooperation with the state. Second, that the psychological consequences of dispossession do not always lead to rebellion but may also lead to resignation. Third, the US did indeed recognize systemic failure and addressed it with the economically more regulatory and redistributive "New Deal." Finally, while the US was already climbing out of the Great Depression, that the Second World War provided a massive government-led demand, which boosted economic production and technological development, allowing the US to overcome the mass unemployment and impoverishment of the Great Depression and setting in train the almost three decade "long boom" that followed.

It was this extended period of postwar growth that, as a denouement of negative material circumstances, posited the earlier period as the systemic aberration, rather than the failure of liberal democracy itself. Fukuyama's proposition did not, however, adequately address the issue of the widening gap between rich and poor, the structural establishment of a working poor underclass, the links between poverty and having a prison population between three and eight times higher than comparable countries (BJS 2005), and the political hegemony of neo-liberal capitalism. This begs the question that if the US is the shining example of liberal democracy then what are examples of its failure? One might have thought that if Fukuyama was looking for genuinely positive examples of liberal democracy he might have chosen the overwhelmingly more egalitarian examples of Scandinavian countries. In this, however, the argument might be raised that these states represent social democracy rather than liberal democracy, assuming the distinction between qualifiers refers to economic orientation. Yet if this is the case, clearly there is a strong case to be made that if history does have an "end," and that such an "end" is more or less present, it is to be found in societies that demonstrate much greater degrees of social tolerance, inclusion and support, along with higher standards of limiting exploitation of their own and other environments and economies, and higher levels of participation in well modulated, regular elections, leading to greater overall representation.[1]

The type of ideological determinism that claimed that history was headed in a necessary linear direction and that its final destination could be known (or had been achieved) was the principle failing of Hegelian idealism, Fukuyama's own version of the "end of history," and Marxian political economy models. Each ignored the fact that decisions may be driven by abstract considerations built on previously accumulated knowledge. As such, decisions may reflect a broadly progressive view of history, but they are taken in a real, human world in which self-interest, greed, lust for power and differing interpretations of the bonded political community can and do rise to the fore. Particular political models may become available as a political consequence of particular sets of economic circumstances. But due to the effects of agency, particular economic circumstances may give rise to and accommodate a variety of political models, only one of which could be meaningfully defined as "democratic."

Agency may, given an opportunity for the rational allocation of popular decisions, edge towards a broadly more participatory, accountable and egalitarian model. It may be sufficient, in many instances, to apply "rational ignorance" to elements of such a process, assuming the systems in place are suitably functional. But when tensions arise over a burden of oppression or systemic failure – when the social contract is either broken or no longer applies – rationality implies not "ignorance" or passive behavior, but activism. Assuming a tension, or competition between structure and agency, in which the default position of structure is to draw to itself as much political authority as possible, any assumption about political development that is passive necessarily plays into the hands of structural interests.

However, agency may also accrue to itself political power and the benefits that arise from such power. Alternatively, political power may be accrued by an agency that is captured by romanticist notions that do not correspond to reality, or which seek to bend reality to its wishes. This latter case gives rise to Spencer's concern that "There is no political alchemy by which you can get golden conduct out of leaden instincts" (Spencer in Lafargue 1884). In more extreme cases, here ideology breaks its bonds with material circumstances, such irrational power becomes dangerous. As noted by Bullock: "The existence of such an organization [in this case the National Socialist Party] was in fact incompatible with the safety of the Republic" (Bullock 1962: 176).

In attempting to understand how ideological irrationality can escape the grounding of material reality, the rise of Germany's Nazi Party and the failure of action against it remain instructive. There were, according to Bullock, three reasons for failure to take action against the rise of Nazism:

1. Tactics of legality designed to win maximum advantage from a democratic constitution. In this, there was little scope to block the rise of a "legal" political organization that was able to exploit weaknesses in the democratic process, for example using freedom of speech to shout down other voices.
2. Challenges to the state remained camouflaged or latent, so there was a strong temptation by the government not to add to its problems by banning potential challenges.
3. The refusal by other parties to sink their differences, unite in the face of emergency and jointly assume responsibility for unpopular but necessary decisions, forced the government to look outside of party politics towards the army, whose support was equivocal.

(Bullock 1962: 176–9)

While Nazism might have been ideologically irrational, its techniques and tactics were often not only highly rational but inventive, extrapolating from mass industrialization to mass socio-psychological organization and manipulation. In this, Nazism differed to all previous dictatorships because it was the first to make full use of modern technical capacity for total domination (Speer in Nuremberg Trials 1947–9: xxii, 406–7). However, the reigns of both Hitler and Stalin were characterized not just by the use of modern technology as a means of ensuring social compliance, but either started with, or created an economic and political tabula rasa in which expressions of industrial efficiency and organization were then applied to society, and were thus the political expression of the mechanistic age in which they arose. Without suggesting a deterministic association between industrialization and totalitarianism, not only was industrialization the rationale for these regime types and the means by which they built their political and military strength, but there were parallels between the regularized methods of mass production and totalitarianism's regularization of mass communication and political control. If political styles reflect the economic conditions upon which they are based, totalitarianism reflected the idea of absolute industrial efficiency, in which individual "cogs" were subsumed by the state machine.

Following from such industrial efficiency was a single minded concept of the national interest that claimed to represent not just sectional interests but the entire community, embodied in and guaranteed by the absolutism of the state (Bullock 1962: 406). Moving towards its most pure expression as an unconnected ideology, "Stripped of their romantic trimmings, all Hitler's ideas can be reduced to a simple claim for power which recognizes only one relationship, that of domination, and only one argument, that of force" (Bullock 1962: 408). That is, agency without regard for material circumstances and reduced to its most efficient, minimalist expression devolves to the greatest will able to take advantage of the greatest capacity.

> I shall give a propagandist reason for starting the war, no matter whether it is plausible or not. The victor will not be asked afterwards whether he told the truth or not. When starting and waging war it is not right that matters, but victory. . . . Close your hearts to pity. Act brutally. . . . The strongest man is right. The greatest harshness.
>
> (Hitler, 22 August 1938)

Conversely, a reflective and representative will seeking to distribute the fruits of capacity avoids domination and the imposition of force. Reflecting on the ideology of power as self-rationalizing, Ortega y Gasset warned that:

> Civilization consists in the attempt to reduce violence to the *ultima ratio*, the final argument. This is now becoming all too clear to us, for direct action reverses the order and proclaims violence as the *prima ratio*, or rather the *unica ratio*, the sole argument. It is the standard that dispenses with all others.
>
> (Ortega y Gasset 1964: Chapter 8)

By establishing power as the sole rationale for the regime and hence the state, totalitarianism can exist only so long as it is able to assert its power. In this, the citizens of the state become alienated from its purpose which in turn strips it of legitimacy and hence a reason for continuing. The regime ends up living on borrowed time, and as soon as its political core – usually the leader – is unable to hold to power by itself, it begins to crumble. The regime thus disappears and, if the state is predicated upon the style of the regime, so it also disappears, perhaps to be reborn in a different form (e.g. Germany as East and West, the Soviet Union as its composite states).

Two approaches to failure

This view of human nature accruing power through authoritarian methods errs towards the negative, and is too often confirmed, especially when goals are not understood in terms of how they are achieved, i.e. that the end result is more important than the means, even though the means contribute to shaping of, and might determine, the ends. The path to democratic failure arising from this perspective is that democracy is singular, it is a given, that it is the only viable option and is thus inevitable, that governments based on other systems will ultimately lose legitimacy and default to the popular desirability of democratization.

This approach might be called "democratic mysticism," in which there is a *belief* in the inevitability of a meaningful democratic outcome without fully or even partially understanding the means by which such an outcome should be achieved. In this sense, democracy takes on a religious or metaphysical quality, or is presented as such to an audience that is encouraged to accept its inevitability on the basis of "rational ignorance"; that the acceptance of its inevitability or continued presence is based on the trust of others (usually an oligarchic elite) to ensure its carriage.

As discussed in Chapter 7, democracy can exist, but it is diminished by claims of curbing its "excesses" – that more complete application is inefficient or divisive – or by way of safeguarding it against its potential for abuses. In this latter respect, the post-2001 "War on Terror" (and many previous conflicts) has produced claims that the "war" requires the sacrifice of certain democratic principles or the limitation of certain liberties, in order to secure the greater well-being. Proponents of the war argue that the threat it opposes is against "our way of life," or against "democracy," yet it is precisely that which is limited in order to "protect" democracy (for example, see Aden 2003; Cole 2003; general US responses to Islam in Nisbett and Shanahan 2004). This has led a number of observers to ask: if a Western way of life is the target of such terrorism, then do such restrictions indicate that the terrorists have been successful in achieving a principle goal? The implication of this is that Western political leaders have either inadvertently defaulted to limitations upon democracy and its putative association with freedom, or that is what most Western elites had wanted all along and were simply taking advantage of post-2001 opportunities to bring this into being. Similarly oligarchic, the increasing hegemony of economic deregulation coupled with limitations on government spending are frequently claimed to require economic sacrifices on the part of those usually least able to afford them. By way of illustration, in 2006 the world's biggest mining company, BHP Billiton, opposed a pay claim by workers at its Escondida copper mine, the world's largest, in Chile, at a time of world record copper prices and as the company announced a massive profit of US$10.4 billion. While the issue of the growing gap between the rich and poor, even within developed (OECD) countries did not reflect on democracy as such (or at least a limited political understanding of democracy), it did illustrate both a growing gap between material interests. This in turn placed pressure on notions of a social contract and an incapacity of the less powerful to have their interests more adequately represented. The cumulative effect of piecemeal diminution of democracy has tended to look like political "death by a thousand cuts."

Alternatively, democracy might be assumed to be broadly representative, rather than the simple equation of "fifty per cent plus one" but in fact constitute a dictatorship of the majority. A genuine functioning democracy should, of course, be inclusive and broadly representative as well as catering to majority views. But these qualities are not a necessary part of a formal democratic process. Belief in the existence of such qualities might reflect a more passive naïvety rather than a cold appreciation of political reality or an active engagement in shaping political processes and outcomes. In this respect, then, an expectation of the "coming" of democracy, in much the same way as the "coming" of a representation of God, leads towards a political parallel to Saint Pio's comforting but ineffective proposal for his parishioners to "pray, hope and don't worry" (attrib.).

Regime change

Regime change is a vulnerable time for political order, and the outcomes of such change comprise a wide range of variables. As discussed, regime change tends to reflect one of two competing political paradigms; democratic liberalism and non-elected authoritarianism although, as mentioned, it is possible to have regime change (or at least a *coup d'état*) within the context of the latter. The following discussion considers the varieties of potential change:

From democratic/liberal to authoritarian

This might take advantage of what Spector referred to as "Machiavellian moments," in which are manifested threats to civic virtue and notions of liberty (Spector in Weinstock and Nadeau 2004). In this, self-serving groups manipulate or take advantage of unstable circumstances to take power while at the same time dispossessing the majority.

From authoritarian to liberal/democratic

Democratic elections have not always guaranteed the continuation of democratic processes. As discussed in Chapter 8, once a party has taken power through electoral means, it may move to functionally or literally eliminate political competition (Diamond *et al.* 1989b: 2). In particular, where political support is deeply divided between strongly opposed political camps, or where political leadership is insufficiently strong, political competition may tear at the political fabric of the state through a process of political deadlocks in decision making, ethnic polarization, political competition spilling over into partisan violence, state repression of dissent, and electoral fraud (Diamond *et al.* 1989b: 2). Not all change towards authoritarian regimes has been exclusively through violence though, with:

> . . . the transition from political pluralism to authoritarianism . . . also marked and consolidated in Senegal and Uganda by constitutional change from parliamentary to presidential systems, with extreme concentration of power in the presidency and a marked diminution of legislative authority. . . . Underlying each of these . . . executive coups was a sense of political insecurity.
>
> (Diamond *et al.* 1989b: 3)

Such "insecurity" is exacerbated by coups and other violent political responses, making the regime harder if more brittle and thus prone to turning on itself. Regime failure has consequently been common, and state failure has followed close behind.

Underlying many of the problems of Sub-Saharan African states has been deep ethnic divisions within post-colonial state structures, which has resulted in a shallow sense of national identity and a consequent lack of political unity. This has been compounded by "thinly established political institutions with little depth of experience, lack of indigenous managerial and technical talent, extreme economic dependence, and revolutionary popular expectations generated by the independence struggle" (Diamond *et al.* 1989b: 5). This latter issue of inflated expectations has frequently been set against a difficult economic and administrative post-independence reality, in which the new state lacked the capacity, resources and in some cases sufficient legitimacy to address such expectations, resulting in political tensions and government tendencies towards suppressing potentially destabilizing dissent. The problem in Sub-Saharan Africa was that, in almost all cases, political suppression became an end in itself, reducing government accountability, creating an unfavorable administrative and investment climate (which further distanced economic reality from political expectations), and reducing pressure on governments to live up to popular expectations. As the Kenyan scholar Ali Marui noted, Sub-Saharan African states were sometimes excessively authoritarian to disguise the fact that they were inadequately authoritative.

As discussed in Chapter 7, not all regime changes are towards democracy. Some simply change from one type of authoritarian regime to another, while others change from democratic models to authoritarian ones. In this respect, "end of history" claims tend to be beset by an uncooperative reality. However, regime change away from authoritarian government does not bring with it an imposed order, and is thus vulnerable to a variety of pressures and influences, all of which can add to instability in the process of political transition and which may court a failure of that process and hence of the transitional regime.

State fragmentation

The fragmentation of the state is by definition perhaps the most critical factor in state failure; if the state loses its territorial integrity it will have failed in its principle functions of maintaining its sovereignty and applying its writ equally and fully up to the extent of its borders. State fragmentation necessarily challenges the claims to authority of the state, to its legitimacy and to its very statehood and, as such, is a direct affront to its existence. For these reasons, challenges to state cohesion are very rarely tolerated by the state or the regime entrusted with its maintenance. The exception to this observation is when a state voluntarily devolves into constituent units, such as the division between the Czech Republic and Slovakia, or the devolution of the Soviet Union into constituent states, which then reconvened under the less tightly structured Commonwealth of Independent States.

Such fragmentation can occur along a number of lines and over a range of issues. As discussed in Chapters 5, 7 and 8, the most common form of political fragmentation is "vertical" claims to separate national identities, usually conceived of as an ethnic identity forming the basis of a political bond associated with a particular territory. Such claims to national identity within existing states are not always, or even often, successful. But such claims do challenge the unity of the state and have the capacity to damage its fabric.

Perhaps the second most common threat to state cohesion is based around religious differentiation, particularly where that differentiation has a specific geographic focus and is linked to other forms of differentiation, such as economic or political status. By way of illustration, Northern Ireland's pro-republic Catholic minority was relatively economically disadvantaged and largely politically distinct from the pro-union Protestant majority, while Sri Lanka's historically slightly economically advantaged Hindu Tamil minority was distinct from the generally slightly economically disadvantaged Buddhist Sinhalese majority. In this case, however, linguistic differences and historical geographic separation were also key factors in national identity creation. As a profound marker of culture or word view, religion has the capacity to parallel other forms of bonded identity, in particular that of nation, or to functionally be a part of such a bonded political identity.

More conventional horizontal divisions, based on economic, educational and class interests, tend to be less territorially distinct, although class groupings do tend to congregate in particular geographic areas. The urban poor, for example, tend to live and work in the poorer sections of industrial cities and in intensely industrialized areas. Similarly, horizontal interests can be identified on the basis of particular regions due to broad geographic commonalities that may produce political interests and electoral outcomes that are inconsistent with wider state trends and tendencies. The Indian states of Kerala, West Bengal and Tripura are cases in point of horizontal distinction manifested in particular geographic areas. Following an immediate postwar rebellion by its predecessor organization, the dominant party of these constituent states, the Communist Party of India (Marxist), did not indicate any desire to separate from the larger state.

State fragmentation can also occur in circumstances where there is a collapse in the rule of law or its consistent application over the territory of the state. Such break down of this central aspect of state capacity was illustrated in Cambodia between 1979 and 1993 (and sporadically thereafter), in Afghanistan ahead of the consolidation of the Taliban, in East Timor between April and May 2006, and in Iraq following the 2003 US-led invasion. The collapse of the rule of law has also led to the subsequent collapse of central authority, among numerous Sub-Saharan African states, where "In a relatively short period of time, virtually all of the formal democratic systems left behind by the departing colonial rulers gave way to authoritarian regimes of one kind or another" (Diamond *et al.* 1989b: 1). The electoral supremacy of ruling parties and often high degree of elite cohesion before independence was followed, in many cases, by repression. Many Sub-Saharan African states established one-party regimes in which political power has often been highly personalized. In other states, there has been one party rule despite the presence of multiple parties, which has in turn reduced opportunities for democratic participation. Electoral instability in such environments has in turn paved the way for military intervention. This in turn has undermined the legitimacy of not just the regime but the state itself and, as such, has contributed to state failure.

The role of the military

The role of the military in state failure and fragmentation is contentious, primarily because of differing understandings of the role of the military, especially in developing states, underpins further assumptions. It has been a common view, for instance, that militaries can and legitimately do play a role in state cohesion, ensuring that threats to the state from both without and within are suppressed. An alternative view, however, is that a military function, especially in relation to internal dissent, is a catalyst for state disintegration and an otherwise contributing factor towards state failure. Militaries potentially have a range of roles and functions in the state, which include the following:

- Guardians from external threat, under civil authority
- Guardians from internal threat, under a mixed civil-military authority (it is rarely purely civil authority in relation to internal matters)
- Guardians from ideological threat, generally under mixed civil-military rule or purely military authority
- Political actors through politico-military institutionalization
- Owners and operators of businesses, usually following self-funded revolutionary activity.

The role of the Indonesian military – *Tentara Nasional Indonesia* (TNI) – in Indonesia's transition to democracy is a case in point. Indonesia is perhaps the most physically fragmented state in the world (mountainous countries such as Afghanistan are physically fragmented in different ways), being spread across some 13,000 inhabited (18,000 claimed) islands, containing more than 300 languages and associated cultural groups, and having no pre-colonial political unity. Given the highly constructed nature of the post-colonial state, Indonesia has had a tendency towards political fragmentation. Following its self-defined role in helping to achieve independence from the colonial Dutch, the TNI has taken upon itself the role of guardian of the state, and has consistently been the principle institution to address tendencies to state fragmentation.

One consequence of the TNI's role was that the capacity for local grievances to be addressed by political means was largely removed from the state agenda, which meant that the underlying issues were mostly not dealt with. In a similar manner, TNI intervention in each aggrieved regions has exacerbated pre-existing problems, and provided new sources of discontent with the Indonesian state.

Through its self-proclaimed role as guardian of the state, the military developed a political capacity independently of the civil state, meaning that it could – and did – intervene in civil political affairs. This had the effect of undermining Indonesia's "national project" of building a civic unity from disparate peoples, as well as undermining its civic institutional capacity (for example, the judiciary, while at the same time establishing a parallel institutional state structure). Similarly, following its self-funding during the war of independence, the TNI continued its private business activities, both legal and illegal, in the post-colonial era. This had the effect of removing the TNI from direct political authority through its capacity to fund non-accountable activities and helped to institutionalize corrupt and criminal practises, including extortion and smuggling among many others.

The conventional view of Indonesian politics and the TNI in the period following May 1998 was that the state was undergoing a process of democratic transition and that the military was itself undergoing a process of reform (for example, see Singh 2001). Elaborations of this view held that, after 40 years of authoritarian military-backed government, Indonesia was following the Latin American example of shedding military intervention in civil affairs through military "professionalization" (for example, see Stepan 1976). Surrounded by the rhetoric of *reformasi* and the TNI's *paradim baru* (new paradigm) it was indeed possible to believe that substantive change was afoot. However, fundamental aspects of Indonesia's political and economic history, ethnic and religious composition and physical geography all contributed to a different context to that of Latin America, and even other countries in the region such as Thailand (see Crone 1986). The TNI itself was compromised by its reliance on private and often illegal business, hence contributing to a different outcome to more successful moves away from military domination in parts of Latin America. Even in Latin America, the success of bringing the military under civilian control was sometimes limited (Farcau 1996: Chapter 5).[2] As Philip succinctly put it: "The military does not behave in any simple or one-dimensional way which can be deduced *a priori*. . . . contemporary observers have been strikingly wrong in their expectations of military behavior" (Philip 1985: 356).

Parallels to the TNI can be seen in a number of developing countries, in which the military is either the guarantor of state cohesion (for example, Burma) or intervenes in internal political disputes (such as large parts of Latin America and Africa). From time to time militaries in developing states also depose civilian governments on the bases of various claims of governmental ideological orientation, inefficiency, corruption or incapacity (for example in Thailand in 2006). In almost all cases, however, military intervention does not lead to any condition that could be included in notions of political development (Portugal's Carnation Revolution of 1974 perhaps being the single exception). Usually, it leads to a diminution of other forms of development through criminal activity and the exacerbation of political instability. In the case of Indonesia, when the negative qualities of a functionally independent military were coupled with a severe economic crisis (to which the TNI was a contributing factor), one province, East Timor, managed to secede and others threatened or attempted to do so. In other provinces, military-linked sectarian religious and ethnic conflict seriously damaged the fabric of the state (see Kingsbury 2005: Chapter 8).

Beyond the role played by militaries in weakening state structures, which in turn may lead to state failure, militaries may also play a role in arresting or reversing state failure by either imposing themselves as the government or by supporting bureaucratic–authoritarian regimes. The conventional claim of such military intervention is that the causes of state failure are essentially "political"; that is, they derive political power from particular ideological orientations, political discord or competitive government inefficiencies. The military response in such cases is to impose a government that is "above" or "free from" politics (O'Donnell and Schmitter 1986: 48), even though this is invariably shorthand for the imposition of a form of political rule that is usually posited as opposite to the range of qualities that might ordinarily be associated with political development.

In states where governments are less accountable, there is a tendency for state elites to engage in practises that do not necessarily reflect the interests of their state citizens. In developing countries, for example, economic neo-liberalism has often been manifested as "Structural Adjustment Programs" (SAPs), which have been imposed as a condition of multilateral economic assistance (primarily from the IMF and the World Bank) and which imply two related policies. The first is to promote export oriented economic development through "comparative advantage," which means that a country produces better or cheaper exports than its competitors. A developing country may do this by focusing investment in a particular field or sector through preferential or low tax investment schemes. The second policy of SAPs is to reduce external (and especially government) debt, which means reducing government spending, reducing taxes, and increasing a "user pay" system of public service. The consequences of SAPs have been mixed. In those countries where there is an established comparative advantage, there has generally been greater efficiency in export production and a reduction in import substitution-related production. The success of export oriented economics has been greatest in East Asia, where other factors (historical, organizational and geographic) have influenced the relative local success. Outcomes have been much more mixed in Latin America and Central Asia, while most of Sub-Saharan Africa has seen an absolute decline in income since the introduction of SAPs, and a reduction in or failure of a number of state functions, especially in terms of health and education.

In many countries where SAPs have been applied there has also been the side effect of increased unemployment and the greater impoverishment of lower income earners. In countries that base their comparative advantage on low incomes and simple technology, the consequence has been a trend towards further downwards pressure on wages. "Liberalized currencies" often effectively increase foreign denominated debt, especially in Sub-Saharan Africa, leading to greater capital outflows, and hence poverty (Moore 2003: Chapter 3). According to the UNDP, aid donor countries spend US$1 billion a day assisting their own agriculture industries, and a further US$1 billion on domestic subsidies that undermine the competitiveness of farmers in developing countries, making a mockery of "free trade" (UNDP 2005: Chapter 4). In this, the general tendency has been for both an increase in the income gap between the rich and poor within countries *and* between richer and poorer countries. Even in the US, the richest 1 per cent of people own 33 per cent of the nation's wealth, the richest 10 per cent own 71 per cent of the nation's wealth, while the bottom 60 per cent own just 4.3 per cent of the national wealth (Wolff 2004). The distribution of wealth within a state as an indicator of the health of a social contract has become one of the key criteria for a state's political legitimacy and that of its government (UNDP 2005: Chapter 2). Without legitimacy, a state is fundamentally compromised and prone to dissent leading to collapse.

The 2005 *Human Development Report* shows that 18 countries (around 9.5 per cent of the global total), with a total of 460 million people (around

14 per cent of the global total), actually became poorer between 1990 and 2005. By 2015, it was predicted that more than 800 million people would still be living in extreme poverty, while 1.7 billion would be living on less than US$2 a day. Sub-Saharan Africa has accounted for half or more of the total failure to meet "Millennium Development Goals" criteria and other basic development benchmarks, and occupies all but 2 of the 31 "low human development" places on the 2005 Human Development Index (UNDP 2005: HDI). In 2005, the poorest 40 per cent of the world's population (around 2.5 billion people) lived on US$2 a day or less, or just 5 per cent of the global income, while the richest 10 per cent accounted for 54 per cent of global income (UNDP 2005: Overview, Chapter 2). The populations of those countries which have the highest concentration of absolute poverty are, not coincidentally, also those at greatest risk from regime and state failure.

Reduced government spending in developed countries also leads to a shortfall in investment in developing countries with a poor domestic investment base, insufficient or diminishing infrastructure, low overall economic stimulus, and inadequate basic social services such as education and health. In countries in which the general population lives a marginal existence, a sudden shift in the environment can (and often does) lead to human catastrophe, such as famine. That is to say, state policies can lead to outcomes that manifest as state failure. It was because of such imposed policies, and mistakes, by the World Bank and the IMF during the Asian economic crisis of 1997–8 that the G8 (Group of Eight) countries expanded to become the G20 (Group of 20) in 2006. For states like Indonesia, however, state failure came perilously close.

State failure and political development

As discussed elsewhere, it is possible to conceive of political development as occurring in other than a formal state context. Localized polities may be able to respond more readily and accurately than larger and more unwieldy structures, while globalized institutions may contain within them rules and standards that promote political development more readily than some states. But as the continuing principle site and conduit of political activity, the state remains critical to the implementation or otherwise of political development. The success of the state, then, is central to the opportunities for, and materialization of, successful political development.

Conversely, and more critically, the failure of the state not only inhibits the state's capacity to implement those normative qualities associated with political development, but such failure is almost always attended by the active diminution of political development. The incapacity of a state to extend its power and authority to the extent of its sovereign territory, for example, implies that the equitable and consistent rule and application of law are reduced or no longer available. This has strong implications for the safety and physical security of the citizens of the state, and has considerable capacity to diminish claims to and respect for human rights, in particular civil and political rights. Similarly, state failure usually means that not only the institutions of the state cease to function effectively, or perhaps function at all, but that non-structural institutions such as the extent of capacity for representation, participation and accountability in political affairs, or the reciprocation of a social contract, are less likely to exist.

Indeed, if the state is taken to be the embodiment and guarantor of the nation, as suggested by Gellner (1983: 44, 110), then state failure goes directly to the viability of the nation as a bonded political identity (although keeping in mind that the failure of a bonded political identity might be a principle reason for state failure in the first place). That is, if the state fails, the structures around which citizens construct their lives – indeed, the very idea of citizenship, including the right to live in a particular place – lose the relative political, social and material certainties that functioning states are otherwise able to offer. State failure is thus the direct antithesis of political development. Avoiding or arresting state failure is, then, a key criterion for political development.

10 Violence and resolution

Politically motivated or inspired violence or the threat of such is the single most significant issue that faces notions of political development. It is the most problematic issue in politics, and over which opinions divide most sharply, not least because it has the most potentially serious consequences. If development is about creating a sense of security in which freedom becomes available, then illegitimate violence is the greatest challenge to that freedom. Conversely, legitimate violence can be freedom's savior. But because violence has such absolute consequences, questions of legitimacy around it use are profoundly contested.

Illegitimate violence can not only preclude political development, but it can define the way in which development might take place by imposing through force a particular ideological outcome. More positively, through acting as a guardian, legitimate political violence can ensure and enhance political development through securing the state and the efficacy of its institutions. In its application, the point between potential and actual violence may only be marginal. Potential violence is experienced as actual violence not yet manifested, but always imminent and hence retaining its coercive quality.

There are four categories of political violence within the context of political development. The first is "legitimate state violence," in which the state is manifested in its political regime. Such regimes retain the reserve power of the state as the legitimate manifestation of the collective will of their citizens to employ violence in support of state goals. "Legitimate state violence" is used to maintain the state's laws, and the state claims a monopoly upon the use of such violence, excluding all others from using violence. By contrast, the second category might be called "legitimate non-state violence," in which violence or the capacity for coercion is employed by non-state actors in pursuit of legitimate goals, in particular where the state is regarded as acting illegitimately, for example where the state employs extra-judicial violence or otherwise behaves unlawfully. This is clearly a much more problematic category than "legitimate state violence," not least because it does not enjoy the legitimizing quality that the state brings to its coercive capacity. As the dominant claimant to legitimacy and to a monopoly on the use of violence, the state by definition characterizes violent non-state actors as illegitimate, regardless of the validity of their claims. The third category is "illegitimate non-state violence," which can range from simple criminal activity to political violence in pursuit of goals that do not accord with prevailing or even common minority views. Non-state actors may also employ particular methods that are held to be delegitimizing, such as "terrorism" (although noting that the definition of this term is open to wide interpretation). Violent non-state actors might claim their actions as legitimate, but as a consequence of the invariably formal non-representative structure of non-state actors, their claim is less able to be substantiated on that basis. They are therefore beholden to establish their legitimacy through weight of other evidence. Finally, there is "illegitimate state violence." Though all states claim legitimacy on the basis of their statehood, they may still exercise violence illegitimately. Illegitimate state violence may be exercised outside a state's own codified legal structures, by ignoring conventional global standards on arbitrary arrest, detention and torture, or by assuming power through illegal or non-representative means. It may also be used to perpetuate a regime that is otherwise lacking in legitimacy, which in turn, abrogates the generally agreed terms of the social contract under which the nation coheres as an agreed political unit.

Legitimate state violence

Traditionally, violence, its threat or its unstated presence has been the primary method by which state interests have been asserted and by which order has been maintained. In such cases, the state as the sovereign authority over a territorially demarcated area, claims a legitimate and exclusive right to the use of violence to compel compliance with its laws, protect its sovereignty and maintain order (see Weber 1948).[1] Assuming popular acceptance of state laws – that is, the establishment of legitimacy – state violence should only exist as a reserve power, in which the police or other state agents only take action against explicit challenges to, or contravention of the law. Implicit in this is that law is an accurate reflection of the values of the society in question. This constitutes legitimate state violence, and as a guarantor of peace and order can be said to be a significant contributor to political development.

Illegitimate state violence

States can also and sometimes do employ violence to compel compliance, and their actions might not always conform to the full range of conceptions of legitimacy. Indeed, the methods employed by the state can resemble non-state methods, particularly in pursuit of narrowly conceived political goals, and may include assassinations, bombings, and so on. Assuming that the state normatively claims to protect all its citizens under an equitably applied law (a basic criterion of state legitimacy), the extra-legal use of violence by the state in the form of torture, murder, rape and other methods that violate basic human rights, not to mention more standard forms of state violence such as conventional warfare (for example, bombing from a distance), offer privileged opportunities for illegitimate state violence (see, for example, Anderson 2001).

More problematically, governments may not be widely perceived as legitimate and lack strong popular support. Alternatively, they may be legitimately elected or otherwise initially accepted as legitimate, but come to act illegitimately or introduce and enact laws that do not represent popular wishes, which may in turn reflect a non-representative and non-participatory political process (for example, presidential decree), or which may run contrary to broadly accepted social and moral codes. Indeed, governments may use state force to control their citizens in a manner that is predatory (see Evans 1995, regarding Sub-Saharan Africa) in order to serve the interests of an oligarchic elite (see Hutchcroft 1991, regarding the Philippines). Alternatively, political dictates may be carried out by state institutions regardless of, or despite the rule of law, or where the law is so poorly codified or enforced that it is inconsistent and incoherent and therefore open to extensive interpretation or disregard (such as in Burma or Indonesia under Suharto). Such violation or re-interpretation of laws may run contrary to the popular will, but can be maintained and indeed further developed, by employing mechanisms that support more popular or conventional law, being the reserve use of violence. In cases where social dissent is deep, governments may employ a range of methods to achieve compliance, including not only conventional police but also political police, intelligence operatives and informers, and military and paramilitary organizations, in widely focused political oppression. This in turn further weakens the legitimacy of the government and possibly the state in the eyes of its citizens. While such actions are invariably justified by the wielders of power on the basis of order, national cohesion or other claims, they are almost invariably a consequence of a non-representative and non-accountable form of government and, as such, cannot be tested. This is to say, in the competition between structure and agency, or economics and politics, while a middle ground can be accommodated via social contract, without active political participation, communication and organization, political development (and its popular manifestation as democratization) cannot progress. The subsequent tensions that arise from this blockage may manifest as conflict, or the illegitimate (that is, partisan) application of state violence.

Within the above is the role of militaries, civil-military relations and military transitions (both to and from democracy). States that have achieved independence by military means, or in which a government has come to power through such means, are more likely to retain a prominent role for the military in political affairs. The military, in such cases, will often see or portray itself as the "guardian of the state," and will reserve its right to intervene militarily in civil affairs if and where it believes that state interests are being threatened; hence, the propensity to *coups d'état* in a number of developing countries.

There are a number of problems with military intervention in political affairs. The first is that the military is rarely the best judge of when or if such intervention is necessary. This is particularly so given the institutional cultures of militaries, which are necessarily strongly hierarchical and driven by an absolute authority rather than a participatory and representative decision-making framework (Huntington 1957). Although the military is an institution of state, its engagement in anti-regime activity may exist partially outside state structures or state constitutional paradigms. Thus, the military may pose more of a threat to the state than the "threats" to the state that they sometimes seek to contain, as demonstrated by the political and often economic failure of military coups.

Militaries in many developing countries further suffer from conflicts of interest, in which political power assists them in maintaining institutional or extra-state power. Conflicting interests could also revolve around economic interests, such as military businesses and criminal enterprises (for example, throughout Latin America, South-East and Central Asia and Sub-Saharan Africa). The extent to which militaries are subordinate to, or outside civilian authority, their ability to protect and enhance their own interests is a direct indicator of the political health of a state, and a primary marker of political development.

Legitimate non-state violence

The use or threat of violence is commonplace by states, and indeed, the legitimate and sole use of violence is widely seen to be one criterion of successful statehood. The critical issues, and over which the debate becomes more divided, revolve around the legitimacy of state and non-state actors. States claim a monopoly on the legitimate use of violence as a primary capacity; *ipso facto* states deny the use of violence to non-state actors, and are obliged to regard such use of violence as *prima facie* illegitimate. This de-legitimizing of non-state violence is sometimes assisted by the methods used by non-state actors, usually as a consequence of their limited capacities. As a leader of the armed separatist Algerian National Liberation Front (FLN) said: "Give us your bombers [planes] and you can have our [bomb] baskets." Personally delivered bombs and other methods of non-state violence may be effective but are not conventional state methods, which further distinguishes non-state from state actors in a negative sense.

Just as states claim legitimacy on the basis of their statehood, non-state actors can also have claims that they regard as legitimate. In asserting these claims in response to state or state-associated violence, non-state actors can claim to legitimately employ reciprocal violence (see, for example, Fanon 1970). For example, the formation of the Liberation Tigers of Tamil Eelam (LTTE) in Sri Lanka and like organizations elsewhere reflects the claim to legitimacy of reciprocal violence following discrimination by the Sri Lankan government and violence by groups that were seen to be aligned with and supported by government institutions (especially the police and army). Both the government of Sri Lanka and organizations associated with it have specifically targeted and used indiscriminate terror against the LTTE, along with more conventional military approaches to violence. The identification of the LTTE as a "terrorist organization," therefore, is inaccurate in that it applies only to the LTTE (although the LTTE also used terror as a tactic), and implies that the LTTE has no function other than as a terrorist organization (within the territory it controls, it fulfills most state functions, including the application of rule of law).

The realm of non-state violence is perhaps the most controversial area within the field of political development in that it constitutes a direct challenge to the legitimacy of the state, to conventional forms of order and, not least, to those institutions and actors that hold state power (the government, military, police, and so on). As noted, non-state violence will always be characterized as illegitimate by states and their representatives and supporters, not because of the legitimacy or otherwise of state violence, but because it is *prima facie* an attack against the legitimacy of the state. It may be claimed, with good reason, that much non-state violence is indeed illegitimate, and it is usually dangerous to defend cases where non-state violence takes place, regardless of the arguments for or against it. This was especially so at the time of writing, when terrorism had gripped the imagination of the Western world and much of the non-Western world. As a consequence, actual or so defined "terrorists" successfully achieved their first aim of bringing attention to their cause. The governments of many countries have not only defined themselves in opposition to such terrorism, but have redefined themselves in relation to their own citizens.

Even a cursory assessment of non-state violence, in particular in relation to domestic insurgencies, will quickly show that what are understood by less subjective audiences as rebellions, revolutions, claims to separate state identity, and so on, are almost always characterized by the government under attack as "terrorism." The use of the term "terrorist" is clearly an emotive one, raising fear of attack outside conventional conflict environments, and hence, lacking that element of predictability that conventional conflict is felt to offer.[2] The term "terrorist" also constitutes an attempt to delegitimize the attacker and, more importantly, to delegitimize their motives. The term "terrorist" also constructs the attacker as a violent sociopath who lacks a coherent agenda, and who is very much one of "them" as opposed to the unifying qualities of "us." Yet the truth – and this is one of the more contested areas in which the term "truth" can be used – is that non-state actors engage in violence for a range of reasons, many of which may seem perfectly rational within a particular political or economic context in which intolerable situations create little space for non-violent methods.

Assuming that "common to all men is the strong desire for fair treatment and justice" (Angiolillio 1979: 5), or the fulfillment of basic elements of a social contract, there is a view that if the law is unjust then there is a moral

obligation to not cooperate or to oppose it, usually through civil disobedience (Locke 1960: 2nd Treatise; Thoreau 1993; Kurland and Lerner
1987: Chapter 3). This perceived moral obligation necessarily establishes
elements of society in direct opposition to the state and its guardians who are
authorized to employ violence. The dispute over legitimate non-state violence
versus illegitimate state violence tends to quickly devolve into a contest of
violence between the opposing parties, with the result either being the suppression of the non-state "uprising," or a change of government (or indeed
change of the state). However, civil disobedience or political violence aimed
against unjust laws or state actions may reflect or evolve into a paradigm that
is itself of questionable moral validity, especially in cases where social
responses are commonly seen as out of balance with the "evil" they seek to
overturn (for example, "the Terror" of the French revolution, or acts of indiscriminate terrorism). Although the claim that political violence is necessary
to adequately institute desired change (for example, Sorel 1970: Chapter 6)
does have an element of truth in it given capacities for resistance and reaction,
it is dangerous to adopt standardized violence as a first response to a variety of
situations (for example, Cambodia's Khmer Rouge 1975–9). Beyond this, the
primary intention of non-state violence might be not to overturn illegitimate
state behavior, but rather, to overturn legitimate state action, such as through
organized crime (illegitimate non-state violence).

Illegitimate non-state violence

Illegitimate non-state violence is that which is formally and morally criminal,
and which is engaged in for reasons that are not connected with preservation
of self or of one's community, resistance against oppression or other more
altruistic motives. There is also a view that the methods employed in non-
state violence can delegitimize it, especially if the targets of such attacks are
indiscriminate and are designed to have a general effect, such as generalized
terror, rather than to achieve a specific goal.

Illegitimate non-state violence can, at the most basic level still be
described as political. It may be engaged in by individuals or groups of
criminals who have declined legitimate, available choices for livelihood and
have instead chosen to prey on their fellow citizens, or who have chosen to
engage in violence for other reasons, such as mental instability. Criminal
gangs, especially those that enjoy a relatively high degree of organization,
engage in violence, or use the threat of violence (coercion), may act well
outside state law but still conform to a different, often poorly articulated (and
more than occasionally broken) code of social behavior (for example, a "code of
silence" or "honor among thieves"). They can and sometimes do function as
elements of a state within a state, particularly where state capacity is weak.
The history of the Italian mafia, by its various names, is a case in point in
which a weak but oppressive feudal state was resisted by local or regional
networks of criminals, who institutionalized their social, economic and even

political role. Various "mafias" that operate in other countries may have different origins. The Russian "mafia," for instance, arose in response to the declining efficacy of the state to provide and protect, but their social role and their relationship to the state is similar to the Italian model. Criminal organizations also function in liberal democracies and constitute a significant threat to state capacity and rule of law. Clearly, any state that either tolerates or has too little capacity to address this type of problem has a low level of political development in regard to its protective function.

Quasi-political gangs

The point at which such organized crime networks more formally insinuate themselves into the political process is the point where one or more aspects of state capacity is also relatively weak. It also indicates a more formal recognition of the value of political power. The means by which criminal gangs or networks insinuate themselves into political processes can include bribing politicians, supporting particular candidates for political office, or entering a criminal organization or its leadership into politics. Further, incipient or marginal political organizations can and do recruit criminals into their ranks, and employ extra-legal violence as a part of their political campaign. Of course, political power was historically often achieved through use of force and the imposition of warlord or mafia-like rule. Europe's history is littered with such examples; that region's fading aristocracy are largely the descendents of robber-barons and other unsavory thugs whose claim to political power was based on their capacity to impose subjugation. Although this type of political persuasion is no longer globally dominant, it still exists among warlords in places such as Afghanistan, Iraq, Liberia, Ivory Coast and Somalia. And, despite representing perhaps the lowest form of political underdevelopment, its European descendents are the inheritors of an imposed myth about divine right, aristocracy, "blue-blood," and so on.[3]

To illustrate, the rise of the Nazi and Fascist parties was accompanied by politically organized extra-legal violence that employed criminal elements. Somewhat differently, many guerrilla (or terrorist) organizations may explicitly employ criminal violence in their political repertoire to sustain their political or military campaigns. The Indonesian revolution was largely predicated upon the now political criminal activities of gangs of revolutionary *preman* (gangsters) (see Cribb 1991), the activities of which continue to dog their successor organization, Indonesia's TNI. Similarly, separatist organizations within Indonesia such as the Free Aceh Movement (*Gerakan Acheh Merdeka* – GAM) were variously accused of (and occasionally admitted to) extortion backed with exemplary violence. Such "extortion" could be characterized and was referred to by GAM and their supporters as *pajak nanggroe* (state tax), which was the principle means by which many GAM fighters survived. But on occasion such extortion was little more than armed robbery, especially if the person who was robbed was unsympathetic to GAM's cause.

By way of comparison, the revolutionary separatist LTTE, which has also been characterized by some[4] as a terrorist organization, imposes a more regularized form of taxation, and also raises funds through the expatriate Tamil community.

Violent political organizations, if successful, usually regularize their political or state support role, legitimizing their previous acts of violence on the grounds of necessity, or rationalizing continuing violence on the grounds of their eventual success. For example, the Jewish paramilitary organization Haganah was the main precursor to the Israeli Defence Force. As a further illustration, the LTTE can be seen as an organization that has regularized its political role as the administrative authority of "Vanni," the district of northern Sri Lanka up to the Jaffna Peninsula, while the Palestinian organization, Hamas (*Harakat al-Muqawama al-Islamiyya*, or Islamic Resistance Movement) has similarly evolved from a military organization (albeit one with active social policies), often claimed as "terrorist," to that of a democratically elected governing authority. Hamas continued to be labeled as a terrorist organization even after having achieved electoral office, while the party that it ousted, Fatah, was portrayed as the more moderate and hence legitimate political organization. Somewhat ironically, Fatah had also been labeled as a terrorist organization by many up until Hamas was elected to office. Similarly, Nelson Mandela was the head of what was labeled by UK Prime Minister Margaret Thatcher as a terrorist organization, yet after his release from prison he was globally hailed as a statesman. If one person's terrorist is another person's freedom fighter, then yesterday's "criminal" might easily become tomorrow's politician.

Terrorism

The issue of, and use of the term, "terrorism" has vexed many other more rational approaches to understanding conflict. There is no absolute definition of the term, although it is generally agreed that it includes, as a minimum, the use of violence or the threat of violence to compel others to undertake activities that they would otherwise be disinclined towards. Such "terrorism" may be employed to change an existing order, to produce a reaction that alienates a population, or section of a population, which in turn changes an existing order, or for its demonstrator or shock value effect.

In identifying terrorism, a focus is often placed on particular methods of violence, in particular the indiscriminate targeting of civilians. There is no doubt that the indiscriminate targeting of civilians creates a sense of terror among those civilians. However, civilians can also be specifically targeted, in particular those who are, or seen to be politically active or militant, or who have a high profile. This specific targeting of civilians does not lessen the sense of terror, but does attempt to compel compliance from a particular group, either for a particular purpose or to enhance the demonstrator effect. As such, "terrorism" can be undertaken by both state and non-state actors.

In the public discussion about terrorism and its ostensible rise ("terrorism" in the modern sense having been a common feature of various political landscapes since 1881),[5] little attention is paid to what is meant by the term. Indeed, contemporary use of the term "terrorism" implies a pejorative, antithetical position rather than a standardized descriptive quality (which applies to the methods rather than to the causes). That is, it is often less the methods employed by "terrorists" that define them, but rather whether or not they are on "our side" (for example, Nicaragua's "Contras"). This intense subjectivity has, perforce, undermined much clarity of analysis.

The driver for terrorism, and indeed for all political claims, is a relative lack of opportunity to realize perceived legitimate interest, which can be understood as (real or perceived) economic or political scarcity, or a structural inability to otherwise change one's perceived circumstances of injustice. As described by one German "terrorist," terrorism is "The power of the powerless" (Baumann 1977: 23). Scarcity is both a contributor to and manifestation of reduced security which, if not adequately addressed, can and often does call forth a reaction. While there are examples of reactions based on more or less purely ideological grounds, even if in such cases they tend to claim to represent the interests of people affected by scarcity (although in some instances the interests being represented are much more personal and reflect a complex of economic considerations, status and power). Recruitment to such causes, however, relies on experience of a real, lived scarcity, which can be channeled into an ideological (explanatory and prescriptive) framework. Experience or awareness of scarcity and acceptance of an ideological explanation logically implies a call for political redress, either by or on behalf of those experiencing such scarcity. Violence has been and remains a widely accepted if politically unsophisticated method of achieving compliance to a particular ideological prescription, and within the context of imbalances of capacity for violence, terrorism can act as a persuasive shortcut.

The specific causes of terrorism, as it is broadly understood, are not consistent, and derive from a range of grievances. Principles causes of terrorism are usually centered around claims of oppression, including domination by a domestic autocratic authority (or hegemonic power, for example, capitalism), colonialism/imperialism, (real or perceived) religious persecution, or vertical (primordial) conflict. In many cases, these issues overlap, such as where religion is mixed with opposition to domestic or external oppression or primordial conflict, or where there is perceived to be an association between a domestic autocratic authority and an external power.

Despite broad acceptance, as noted, of the usual idea of "terrorism" being intended to obtain compliance, there remains no finite definition of "terrorism"; nor are its actors limited by position. The term "terror" within a political context usually means to attempt to persuade others of one's own political position by the use of exemplary violence, or the threat of violence, instilling in the audience a state of heightened or absolute fear, or terror. But terrorism can also be used to persuade others not to accept a particular political perspective but simply to engage in action in accordance with the "terrorist's" political desires (for example, the release of political prisoners or the establishment of a material "good"). It may also aim to encourage a public response that in turn supports the goals of the terrorists (such as increased generalized repression that may lead to broad-based anti-repressive sentiment). The term "terrorist" is further usually applied to individual or collective violent non-state actors, though state or state-sponsored actors can and do also conform to either the methods or purposes of non-state terrorists.

While some so-called terrorist organizations such as Hamas and the LTTE have a clear political agenda in relation to a specific territory, others such as Al Qaeda have a more universal, if specifically applied, agenda which ambitiously seeks to change the political, economic and religious world order. In the case of Hamas and the LTTE, the goal is to achieve the liberation of a specific territory for a specific people; in the case of Al Qaeda and its affiliated organizations, the goal might focus on specific conflicts such as in Afghanistan or Iraq, but its ultimate purpose is to engender a response that divides the world into two opposing camps, in which one will be dominated by a specific religious-political agenda. Where the goal of Hamas and the LTTE is to become the government of an independent state, and their political organizations reflect a more or less conventional party structure, Al Qaeda and linked organizations do not have any formal structure, being formed through networks of personal and familial allegiances and the "dog whistle" effect in which the appeal of the movement is communicated by common calls that are only heard in a specific way by those attuned to such calls. This type of structure, or non-structure, is referred to as "leaderless resistance" (see Fernandes and Kingsbury 2005: 17–18). First expounded by the former US Army Colonel Ulius Louis Amoss, the idea of leaderless resistance was later developed by white supremacist Louis Beam (1992) and employed by organizations such as the Ku Klux Klan and Aryan Nations (Norwitz in Bolt *et al.* 2005: 431, nb24; Snow 1999: 132). The main principle of leaderless resistance is that it does not rely on a formal hierarchy and is largely or entirely composed of quasi-independent cells. This type of organization makes it extremely difficult to infiltrate or destroy, given limited links between cells and the lack of a coherent chain of command. However, such organizations also generally have a relatively incoherent ideology or plan beyond ideologically motivated attacks and their own survival.

The truism that one person's terrorist is another person's freedom fighter points out, if nothing else, that the issue of terrorism remains, as noted, intensely subjective. Competing political claims will always produce conflict, but it is the point at which such conflict becomes violent that "the rules of the game" have been abandoned. Assuming a normative state legitimacy, terrorism is nothing if not illegitimate criminal activity. While a highly organized terrorist organization might require a higher level state response, it is its motives that present the greatest continuing state challenge. However, where the state has lost, or never had, legitimacy, the role of political violence is more complex and nuanced. Rebellions are failed revolutions, and successful revolutions are self-legitimizing. There is little doubt that the British government considered American rebels as little more than terrorists, at least until they could organize on a conventional scale, and there is no doubt that the US Founding Fathers considered violence to be a perfectly legitimate expression of their political claims. Perhaps very little political violence can be justified, or regarded as legitimate, either by state or non-state actors. But equally, potential or actual violence in support of laws by a legitimate state is almost universally regarded as acceptable. The challenge is to understand if and when non-state violence represents legitimate political claims.

The resolution of conflict

It is axiomatic that killing, destruction, repression and fear – the key ingredients of war – are the antithesis of political development. The implementation of development programs of any type is difficult, and often impossible, in war zones, while the political conditions necessary for the prosecution of war entails the greatest limitation on personal and social freedoms. Yet warfare is a common affliction between states, and, more commonly, within developing countries. For the peaceful resolution of conflict, then, the first step that must be taken in the pursuit of development, especially political development.

The most desirable solution to conflict is to remove the conditions that make it more likely which, as noted, refer to scarcity. In a simple economic sense, while there is not an absolute structural link between poverty and conflict, there is a high ratio of connectedness, and it would appear that poverty not only creates desperation that can lead to conflict but that the general social weakness that accompanies much poverty also tends to encourage conflict. For example, the global order is more likely to be maintained and potential for war reduced through a decrease rather than increase in material disparities, as indicated by the evidence of global conflict relative to periods of global inequality. By way of illustration, a survey of security and conflict showed that there was a rapid decline in the probability of war within five years (from the point of measurement) from around 15 per cent in cases where per capita GDP was US$250 or less, to 6 per cent where per capita GDP was US$750. Conflict potential within five years was further reduced to 4 per cent where income was US$1,250 and to 2 per cent or under where GDP was US$2,500 or above. From the point of around 2 per cent it appeared that the probability of warfare within five years, was influenced by other factors beyond poverty. According to the authors: "Poverty is associated with weak state capacity. The greater the poverty and the lower the state capacity, the higher the risk of war" (Mack 2005: figure 5.4; Humphrey and Vershy 2003). In both cases, Huntington's broad thesis that state capacity, or institutions, are necessary to appropriately channel political participation towards constructive ends appears valid.

The ending of conflict and the achievement of peace are commonly achieved by one of two primary methods. In the first instance one side is victorious and the other defeated, in which case the conditions of surrender determine the opportunities remaining to the vanquished party. The second method is through negotiated resolution.

Assuming that the qualities of victory and defeat are more or less absolute, the conditions of surrender and its acceptance are generally limited, or are unconditional. The victor may, of their own accord, decide to punish the losing party for real or perceived transgressions or reparations. Historically, the former has been done through a policy of destruction, perhaps the outstanding historical example of which was the policy of Genghis Khan towards communities that did not agree to submission. Similarly brutal policies or purges have also been practiced against opponents by absolutist or totalitarian regimes, including by Germany's National Socialist Party, Stalin's Soviet Union, Mao's China and Pol Pot's Cambodia.

Absolute domination may lead to complete submission, but where a society is left largely intact it may also fuel deep resentment. Germany in the period following the First World War was rife with such resentment which, along with economic instability, led to the development of policies of returning lost territories and ending war reparations as well as rearmament. The extension of such claims was territorial expansion, which ultimately led to an even more devastating conflict, being the Second World War.

Given the risk of the imposition of absolute authority inviting social reaction, victors might in some instances choose to implement development programs in order to stabilize the political environment of the vanquished society as a means of reducing the grounds for a resumption of hostilities and to make political stability more sustainable. The economic and later political redevelopment of West Germany following the end of the Second World War had the focus of building the western half of the country as a bulwark against the advance of Soviet-style communism in the east, and of political controlling East Germany through economic redevelopment. The development of East Germany was by contrast intended to strengthen the claims of Soviet-style communism while at the same time ensuring that the Soviet Union would not again be prone to the type of attack that had devastated much of the country and left some 20 million people dead between 1941 and 1945.

In the second instance, conflict may be ended not by victory or defeat, but by negotiated settlement. In this, a functional victory or defeat might lie behind a negotiated outcome because the victor does not regard as desirable or even possible the absolute destruction or domination of their opponent. In other instances, both parties may recognize that the conflict has reached a practical stalemate in that either side might have achieved some advantage but is unlikely to substantially or permanently alter the balance of power over a given territory, especially when the cost of a war by attrition is more than either side can, or is willing to bear. To achieve a negotiated settlement and for such a settlement to be sustainable, a range of criteria must be put in place, the composition of which will vary according to the specific circumstances. However, as a rule of thumb, there are at least three criteria for achieving such an outcome.

The first criterion is that both parties must want to achieve a negotiated settlement. That is, the cost of continuing a conflict must be recognized by both parties as too great to want to continue. In this, both parties must also recognize the futility of continuing a military stalemate, or that there has been a sufficient change in the outlook of one or both parties about the undesirability of conflict and the possibility of an alterative method of achieving a political settlement. This implies that the dividends of peace also have to be sufficiently high. The second criterion is that both parties must be sufficiently representative of the constituencies that are at conflict. Each of these constituencies and their representative parties must therefore be sufficiently united in order to ensure that agreement is possible, that there is not internal dissent over fundamental aspects of the negotiations, and that once achieved, an agreement will be sufficiently supported to be sustainable. The third criterion is that there must be enough compelling reasons for the parties to want to reach a sustainable settlement. This last element goes beyond the first criterion of desire to address the issue of structural necessity of conflict resolution in that it considers sustainable methods for avoiding or redressing economic or political collapse.

In working towards negotiated outcomes, the "all or nothing" approach is probably best if both sides are committed to peace, and just need to work out the details. But if one or both parties are less than committed, then an incremental approach appears to work best, so long as it is built on "levers" which can pry open further negotiable space. Short-term increments such as ceasefires do not in themselves achieve much of substance, and may simply offer a distraction rather than part of a solution. The "levers" approach, of course, assumes that influential actors in the negotiating process have a realistic plan or vision for a negotiated outcome, as levers must be used towards a particular end and play the politics of both sides the right way.

Within negotiations, perhaps the most critical issue is the capacity of the respective parties to impose their will to realize their interests. This capacity may derive from military strength, the capacity to impose will through force of arms, the strategic positioning of the combatant forces and the capacities and motivations of commanders and troops. It has long been clear that despite many other disadvantages, soldiers fighting for a cause they deeply believe in will sustain their commitment to the conflict much longer and more completely than soldiers whose commitment is based on a doubtful political order or personal financial gain. These respective capacities are buttressed by external interest, which may enhance or limit military capacity, or the political will to support military capacity. Such buttressing may take the form of financing, moral or diplomatic support, a physical military or logistical base, the supply of arms or other resources, training or, less commonly, direct intervention.

The capacity to negotiate is underpinned by military capacity in that withdrawal or loss of territory equals defeat. Conversely, especially for a guerrilla force, even the basic capacity to survive equals a victory of sorts. Mere survival can be proof sufficient of the force of a claim. This recognition of capacity to secure particular interests in turn tends to imply the intention of the negotiating party. That is, determining actual or self-perceived capacity is a fair guide to intention. This arranging of interest and capacity is complicated by the intellectual and organizational capacity of the negotiators and their support teams. The potential capacity to impose will and the interest of each party may be reduced by a lack of planning, coordination, discipline or intellectual resources. In this, each team must know the strengths and weaknesses of their own members, be able to use them at a given time, or hide them where they could reveal weakness or personal flaws (such as over-emotionalism, a desire for acceptance, anger, and so on). In large part, negotiating is about bluff and gamble, and not betraying one's emotions, or intentionally betraying them (or being seen to betray them) only for specific effect.

The imposition of will is not just measured by capacity. It can also be measured by resilience, or the capacity of the respective parties to resist. As with capacity to impose will, capacity to resist reflects political and military strength and positioning, external support or constraints, and the various capacities of negotiating teams and the individuals who comprise them. A negotiating team that enjoys a strong political or military position may still not be able to fully press its advantages in the field at the negotiating table if its negotiators are lacking in skill or expertise. Conversely, a strong negotiating team may be able to actually increase the advantages it enjoys from the field, or compensate for some disadvantages. Again with a guerrilla force, to resist is a functional statement of survival, and survival equals victory.

Assuming, however, a relative balance in negotiating capacities, but a significant imbalance in military force, if one party is determined to dominate the other then no meaningful accommodation is possible. Invariably, the militarily stronger party will attempt to impose this outcome as a part of the negotiating process. But assuming that negotiations in fact proceed, the existence of negotiations would tend to indicate that claims to such overwhelming capacity in turn do not exist. Thus, the supposedly stronger party will assert their claimed strength and demand compliance upon pain of reprisal. But if the stronger party lacks the capacity to fulfill such a threat, or the capacity for resistance militates against it, then bluff is called and the bluffing party must move to reassess and restate its position.

Once the process of negotiation has begun, it is standard for the respective parties to ask for more than they believe can reasonably be agreed to, so that they might be able to later make less painful sacrifices, or so that later concessions can appear to be generously offered. In this, a negotiating team must know and equally understand what outcome it wants, the strategy for achieving it, the customs or form of the negotiating process, the concessions or sacrifices that it is prepared to make, and the limits beyond which it will not negotiate. In terms of customs of negotiation, while there are general rules for behavior, these only apply to the extent that they can be compelled, usually by a mediating body or by mutual agreement, and can be abrogated if and when it suits the interest of a negotiating party that has the capacity to sustain the abrogation.

In negotiating peace, in which there is a specific scaling back of personnel or military equipment as the final point of negotiation, disarmament is only undertaken to the lowest point necessary to ensure the safety of combatants and to protect the political institutions that give rise to the combatant force. It is unrealistic to expect that the claims made by the respective forces are frank and transparent, as each will seek to hide an advantage in any declaration of demilitarization. The question then devolves to intelligence capacities of each force, the monitoring of commitments, and the transparency of the demilitarization process.

In any peace agreement that has a preamble, the preamble appears to define its terms, but is rarely binding. Preambles simply state the purpose and spirit of the agreement to which both parties are expected to comply. Compliance with an agreement is only valid in so far as the parties are so weakened they have no choice but to comply, there is sufficient external pressure, or the agreement is to their advantage. In any other case, it should be expected that a party to an agreement will seek to avoid or undermine it, or break it as soon as is practical. In this sense, negotiating is like a game of chess, in which all moves must be planned well in advance, including the potential moves of the opposition. The primary difference between negotiating and chess is that in a practical sense, the only rules of negotiating are those which can be imposed on the game by one of the parties to it.

The success of a negotiating process relies much less on the negotiating skills of the participants to the process or of the quality of mediation, as the context for the negotiations. Indeed, were the alternative the case, there is little likelihood that the Aceh peace process of 2005 would have been successful. Success in negotiating relies heavily on structural circumstances, in which one or both of the parties feel compelled to reach some sort of a settlement. Once the structural circumstances dictate the necessity of a settlement, agreement is still not a given, as the process of actually achieving an agreement is itself fraught with problems (as indeed was the case in the Aceh peace process). But compelling structural circumstances – a sense of impending necessity on the part of both parties – make a successful outcome possible. The reverse is also true; if there are insufficient structural conditions in place then even goodwill or a great deal of skill on the part of the negotiators or mediators will almost certainly not be enough to secure a sustainable peaceful outcome.

Finally, negotiating, like diplomacy, is not so much war by other means, rather it is a form of war, with winners and losers, and high costs in human lives before, during and often after the process. It should therefore never be assumed that negotiation equates with friendship, as there are only interests. When those interests coincide, and can be reasonably expected to continue to coincide, alliances can form for the period of assumed continuation. There are and can be no friends across a negotiating table. The only "friendship" that is possible is that which is born of a common interest that is too deep and fundamental to divide, which may occur at the end of a negotiating process, but is most unlikely to be able to occur during it. This, then, is less a case of either alliance or friendship, but rather recognition and acceptance of the possibility of a common fundamental bond, for any sense of separation to be replaced by genuine unity. This implies trust in both intentions and capacities. Trust is the most hard earned, and most easily dissipated, of commodities.

To illustrate the issue of conflict resolution, the case of Indonesia and three of its internal conflicts in East Timor, Aceh and West Papua is instructive.[6] In East Timor, the National Council for Timorese Resistance (Conselho Nacional de Resistência Timorense – CNRT), existed to achieve East Timor's independence, and its principle method was through international pressure on Indonesia to grant the territory a ballot on self-determination. In this sense, the CNRT did not want a negotiated settlement as such, but worked towards a negotiated settlement that would allow East Timor's people an act of self-determination. The continuation of the military conflict in East Timor by the resistance force Falintil (Forcas Armadas para la Liberacao Nacional de Timor Leste – Armed Forces for National Liberation of East Timor) was in large part aimed at sustaining international interest in East Timor to pressure the government of Indonesia. The Indonesian government, on the other hand, was looking to resolve an outstanding internal and international problem within the context of its own, then still new, process of reform from its previously authoritarian political system. As such, it finally did allow a vote on self-determination in East Timor.

In Aceh, following 28 years of conflict, and intensified military campaign from May 2003 and previously failed ceasefire agreements, the Free Aceh Movement (*Gerakan Acheh Merdeka* – GAM) sought a ceasefire in which to create suitable conditions for a possible negotiated settlement. However, until the advent of the massively destructive Asian tsunami on 26 December 2004 (and for some months after it), GAM's single and non-negotiable goal was the independence of Aceh from Indonesia, either through military means or through conflict creating suitable conditions for a negotiated method. The Indonesian government, on the other hand, wanted to enter negotiations to force GAM to accept its offer of "special autonomy," which had been implemented in 2001 but not accepted by GAM. In theory, special autonomy was supposed to provide Aceh with a greater level of functional self-determination (but which had failed to do so in practise).

In West Papua, the Free Papua Organization (*Organisasi Papua Merdeka* – OPM) and its sympathizers were moving by 2006 towards a consistent position on wanting to work towards a negotiated settlement to resolve problems stemming from the incorporation of West Papua into the Indonesian state in 1963. This orientation marked a substantive shift away from the previously military-oriented goal of the OPM, which like the CNRT, had struggled to keep alive its claims in the international community. The Indonesian government, on the other hand, promoted West Papua's acceptance of its questionable offer and relatively hollow implementation of "special autonomy," also in 2001, although this was complicated from 2004 by the division of the province into three provinces, which was a legacy of the previous administration.

Sufficient representation

In East Timor, the CNRT comprised a broad coalition of East Timor's key political parties, student and other civil society organizations, and the military resistance organization, Falintil, and its clandestine, civilian-based Internal Political Front (Frente da Politica Interna – FPI). As such, it could legitimately claim to be widely representative of the East Timorese people. The government of Indonesia had a constitutional mandate following the resignation of President Suharto and the promotion to president of his vice-president, Bacharuddin Jusuf Habibie, in May 1998. However, the difficulties of regime transition, questions over the legitimacy of the interim government, Habibie's lack of popularity and the formalizing of pre-existing political divisions following legislative elections in June 1999 meant that while the Indonesian government could enter into negotiations towards a settlement of the East Timor conflict, this process was not well accepted by a number of Indonesia's key political actors. The major consequence of this was the quasi-official organization of an effort to derail East Timor's ballot process, principally through intimidation, destruction and violence.

On the question of Aceh, GAM claimed to be the principle representative organization of the Acehnese people, and while it claimed majority representation this could not be tested. However, after agreeing to engage in negotiations with the Indonesian government in 2005, GAM quickly moved to establish more complete working relations with Acehnese civil society groups, including NGOs, *ulama* (Islamic religious leaders), academics, business people, and so on. Towards the end of the negotiations process, GAM could claim overwhelming support for its commitment towards peace, which was confirmed during the implementation of the agreement. The Indonesian administration, on the other hand, could claim a mandate on the basis of the Aceh peace process as an election issue, and had around 53 per cent support in the national legislature for legislation required to implement its part of the agreement. However, it also faced stiff political opposition, although this opposition appeared to be largely opportunistic and was ultimately unable to derail the government's position. The government's main difficulty lay with its military, which saw the Aceh peace process as in part being aimed at reducing its political influence and economic reach.

The position of West Papua was similar to Aceh in that the Indonesian government faced national political and military opposition, but on the basis of its electoral mandate and representative majority was in a generally sound position to put through any agreement it might reach. The West Papuans, on the other hand, had a history of generalized opposition to Indonesian authority due to the latter's exploitation of its natural resources, military domination of the province and the constant level of oppression of local people who expressed grievance. However, the key opposition movement, the OPM suffered from regional factionalism based largely on pre-existing tribalism, while political and NGO leaders were often divided along similar lines, as well as by the extent that some of them had been bought off by Indonesian political and economic interests. This tendency towards fragmentation was exacerbated by the loss of West Papuan leadership, with local leaders having been targeted by Indonesian security forces and either being killed or fleeing into exile. However, from mid-2005, West Papuan groups again began to coalesce and by 2006 appeared to present a united and coherent front from which to enter a negotiation process.

Compelling reasons to negotiate

The most clear, simple and compelling reason for parties to negotiate is that conflict is always destructive, usually mutually, and rarely produces clear winners. The real issue in conflict is its apparent compelling necessity from the outset of who loses the least. When two or more parties are locked in what is, or what appears to be, a life and death struggle, the option of disengagement carries with it the prospect of the diminution or termination of one of the parties. Of course, often the fear of loss or failure exceed their actual import, and this fear very often less negative than the continuation of conflict. A negotiated settlement generally avoids the "winner-take-all" outcome of conflicts, and is thus a constructive alternative to such an absolute eventuality. In other words, the costs of sustaining conflict invariably outweigh any potential benefits that might be perceived to be available through it.

In East Timor in 1999, there was a strong desire to politically resolve the territory's 24 years of bloodshed and mayhem. Some scholars of genocide have asked whether there were distinct phases of mass killings in East Timor under Indonesia, or if there was just one long period of killing marked by relative peaks and troughs in the level of atrocities. What was clear, however, was that the situation in East Timor was both very bad and that it was continuing. Following pressure from the international community and reformist political changes within Indonesia, the option was finally put to the East Timorese people of a ballot on accepting a proposed high level of autonomy within the Indonesian state or, under UN supervision, independence. The option of independence was always going to be a part of any agreement by the Indonesian government given that, under international law, East Timor was never recognized as a part of Indonesian sovereign territory. For the CNRT, the prospect of a ballot to determine the future of the territory of East Timor, set against the alternative of continuing atrocities and repression under Indonesia, constituted the practical fulfillment of its long-standing political campaign.

In Aceh, three factors combined to push GAM towards a negotiated settlement. The first was that the people of Aceh had suffered terribly as a consequence of the war and that the period from May 2003 until August 2005 marked a major escalation in the conflict, which GAM had some difficulty in sustaining. It has been claimed, with considerable justification, that regardless of the losses to GAM, it would have continued to be able to find new recruits from its large support base, or that it would have been able to eventually rebuild after a de-escalation of the conflict. However, there was little doubt that GAM had not only lost a large number of its key personnel during the previous two years, but that its fighters, cut off from their regular supplies, had in many cases been pushed to the margins of survival. The second main factor was the election of Susilo Bambang Yudhoyono as president, and his commitment towards resolving the Aceh conflict as part of his reform program and Indonesia's continuing if at times limited process of democratization. This in turn opened up the possibility for GAM to achieve a number of its key claims on behalf of the people of Aceh, and, even if its claim of independence was not among them, many of the supposed benefits of independence could be. The third main factor was the destructive impact of the tsunami on Aceh and the related loss of life, which caused both GAM and the Indonesian government to take stock of the situation and eventually resulted in a change of position on the part of both parties. The tsunami required massive rebuilding which was not possible while the conflict continued, and that the people of Aceh had suffered enough.

In West Papua, the prospect on one hand of continuing military repression, political and social alienation and structural dispossession, and, on the other, of dealing with a government that, based on the Aceh settlement, for the first time appeared genuine in its commitment to negotiations, was sufficient reason for West Papuan groups to move towards consensus on the need for a negotiated outcome. This growing unity among West Papuan leaders from late 2005 was also built on compromise, in which the more extended claims of some were moderated by the limited claims of others. Like in Aceh, the central question for West Papuan leaders was whether achieving many and perhaps most of the claims intended to improve the lives of ordinary West Papuans be sufficient? This question was set against the threat of continuing external migration which complicated and limited real prospects for a non-military outcome, and the belligerence of the Indonesian military. Even a "window of opportunity" offered by a political administration in Jakarta that appeared in favor of negotiations, could not be guaranteed beyond the end of its term.

In the case of Indonesia and its three troubled provinces of East Timor, Aceh and West Papua, the compelling reasons to negotiate were, at one level, the same or similar. Indonesia could not afford to continue to be at war with itself; nor could it continue to seek military solutions to political problems if it was to continue the process of democratization by limiting or ending the political role of the military. More specifically, in the case of East Timor, then President Habibie saw the option of a ballot on national self-determination as a means of resolving a long-standing problem Indonesia faced with the international community. It also provided opportunities to cap the constant and ill-affordable drain on the country's development and military budgets, and also to establish Habibie's own credentials as a reformist president. If Habibie actually believed that the vote would go in favor of East Timor staying within Indonesia, then he and many others could not have been more mistaken. (Creating such an impression was in part a strategy of the CNRT, notably in the 1999 general elections, in which the vote in favor of Habibie's party, Golkar, was intended to create a sense of complacency.) The final decision, however, to respect the outcome of the ballot in favor of East Timor's independence only followed widespread killings and massive destruction, which in turn prompted the US to push the World Bank to refuse the allocation of further funds intended to help bail out the ailing Indonesian economy unless it agreed to intervention by an Australian-led multinational peace keeping force. That is, the final resolution was brought about by externally driven economic considerations and external military intervention.

In the cases of Aceh and West Papua, there were equally compelling, albeit somewhat different, reasons to negotiate. By 2005, Indonesia had gone from being a major oil exporting country to one that imported oil (during a world record peak in oil prices), due almost entirely to a lack of foreign investment in oil infrastructure and poor foreign investment generally. More generally, foreign investment had also largely stagnated, and it was this gap in foreign investment that comprised the gap in economic growth between that below that sufficient to stay abreast of population growth and that which could match or exceed population growth. The foreign investment downturn in turn reflected on Indonesia's internal security problems, such as the conflicts in Aceh and West Papua, as well as Islamist terrorism. In addition, Indonesia continued to face numerous other problems. There were high levels of official corruption (notably in the judiciary, which in turn compromised the application of law in conflict zones). Also importantly, there remained military extortion of foreign businesses, the prevalence of a military-led black market, and the significant drain on the Indonesian budget of the increased military campaign in Aceh (and later a military build-up in West Papua). This in turn led the military to seek unofficial funding through other government departments. In the case of post-tsunami Aceh, the international community also became increasingly reluctant to provide much of its promised US$ five billion in reconstruction aid, citing concerns over the conflict, military theft and generalized corruption. That is, there were strong political and economic reasons for the Indonesian government to seek negotiated solutions to the conflicts in Aceh and West Papua, which were in large part driven by the views of the international community. In the cases of East Timor and Aceh, the intervention of the international community was not only critical in bringing about a move towards conflict resolution but, set against a backdrop of military-backed provocations, it also provided a greater guarantee of sustaining the different agreements that were eventually reached.

The principles, then, of interest, capacity and compelling reason or opportunity to negotiate in Aceh and East Timor were critical to the successful end to military conflict. These principles could also be claimed to apply to other conflicts, not least to West Papua. In the case of Sri Lanka, the failure to reach a negotiated settlement (at the time of writing) appeared to be due to an incomplete desire by both the Sri Lankan government and the LTTE to reach such a negotiated settlement. This could be attributed in part to a degree of government factionalism and the lack of discipline this implied in the field, and in part to a lack of internally driven or externally motivated compelling reason, especially on the part of the government. Similarly, in the Israel-Palestine conflict, the desire for peace has been beset by a lack of political unity on both sides, which in turn points to a clash of fundamental aims and default positions, and insufficient structural flexibility to ensure that both sides are able to seek peace for economic or other material reasons. The Israeli response to cutting off the supply of tax-based funds following the success of Hamas in the 2006 elections did not push Hamas towards negotiations. Rather, it reinforced Hamas' pre-existing position against Israel, and counter-productively perpetuated its reliance on other financial sources, such as Iran. While the conditions for negotiations may or may not be favorable, how the political relationship is handled, both within and as a context for the negotiating process, is critical to its success or failure.

External intervention to end conflict

There are occasions when there is a desire to end conflict but there is a lack of capacity to do so. It may be that the recognized government does not have the capacity to compel another warring party or parties towards negotiation. Alternatively, the government in question may have lost legitimacy and external intervention is sought by non-state parties whose claims to legitimacy are perceived as greater by the international community, or a significant section of it. An invitation to an external body by a legitimate or recognized authority within the state is usually the criteria by which intervention occurs. However, it is also possible for the UN Security Council to approve a resolution in favor of unilateral, usually "humanitarian," intervention, "to maintain or restore international peace and security" (UN 1945: 7: 42), such as occurred in the case of the UN Security Council's approval for NATO's intervention in Kosovo (NATO 1999). Such intervention was claimed by the US and its allies in the case of the war in Iraq, even though the UN secretary-general said that there needed to be a further Security Council resolution before action in Iraq could be taken.

However, non-UN sanctioned intervention has also occurred on a number of occasions, mostly to "protect" foreign nationals living in the country in question (for example, the French intervention in Cote d'Ivoire in 2004, and several US interventions – not including wars or official invitation – since 1945).[7] In such cases, a capacity to impose a political or military will continued to exist even where a more seemingly legitimate rationale did not.

War or peace?

War and other forms of conflict are by definition materially destructive, and frequently produce negative political outcomes as well. This is not least because war has its own internal logic of survival at any cost, which in turn can mean the rationalization of any level of death or destruction. There is similarly much to suggest that peace does indeed produce substantial dividends. But the options for war and for peace are often not simple or always available.

Both external and internal aggression can result from competing political and economic interests, conceptions of ethnic, religious or other forms of supremacy, and claims to territorial ownership. If basic survival is threatened, such aggression is usually met with an equal response. However, sometimes threats are not blatant, or may build up over a period of time, which can constitute either a political or violent response to what might be seen as an institutionalization of injustice. In cases where there is little or no recourse to a political response and violence used, if the warring parties had known in advance the cost of such violence, it is likely that it would have been precluded by negotiation. Even proponents of ideologies that glory in war usually do so only rhetorically, and generally choose to avoid it if their goals can be reached by non-violent means. Having said that, advocates of ideologies that glorify war usually engage in conflict most readily when its intended victims are at a significant disadvantage (the cost of glory is not too high) and where the leading ideologues are not likely to be forced to directly face the consequences of their actions. There is a tendency for pro-war activists to fight to the last drop of someone else's blood. Of course, there are exceptions to political decision makers going directly into battle,[8] but these have always been rare, especially in larger political organizations and in contemporary conflict.

It may be, however, that conflict must be entered into in order to remove a malignant power before political development can take place. Reason and moderation do not always produce desired outcomes, and negotiation is not always possible. Given the human costs of conflict, it is tempting to say that all conflict is simply bad and should be avoided at all costs; pacifism and its many adherents do indeed present compelling arguments. But human beings do not have, and cannot be expected to display, unlimited tolerance in intolerable conditions. Material conditions may be prevalent in providing grounds for conflict, along with political oppression or similar types of grievances. And even seeking to avoid conflict, turning the other cheek is not always possible when the blow is directed not at oneself, but at a loved one. It may be the point at which one is compelled to defend oneself, a loved one or one's community that war becomes inevitable. But war is never desirable, and nearly always avoidable if the parties to it genuinely wish to avoid it. The problem is that political will is all too often in favor of rather than against war.

Conclusion

This book has attempted to address a number of criteria which it has proposed are fundamental to the issue of political development. It may be that these criteria are not exhaustive, and that greater treatment could be given to specific issues raised both by and within them. But the book has proposed that if there is to be any progress towards political development, then it must address at least the criteria enumerated here in order to sustain its claims. In a general sense, these criteria revolve around a benign form of political organization that has as its first concern the welfare of the people for which it is responsible, an accurate means of ensuring reflection of their wishes, and a process of accountability in doing so. Within this are the issues raised in this book.

The issue of political violence is both vexed and vexing, calling forth as it does both the worst aspects of inhumanity as well as the greatest needs to end injustice. In its extreme application, political violence is used to settle political disputes not through reason but through power. The profound consequences that political violence can have for its participants (active and passive alike), sets it outside most discussion of political development, and paints its proponents as certainly dangerous and probably unstable. Yet state potential or actual state violence is widely regarded as the acceptable and necessary expression of the rational state in pursuit of the common interests of its citizens, even though states can and do act against their own citizens as well as in ways that diminish the interests of others. This, raises challenging questions about legitimacy. Counter-posed against the rational and legitimate state, violent non-state actors are, perforce, irrational and illegitimate. But in cases where the state has compromised or lost legitimacy, and where there is widespread acknowledgement of that loss, the question arises of whether and in what circumstances non-state violence becomes rational and, hence, legitimate.

There is no clear answer to the point at which violence can be a rational response to illegitimacy, but claims to "legitimate violence" have been embodied in many great political philosophies of differing ideological persuasions; there have been few polities throughout history that do not accept the right to violence in self-defense. Even where violence may be legitimate and necessary, the option of negotiated conflict resolution is always preferable, at least where it is available. The contradiction in this, though, is that negotiation is often undertaken in an unequal power environment, and implies a type of violence by another means. If there is an answer, it lies with creating conditions which preclude violence.

Functioning state capacity and state institutions that are predicated upon the principle of their serving citizens, including the equal and consistent application of rule of law, appear to be the principle requirements for a functioning political society, and a safe guard against lawlessness and violence. As a mechanism for applying the rule of law, multilateral bodies may play a significant role in preventing conflict and lawlessness between states, as well as ensuring that individual states maintain minimum standards in relation to their own citizens. In practise, however, the role of multilateral bodies and organizations is at best incomplete, and states continue to intervene in the affairs of others in ways that do not always comply with international law. These bodies have also stood by while predatory governments devour their own citizens. As a model, of the common interests of citizens within a particular territory, the state at its most benign, remains the most viable mechanism for ensuring political development. At its most malignant, however, the state is but a mechanism for repression, employed against the interests of its citizens and a danger to others. The form the state takes and how it interacts with its citizens are critical to this outcome.

In a normative sense, the state is the manifestation of the collective political will of a people in relation to a given territory. While there are a number of potential political forms that can comply with a specific territory, the state is the basic organizational model for all groups claiming national identity in relation to a specific territorial claim by a state, even if all groups are not successful in securing this claim. The core question, then, is about the relationship between the state and the nation. In this, there is a tension between the nation as a bonded group based on language, cultural, historical and other signifiers, and their common purpose (such as self-preservation), and the nation based on common purpose, such as commitment to shared civic values developed on the basis of equity and justice. While national identity can be molded by state institutions, it seems less plausible that national identities can be successfully imposed, or that compulsion will produce a positive political outcome. That is, civic nationalism can apply across cultural groups, but without a civic basis – its reflection as a state under rule of law – then nationalism devolves to its geographically specific ethnic origins. If a people cannot find a shared civic identity with others in relation to the state, then they may reasonably seek to find it alone.

Similarly, governments that genuinely represent the wishes of the majority of citizens, which allow and encourage citizens to participate in decision-making processes, and which are accountable in their processes and decisions, have a much lower tendency to engage in violent behavior towards their own citizens and in conflict with other polities. Moreover, such governments are much more likely to promote policies that assist in the broader development of their own societies because they are both representative and accountable. The methods of achieving such political outcomes, however, are not a given and are often fraught with traps for the naïve and unprepared. The process of the transition to a state of political development, presumably represented by a meaningful form of liberal democracy, is perhaps the key element of the "development" component of political development. Not only is the method by which democratic change is achieved important for the character of the process of change, but the process itself and its continuation remain central to the maintenance and expansion of political development.

As a guiding principle, or set of principles, for political development, civil and political rights as first order human rights appear to contain within them the basic conditions necessary for a harmonious functioning society that has as its own best interests a community of equal citizens. The "rights to" and "rights from" logically implied within civil and political rights offer citizens guarantees of protection to go about their business unhindered by others or the state. Most importantly, "rights to" imply the freedom to which development must be aimed if, as discussed by Sen (1999), in order to give itself meaning. Recapping the claims of positive liberty as noted by Berlin (1958), in which citizens fulfill their freedom through active political participation and consequently guard their liberty and affirm their autonomy, global citizens must be active within this larger framework. Positive freedom – "freedom to" – is usually seen as a civic ideal where citizens fulfill their freedom through active participation in political institutions. Participation is seen as the guardian of liberty, since it is the medium by which citizens affirm their autonomy as both citizens of a state and as their own masters.

Within "freedom to" is the voluntary commitment of the individual to the communitarian ideal, as opposed to the imposed or compelled requirement; or the voluntary giving of self, as opposed to the forced taking. This implies that the availability of liberty is the end goal of political development. But this liberty is not an absolute; it exists within the contexts of the material constraints and individual human circumstances within which people live. In order for individuals to enjoy liberty there must be reciprocal respect which entails a just allocation of material opportunity. Given that individual notions of justice will vary according to time, place and personal interest, there must be a consistent underlying understanding of justice and rule of law in order to provide a benchmark for individuals seeking to test the parameters and to know what they can legitimately claim. This then goes to questions of what is required to constitute the "good" society.

In the wider debate about what is broadly understood as development, there is a continuing, if somewhat shifting, focus on economic outcomes. The issue of whether material circumstances determine social outcomes such as political development is at best a moot point. There is little doubt that positive or negative material circumstances either assist or discourage political development, and that particular forms of economic relations can find equivalence in political and social relations. The self-interest of elites in all states across the entire development spectrum constitute perhaps the most significant barrier to political development. Having said that, it could reasonably be claimed that many ordinary citizens in developed countries also constitute a sort of global elite, relative to the great mass of the world's population. One does not have to be part of the economic or political elite of a developed country in order to enjoy a relatively comfortable standard of living that would be vastly beyond the realistic options of most of the world's population. This is not to suggest that there are not serious economic and political imbalances within developed countries; there are, and the gaps have been growing wider for many years. But the "comfortable classes" of these countries, though perhaps less wealthy in terms relative to their own elites, are more wealthy in absolute terms and especially relative to the great majority of people living in the least or less developed countries, and even in developing countries.

Standards of living are in significant part underpinned not just by the ingenuity, hard work and natural resources of developed countries and their people, but also by a distinctly imbalanced global trading system, which in turn arranges its political preferences in ways that support its economic position. People in developing countries also toil under often oppressive conditions and have a capacity for ingenuity, often unrealized because of their structural circumstances. It is but a short step to criticism of major developed countries and the way in which they order global affairs to suit their own interests. But while such a critique is legitimate, the full set of global arrangements that produce a wide variety of outcomes is vastly more complex and subject to agency than is easily allowed. That is, such a critique must be detailed and nuanced, as well as recognizing the great and often varied forces at play. Acknowledging structural arrangements, there remains the question about the extent to which material circumstances structurally determine social outcomes, and the capacities of individuals and groups to change social outcomes based on their knowledge of alternatives.

One can argue that knowledge of alternatives can itself be materially determined, and there is little doubt that hegemonic frameworks, as they are generally understood being habituated as "culture," do have a basis in primarily material or economic interest. Arguments in favor of the status quo based on economic or cultural circumstances are in politically less or least developed societies usually code for the reification of illiberal and undemocratic models. This argument, often in defense of cultural legitimacy, is that because of the ways things are done in a particular place justifies their continuation. That people in least or less developed countries are or should be satisfied with more restrictive forms of government is tantamount to an external imposition of superior claims that "other" people do not deserve freer and more responsive forms of government, or that poverty condemns them not just to limited material goods, but also to limited political goods. This unenlightened cultural determinism reinforces not just material poverty but social and political poverty as well. One might further venture that it also implies institutionalized racism.

Ideas, especially good ideas, do not acknowledge borders and have a way of undermining hegemony. A capacity to think is not exclusively defined by one's wealth or poverty, even though capacity to act on ideas may be, and often is. Nor is culture fixed or permanent. Not all aspects of all cultures are worth preserving; many acculturated acts of barbarity are worth being relegated to the dustbin of history, and if that observation offends cultural relativists then one need only ask the recipient – the victim – of barbaric "cultural" acts whether they willingly and freely agree to them. In this, abuses of power should not be mistaken for culture. In that the act of communication and exchange of ideas imply a capacity to develop thinking about organizing social relations, it should not be imposed by notions of cultural superiority, but by identifying within the varying conceptual frameworks that define cultures of the common elements based on mutual interest and humanity. Communication, especially about political ideas, is not to lead, but to share.

The international order in which such sharing takes place is characterized by growing webs of structural interdependency at numerous levels (economic, political, technological, environmental and cultural) from which individuals, as well as states, can no longer escape. The world is developing and changing rapidly, globalization challenges previous orders, and the confluence of events is accelerating so that most people do not feel relatively unchallenged or insecure. The challenge for political development is for people who are the constituent members of polities to work through this cautiously and carefully and with the best agreed intentions possible, or at least in agreement that agreement is not necessary. No-one has the absolute answer and the only honest answer is to acknowledge this. This end point is the beginning. We are all different and we are all ourselves. But we are all of a common humanity. This then implies what could be referred to as a civic cosmopolitanism, or global citizenship, in which the ideals of the citizen in the benign, concerned and accountable, that is "virtuous," state are developed and applied globally. If the state is constructed along common civic lines, there is then no rational reason to limit an understanding of those civic values to within a particular geographic territory.

The view that has been presented here is that there is no end to human politics, history or evolution or, short of global annihilation, can there be one. What is important, then, is not that societies aspire to (or struggle for) a particular destination for political development, or that they guard and maintain such a destination should they believe that it has already been achieved. What is important is that the focus be placed on the *process* of political development, and that the process is understood as defining the type of future into which it leads. This suggests a continuous and critical reappraisal of the past and present in order to facilitate such progress. A critical question, of course, is the direction of this process. If the process itself implies that there is no single answer to this question, then the answer is ideally defined by its plurality and attendant qualities of balance, tolerance, respect and relative social generosity. The process of working towards balance, tolerance, respect and social generosity within an accountable plural political framework is, for political development, its own goal.

Notes

1 An outline of political development

1 This idea of "common good" has a long history, and has been frequently articulated in the archaic term "commonweal" or, more contemporarily "commonwealth"; a community of shared interests.
2 Cultural issues may influence specific conditions but claims to cultural specificity, especially by power holders, are usually a blind for subverting the rights of others. Further, the relativization of culture as a conditionality logically implies that cultural deconstruction continues beyond the key political site (usually the state) and devolves to the local, both vertically (geographically/culturally) and horizontally (across commonalities of economic interest).
3 This conforms to the judicial maxim that "justice delayed is justice denied." That is, justice cannot be said to be done if it is not actually done.
4 The title of Sen's book *Rationality and Freedom* perhaps should better be *Rationality AS Freedom*. No doubt, however, such a title would have been seen to be too close to his earlier book *Development As Freedom* (1999).

2 Structure and agency

1 The 2006 military coup in Thailand was claimed to be against political corruption and the subversion of democracy.

3 The nation

1 An alternative view is that the state is just the sovereign institutions, and that the "country" refers to its geographic quality.
2 This principle was enunciated by US President Woodrow Wilson in 1918 in his "14 Points Speech" to Congress, which set US goals for the conclusion of the First World War. His position was that further war could be prevented if the peoples of Europe (other than ethnic Germans) were granted states on the basis of nationality. He also argued for foreign policy based on ethical principles. Lenin had a parallel if not identical view.
3 This is not intended to equate with "organicist," which implies a very different meaning.
4 So named after the earlier, ethnically distinct, Cham state, this remainder of it is located on the Bassak River (a.k.a. Mekong).
5 This is somewhat different to the idea of "national interest," which is commonly defined by governments nominally or actually on behalf of the state and its people, but also often reflecting specific interests within that often broad and fragmented social structure.

6 "Aryan" is originally a Sanscrit word meaning "noble" and is not related to European peoples as such, much less the Nordic peoples to whom it was applied and, if it has a contemporary meaning, applies to proto-Indo-Iranian people.

7 That is, religious rather than "cultural" Jews.

8 It should be noted that while some states are officially bi- or multi-lingual, most continue to have problems around "national" identity, which in turn can impact on the efficacy of the state, for example Canada, Belgium and East Timor.

9 By "reiterated states" I mean states that have continued to exist but which had more or less collapsed and been reinvented on the base of the former state territory.

10 The threat of flood was a particularly noticeable bonding agent in "hydraulic" societies, such as eastern (Han) China, Vietnam, Cambodia and Java.

11 Especially where communities bond together to construct grain storage silos and centralize grain collection and distribution.

12 This is less a bond for national identity, but a strong bond for local communities.

13 In the Indonesian case, it can be claimed with considerable justification that the Indonesian Communist Party (PKI) represented the establishment of a large horizontal grouping. However, despite representing a particular socio-economic group, this was largely based on *abangan* (nominally Muslim) Javanese and did not enjoy much support outside the *abangan* heartland.

4 The state

1 This is ideally separated from government authority, although judiciaries do operate as state institutions and adjudicate on state law.

2 There are limited and debatable examples of where democratic states have gone to war with each other (for example, UK and Finland, India and Pakistan), although these do not affect the substance of the assertion.

3 Permanent residency usually allows citizenship to be applied for, or is part of a process towards such citizenship.

4 The main author of the US *Declaration of Independence* and clearest orator on citizenship and related matters was Thomas Jefferson.

5 This is the complete translated text of *Declaration of the Rights of Man and the Citizen* of 1789.

6 For the purpose of this discussion, the "modern era" in politics can be ascribed to particular periods in the histories of specific states, such as England's Glorious Revolution of 1688, the French Revolution of 1787–99, or the post-Second World War period for post-colonial states. That is, the modern era conforms to the introduction of modern political institutions, including external recognition of self-determination within a sovereign, demarcated territory and a functioning government and state institutions with reciprocal internal political relations.

7 This constitutes the full text of Lenin's booklet *What Is To Be Done?* (1902).

8 These observations reflect an indebtedness to Michelle Miller, who initially outlined this assessment of state capacity in her PhD thesis (Miller 2006).

9 In some cases, the state might claim part of the nation has not been included within, or has been excised from its territories, and that it is the duty of the state as the representative institution of the nation to reclaim the territory occupied by the excised part of the nation. This irredentism may reflect a legitimate national grievance, but sometimes leads to conflict between states.

10 This was to be territory into which the German population could expand.

5 Civil and political rights

1 Second generation rights include economic, social and cultural rights, with third generation rights including peace and a sustainable environment.

2   Howard and Donnelly support universal human rights claims, but appear to have been unclear on the point of the universality of their moral assertion.
3   This general assertion is based on personal experience in a range of geographic, cultural and political contexts.
4   This brief assessment closely follows that of Lukes 1993.
5   Islam, Christianity and Judaism in particular express such codes.

6 Democracy

1   At the time of writing, legislation had been passed to allow locally based parties in the province of Aceh, as the key element of a peace deal to end a separatist struggle there.
2   The distinction here is between social liberalism or its opposite, which may not necessarily impinge on political liberalism. That is, one may be socially conservative but still agree with a liberal political structure.
3   By way of illustration, a political liberal might promote taxation for education as a means of increasing social opportunity, while a libertarian would tend to see taxation (and arguably education) as government imposition.
4   Interestingly, in Marx's own earlier writings, he advocated democracy as the constitutional self-expression of the people (Marx 1967: 65, 1970: 120) although, presaging "people's democracies," he also noted that universal suffrage was to serve the people, constituted in Communes' (quoted from *The Civil War in France* p53, and by Lenin 1965: Chapter 5, notably p35). In this, Marx made a distinction between universal suffrage and individual suffrage, or promoted communitarianism over libertarianism.
5   See http://www.mnsu.edu/emuseum/information/population/n for a live count of population figures.

7 Democratization

1   This is the complete text of *One Step Forward Two Steps Back (The Crisis in Our Party)*.
2   Based, in the US, on low voter turnout, inconsistent political allegiances and a lower sense of civic participation.
3   Interestingly, a similar sort of triumphalism – or "politics of self-congratulation" – greeted the Asian economic crisis of the late 1990s, implying that the West was relieved to know it would not immediately be overtaken by East Asian capitalism. Triumphalism as such appears to have more to do with perceived "victory" and its associated sense of relief rather than addressing the fundamental challenge in question.
4   Iraq had earlier been regarded, if not as a "friendly" state, then at least as one worth supporting with military hardware.
5   Schmitter and Schneider (2003) also identified 1974 as being the starting point of a cycle of democratization.
6   Note how the term is employed, for example, in the "New Order" of Germany and Indonesia, and by the State Law and Order Council of Burma. "Order" was also a central theme in later Confucianism and under Japan's Tokugawa Shogunate.

8 Institution building

1   This is not to suggest the police or military are necessarily violent, but that they have a legal capacity for violence which underpins their authority.
2   I use the term "freedom from law" to denote legislative deregulation on one hand,

and on the other a metaphor to indicate law's limitations on inappropriate behavior for the wider social benefit.

3 The contemporary use of the term "stakeholder" means actively interested parties, in particular those that have a vested interest. It is an somewhat overused term and, like much other "management speak," tends to preclude general public interest.

4 This position effectively contradicted Fukuyama's own work on the "End of History."

5 Nationalism produced both liberal and reactionary tendencies. While colonialism was generally politically regressive, in some cases it introduced more enlightened political ideas that had longer-term liberal consequences.

6 Fukuyama was a Freedom House "Century Project Team" member for this exercise.

7 This is not to suggest the appropriateness of male only suffrage, but rather that the allocation of the vote was socially inclusive other than along the lines of sex.

8 Indonesia abandoned federalism in 1950, a year after independence, while the Burmese government rejected calls for independence or functional federalism as per the constitution in 1958.

9 There are five regionalist political parties in the UK, with a further 20 in Scotland.

10 Lega Nord (Northern League).

11 For example, the southern states' "Dixiecrats."

12 Egypt technically allows parties other than the governing National Democratic Party, but these must be approved by the government, and the electoral process guarantees the success of the governing party (although by 2005 there were indications of a potential future loosening of the political process).

13 It could be argued that glorification of "nation" was central to Nazi ideology and that had it not been expansionist it would not have been the party it was. However, the party could have pursued a more rhetorical than militaristic glorification of nation while maintaining authority within the state.

14 The Falangists had a more limited nationalist goal than Germany's Nazis in that they did not embark on extended external occupation and, consequently, survived until shortly after the natural death of their leader, General Francisco Franco, when internal contradictions and lack of strong leadership led to their demise.

15 If the policy distinction is too fundamental and consensus is unavailable, such a distinction could lead to a split in the party and the formation of new or breakaway parties. For example, formation of breakaway Kadima party from former Likud party in Israel.

16 In 1986, Huntington was proposed for membership of the US National Academy of Science, and was twice rejected on the basis that he had misused mathematics in support of his work.

9 State and regime failure

1 All Scandinavian countries averaged above 80 per cent voter turn out, although this figure almost universally declined between 1990 and 2000. By comparison, US voter turn out between 1960 and 2000 averaged less than 50 per cent (often less than 40 per cent) for legislative elections and less than 60 per cent for presidential elections (source: Population Resource Center http://www.prcdc.org/summaries/voting/voting.html accessed 16 November 2005).

2 In 2002, Venezuela underwent a failed military coup; its failure was a sign of military weakness, but its attempt was a sign that the military had not entirely given up belief in the legitimacy of its political intervention. Up until the time of writing, Latin American militaries continued to be involved in domestic

political issues, generally on behalf of oligarchies. In 1999, Pakistan underwent a successful military coup, while military or military-dominated or backed governments continued throughout the developing world.

10 Violence and resolution

1   Weber first enunciated this idea in the modern era, although the legitimacy of state violence was a given of prior state rule, and has since become commonplace in political theory.

2   The word "felt" is used intentionally here, as this is a sub-rational response to conflict, which in reality can strike almost anywhere, especially in an age of long-range aircraft and missiles.

3   The term "blue blood" implies aristocratic heritage but originated in the northern European invasions of southern Europe, in which the conquerors' fairer skin more easily showed the "blue" blood in their veins, also pre-figuring the culturally constructed attraction of fair skin among some, especially Spanish or Hispanic influenced, darker skinned peoples.

4   For example, the government of the US and the EU.

5   The anarchist assassination of Tsar Alexander I. Of course, the use of "terror" for political purposes is as old as politics itself.

6   These are common names and spelling for this independent state and two Indonesian provinces. East Timor is, in English, formally the "Democratic Republic of East Timor," though it is more commonly referred to by its shorter name of East Timor, which is also the English translation of its former Indonesian provincial name (*Timor Timur*). Aceh is generally spelled as such, including by the Indonesian government, but is spelled as "Acheh" by the Free Acheh Movement. According to the 2005 peace agreement, the name of Aceh is to be determined by the local legislature. The formal name of West Papua is "Papua," the addition of "West" implying that it is first part of a whole island (including Papua New Guinea) rather than a province of Indonesia. It is also asserted by indigenous West Papuans and their supporters who are critical of the province's incorporation into the Indonesian state.

7   The more supportable claims include Ecuador 1961 and 1963, Congo 1964, Dominican Republic 1965, Greece 1967, Guatemala 1982, Yemen 1979–84, Libya 1986, Panama 1989–90, Bulgaria 1990, Albania 1991, Haiti 1991, Liberia 1996, Central African Republic 1996, Sierra Leone 1997, Congo and Gabon 1997, Guinea-Bissau 1998, Afghanistan 1998, Sudan 1998, Yemen 2000, Venezuela 2002, Cote d'Ivoire 2002, Haiti 2004, Pakistan 2006.

8   Most recent examples come from revolutionary or separatist movements including Fidel Castro's leadership of the Cuban revolution, and Xanana Gusmao's leadership in East Timor, although the latter inherited political leadership while already a military commander.

References

Acemoglu, D. and Robinson, J. 2006. *Economic Origins of Dictatorship and Democracy*. Cambridge University Press: Cambridge.

Aden, S. 2003. "Taking Liberties in the War on Terror: The Justice department's Patriot Act II," The Rutherford Institute: Vancouver.

Althusser, L. 2003. *The Humanist Controversy and Other Texts*, Mathson, F. (ed.) Goshgaria, G. trans. Verso: London.

Althusser, L. 2006. *Philosophy of the Encounter: Late writing, 1978–87*, Mathson, F. (ed.) Goshgaria, G. trans. Verso: London.

Anderson, B. 1991. *Imagined Communities*. Verso: London.

Anderson, B. (ed.) 2001. *Violence and the State in Suharto's New Order Indonesia*. Cornell University Press: Ithaca, NY.

Anderson, C., Mehden, F. and Young, C. 1967. *Issues of Political Development*. Prentice Hall: Englewood Cliffs, NJ.

Angiolillo, P. 1979. *A Criminal As Hero*. The Regents Press of Kansas: Lawrence, KS.

Archibugi, D. and Held, D. 1995. *Cosmopolitian Democracy*. Polity Press: Cambridge.

Aristotle 1905. *Politics*. Jowett, B. trans. Oxford University Press: Oxford.

Aristotle 1953. *Ethics*. Thompson, J. trans. Penguin Classics: Harmondsworth.

Aristotle 1997. Simpson, P. (ed.) trans. *The Politics of Aristotle*. University of North Carolina Press: Charlotte, NC.

ASC, TI, CSS, PRC 2003. *Failed and Collapsed State in the International System*. The African Studies Center, Leiden, The Transnational Institute, Amsterdam, The Center for Social Studies, Coimbra University, The Peace Research Center-CIP-FUHEM: Madrid, December 2003.

Ba, A. and Hoffman, M. 2005. (eds) *Contending Perspectives on Global Governance: Coherence, contestation and world order*. Routledge: London.

Bachrach, P. and Baratz, M.S. 1962. "Two Faces of Power," *American Political Science Review*, 56.

Bakker, J. and Ferrazzi, G. 1997. "Weber's Pure Ideal Type Model of Patrimonial Prebendalism: Testing the applicability of the model in Indonesia," unpublished paper to the 92nd annual meeting of the American Sociological Association, Toronto, 9–13 August.

Barongo, Y. 1984. "Alternative Approaches to African Politics," in Barongo, Y. ed. *Political Science in Africa: A critical review*. Zed Books: London.

Baumann, B. 1977. *Wie Alles Anfing (How it All Began)*. Pulp Press: Vancouver.

BBC 2006. "Profile: Alexander Lukashenko," BBC News, 20 March 2006.

Beam, L. 1992. "Leaderless Resistance," *The Seditionist*, 12 February 1992; http://www.louisbeam.com/leaderless.htm accessed 14 July 2006.

Beetham, D. 1999. *Democracy and Human Rights*. Blackwell Publishers: Oxford.

Belo, W., Docena, H., de Guzman, M. and Malig, M. 2005. *The Anti-Development State: The political economy of permanent crisis in the Philippines*. Zed Books: London.

Bentham, J. 1781. *The Principles of Morals and Legislation* http://www.constitution.org/jb/pml.htm accessed 8 August 2006.

Berlin, I. 1958. *Two Concepts of Liberty*. Oxford University Press: Oxford.

Berlin, I. 1969. *Four Essays on Liberty*. Oxford University Press: Oxford.

Bernholz, P. 1997. "Necessary and sufficient conditions for a viable democracy," in Breton, A., Galeoti, G., Salmon, P. and Wintrobe, R. (eds) *Understanding Democracy*. Cambridge University Press: Cambridge.

BJS 2005. *Prison Statistics*. Bureau of Justice Statistics, US Department of Justice: Washington, DC.

Blau, P. 1970. "A Formal Theory of Differentiation on Organizations', *American Social Review*, 35(2): 201–18.

Bolt, P., Coletta, D. and Shackleford, C. (eds) 2005. *American Defense Policy*. Johns Hopkins University Press: Baltimore, MD.

Brabant, J. van 1990. *Remaking Eastern Europe – On the Political Economy of Transition*. Kluwer Academic Publishers: Dordrecht.

Bremmer, I. and Taras, R. (eds) 1997. *New States, New Politics*. Cambridge University Press: Cambridge.

Brubaker, R. 2004. *Ethnicity Without Groups*. Harvard University Press: Harvard, MS.

Bullock, A. 1962. *Hitler: A Study in Tyranny*. Penguin Books: Harmondsworth.

Burton, M., Gunther, R. and Higley, J. (eds) 1992. *Elites and Democratic Consolidation in Latin America and Southern Europe*. Cambridge University Press: Cambridge.

Camilleri, J. 1994. "Reflections on the State in Transition," *Arena*, Melbourne.

Camilleri, J. and Falk, J. 1992. *The End of Sovereignty? The politics of a shrinking and fragmenting world*. Edward Elgar: London.

Campbell, T. 1983. *The Left and Rights*. Routledge and Kegan Paul: London.

Carothers, T. 2002. "The End of the Transition Paradigm," *Journal of Democracy*, 13(1), 5–21.

Chee, S.J. 1998. *To Be Free: Stories from Asia's struggle against oppression*. Monash Asia Institute: Melbourne.

Churchill, W. 1947. Speech to the House of Commons, London, 11 November. *CIDA Review*, Ottawa, 1995.

CIA 2006. *World Fact Book: Afghanistan* http://www.cia.gov/cia/publications/factbook/fields/2128.html accessed 3 July 2006.

Cicero, M. 1998. *The Republic, The Laws* (ed.) Powell, J. trans. Rudd, N. Oxford University Press: Oxford.

Clapham, C. 2001. "Rethinking African States," *African Security Review*, 10(3), 2001.

Cole, D. 2003. "What Patriot II Proposes To Do," Law center, Georgetown University; http://www.cdt.org/security/usapatriot/030210cole.pdf accessed 28 August 2006.

Collier, D. and Levitsky, S. 1997. "Democracy with Adjectives: Conceptual innovation in comparative research," *World Politics*, 49(3).

Connor, W. 1994. *Ethnonationalism: The quest for understanding*. Princeton University Press: Princeton, NJ.

Continental Congress, 2nd (US). 1776. *Declaration of Independence*.

Cribb, R. 1991. *Gangsters and Revolutionaries: The Jakarta people's militia and the Indonesian revolution 1945–1949*. Allen and Unwin: Sydney.

Crone, P. 1986. "The tribe and the state," in Hall, J. (ed.) *States in History*. Basil Blackwell: London.

Daems, J. and Nebo, H. (eds) 2005. *Eikon Basilike with Selections from Eikonoklestes*. Broadview Press: Toronto.

Dahl, R. 1970. *After the Revolution: Authority in good society*. Yale University Press: New Haven, CT.

Dahl, R. 1971. *Polyarchy and Opposition: Participation and opposition*. Yale University Press: New Haven, CT.

Dahl, R. 1989. *Democracy and Its Critics*. Yale University Press: New Haven, CT.

Dahl, R. 2000. *On Democracy*. Yale University Press: New Haven, CT.

Dashwood, H. 2000. *Zimbabwe: The political economy of transformation*. University of Toronto Press: Toronto.

Dauvergne, P. 1998. "Weak States, Strong States: A state-in-society perspective," in Peter Dauvergne (ed.) *Weak and Strong States in Asia-Pacific Societies*. Allen & Unwin: Sydney.

Derrida, J. 1980. *Writing and Difference*. University of Chicago Press: Chicago, IL.

Derrida, J. 1997. *Of Grammatology*. The Johns Hopkins University Press: Baltimore, MD.

Desai, P. 1989. *Perestroika in Perspective*. Princeton University Press: Princeton, NJ.

de Tocqueville, A. 2003. *Democracy in America*. Penguin Classics: Harmondsworth.

Diamond, L. 1999. *Developing Democracy: Towards consolidation*. The Johns Hopkins University Press: Baltimore, MD.

Diamond, L., Linz, J. and Lipset, S. (eds) 1989a. *Democracy in Developing Countries: Asia*. Lynne Reinner Publishers: Boulder, CO.

Diamond, L., Linz, J. and Lipset, S. (eds) 1989b. *Democracy in Developing Countries: Africa*. Lynne Reinner Publishers: Boulder, CO.

Diamond, L., Linz, J. and Lipset, S. (eds) 1989c. *Democracy in Developing Countries: Latin America*. Lynne Reinner Publishers: Boulder, CO.

Digeser, E. 2004. "Citizenship and the Roman Res Publica: Cicero and the Christian corollary," in Weinstock, D. and Nadeau, C. *Republicanism: History, theory and practise*. Frank Cass: London and Portland, OR.

Di Palma, G. 1982. "Italy: Is there a legacy and is it fascist?" in Herz, J. (ed.) *From Dictatorship to Democracy*. Greenwood Press: Westport, CT.

Di Palma, G. 1991. *To Craft Democracies: An essay on democratic transition*. University of California Press: Berkeley, CA.

Dodd, C. 1972. *Political Development*. Macmillan: London.

Donnelly, S. 1984. "Human Rights and Development: Complimentary or competing concerns," *World Politics*, 36(2), January.

Downs, A. 1957. *An Economic Theory of Democracy*. Harper: New York.

Editors, The 1985. "On the Road Towards a More Adequate Understanding of the State," in Evans, P., Rueschemeyer, D. and Skocpol, T. (eds) *Bringing the State Back In*. Cambridge University Press: Cambridge.

Elklit, J. 1994. "Is the Degree of Electoral Democracy Measurable? Experiences from Bulgaria, Kenya, Latvia, Mongolia and Nepal," in Beetham, D. *Defining and Measuring Democracy*. Sage Publications: London.

Ellul, J. 1964. *The Technological Society*. Vintage: New York.

Engels, F. 1989. *Socialism: Utopian and scientific*, 2nd ed. Pathfinder Press: New York.

Errson, S. and Lane, J. 1996. "Democracy and Development: A statistical exploration," in Leftwich, A. *Democracy and Development*. Polity Press: Cambridge.

Evans, P. 1995. *Embedded Autonomy*. Princeton University Press: Princeton, NJ.

Fanon, F. 1970. *A Dying Colonialism*. Pelican Books: Harmondsworth.

Farcau, B. 1996. *The Transition to Democracy in Latin America*. Praeger, Westport, CT and London.

Fernandes, C. and Kingsbury, D. 2005. "Terrorism in archipelagic Southeast Asia," in Kingsbury, D. ed. *Violence in Between: Conflict and security in archipelagic Southeast Asia*. Monash Asia Institute/Institute for Southeast Asian Studies: Melbourne/Singapore.

Fowler, M. and Bunck, J. 1995. *Law, Power and the Sovereign State*. University of Pennsylvania Press: University Park, PA.

FfP 2006. *Failed State Index 2006* Fund for Peace http://www.fundforpeace.org/programs/fsi/fsindex2006.php (accessed 23 October 2006).

Foucault, M. 1982. *The Archeology of Knowledge and The Discourse on Language* trans. Swyer, R. Pantheon Books: New York.

FP 2005. "The Failed State Index Rankings," *Foreign Policy*, July/August 2005.

Freedom House 1999. *Democracy's Century: A survey of global political change in the 20th century*. Freedom House: New York.

Freire, P. 1973. *Pedagogy of the Oppressed*. Seabury Press: New York.

Fukuyama, F. 1992. *The End of History and the Last Man*. The Free Press: New York.

Fukuyama, F. 2004. *State Building*. Profile Books: London.

Fung, A. and Wright, E. (2000) "Deepening Democracy: Innovations in empowered participatory governance," *Politics and Society*, September.

Galbraith, J. 1967. *The New Industrial State*. Pelican: London.

Gamble, C. 1986. "Hunter-gatherers and the origins of states," in Hall, J. (ed.) *States in History*. Basil Blackwell: London

Gans, C. 2003. *The Limits of Nationalism*. Cambridge University Press: Cambridge.

Geertz, C. 1989. *Works and Lives: The anthropologist as author*. Polity Press: Cambridge.

Geertz, C. 1993. *The Interpretation of Cultures*. Fontana Press: London.

Gellner, E. 1983. *Nations and Nationalism*. Cornell University Press: Ithaca, NY.

Goenewan, M. 2002. *Conversations With Difference: Essays from TEMPO Magazine*. Lindsey, J. trans. PT Tempo Inti Media: Jakarta.

Goodin, R. 1979. "The Development–Rights Trade Off: Some unwarranted economics and political assumptions," *Universal Human Rights*, 1(2), April–June.

Gramsci, A. 1971. *Selections from Prison Notebooks*. Q. Hoare and G. Smith (eds) trans. Lawrence and Wishart: London.

Grimsley, R. 1973. *The Philosophy of Rousseau*. Oxford University Press: London.

Grugel, J. 2002. *Democratization: A critical introduction*. Palgrave: Houndmills, Hampshire, NJ.

Habermas, J. 2001a. "A Constitution for Europe?" *New Left Review*, 11, 5–26

Habermas, J. 2001b. *A Postnational Constellation*. MIT Press: Cambridge, MA.

Harrington, J. 1992. J. Pocock (ed.) *The Commonwealth of Oceana and A System of Politics*. Cambridge University Press: Cambridge.

Hayek, F. 1960. *The Constitution of Liberty*. University of Chicago Press: Chicago, IL.

Hayek, F. 1976. *The Road to Serfdom*, 5th edn. intro. Friedman, M. University of Chicago Press: Chicago, IL.

Hayek, F. 1988. *The Fatal Conceit: The errors of socialism (The Collected Works of F. A. Hayek)* Bartley, W. (ed.) University of Chicago Press: Chicago, IL.

Hegel, G. 1967. *Hegel's Philosophy of Right*. Knox, T. trans. Oxford University Press: London.

Held, D. 1996. *Models of Democracy*, 2nd edn. Polity Press: Cambridge.

Hellman J. Jones, G, Kaufmann, D. and Schankerman, M. 2000. *Measuring Governance, Corruption, and State Capture: How firms and bureaucrats shape the business environment in transition economies*. World Bank Policy Research Working Paper 2312, World Bank: Washington, DC.

Herz, J. 1982. "Denazification and related policies," in Herz, J. (ed.) *From Dictatorship to Democracy*. Greenwood Press, Westport: CT.

Hewison, K. 2006. *A Short History of Thailand*. Allen and Unwin: Sydney.

Heywood, A. 2003. *Political Ideologies: An introduction*, 3rd edn. Palgrave: Houndmills, Hampshire, NJ.

Hinsley, F. 1978, *Sovereignty*, 2nd edn. Cambridge University Press: Cambridge.

Hobbes, T. 1962. *Leviathan, or the Matter, Forme and Power of a Commonwealth Ecclesiasticall and Civil*. Collier: New York.

Hobsbawm, E. 1983. In Hobsbawm, E. and Ranger, E. (eds) *The Invention of Traditions*. Cambridge University Press: Cambridge.

Hobsbawm, E. 1990. *Nations and Nationalism Since 1870: Programme, myth, reality*. Cambridge University Press: Cambridge.

Holden, B. 2000. *Global Democracy: Key debates*. Routledge: London.

Howard, R. 1983. "The Full Bellies Thesis," *Human Rights Quarterly*, 5(4), November.

Howard, R. and Donnelly, J. 1996. "Liberalism and Human Rights: A necessary connection," in Ishay, M. (ed.) *The Human Rights Reader*. Routledge: New York.

Htin, A. 1967. *A History of Burma*. Columbia University Press: New York.

Humphrey, M. and Vershy, A. 2003. *Violent Conflict and Millennium Goals: Diagnosis and recommendations*, paper to the Millennium Development Goals Task Force Workshop, Bangkok, June 2004.

Huntington, S. 1957. *The Soldier and the State: The theory and politics of civil-military relations*. Harvard University Press: Cambridge, MA.

Huntington, S. 1968. *Political Order in Changing Societies*. Yale University Press: Cambridge, MA.

Huntington. S. 1993. "The clash of civilizations," *Foreign Affairs*, 72(3): 22–49.

Huntington, S. 1996. *The Clash of Civilizations and the Remaking of World Order*. Simon and Schuster: New York.

Huntington, S. 2000. "The Future of the Third Wave," in Plattner, M. and Espada, J. (eds.) *The Democratic Invention*. The Johns Hopkins University Press: Baltimore, MD.

Hutchcroft, P. 1991. "Oligarchs and Cronies in the Philippine State: The politics of patrimonial plunder," *World Politics*, 43(3), April 1991.

Hutchcroft, P. 1998. *Booty Capitalism: The politics of banking in the Philippines*. Cornell University Press: Ithaca, NY.

Hutchinson, J. and Smith, A. 1994. *Nationalism*. Oxford University Press: New York.

Jaguaribe, H. 1968. *Economic and Political Development*. Harvard University Press: Cambridge, MA.

Jupp, J. 1968. *Political Parties*. Routledge and Kegan Paul: New York.

Jutting, J. 2003. *Institutions and Development: A critical review*. OECD Development Center, Working Paper No 210. OECD: Paris.

Kaldor, M. 2004. "Nationalism and Globalisation," in *Nations and Nationalism*, 10(1/2): 161–77.

Kant, I. 1997. *Critique of Practical Reason*. Cambridge University Press: Cambridge.

Kaufmann, D. 2004. "Governance Redux: The empirical challenge" in *Global Competitiveness Report 2003–2004*. World Economic Forum.

Kaufmann, D., Kraay, A. and Mastruzzi, M. 2003. *Governance Matters III: Governance indicators for 1996–2002*. World Bank, Washington, DC.

Kaufmann, D., Kraay, A. and Mastruzzi, M. 2005. *Governance Matters IV: Governance indicators for 1996–2004*. World Bank: Washington, DC.

Kaufmann, D., Kraay, A. and Zoido-Lobatón, P. 1999. *Governance Matters*. World Bank Policy Research Working Paper 2196, World Bank: Washington, DC.

Kaufmann, D., Kraay, A. and P. Zoido-Lobatón, P. 2000. "Governance Matters: From measurement to action," in *Finance and Development*. International Monetary Fund: Washington, DC.

Keane, J. 2006. *Democracy: A short history*. Evatt Foundation: Canberra.

Kearney, A. 2001. "Measuring Globalisation," *Foreign Policy*, Washington, DC, May–June.

Keohane, R. 2002. *Power and Governance in a Partially Globalized World*. Routledge: London and New York.

Kingsbury, D. 2005. *The Politics of Indonesia*, 3rd edn. Oxford University Press: Melbourne.

Kohli, A. and Shue, V. 1994. "State Power and Social Forces: On political contention and accommodation in the Third World" in Migdal, J., Kohli, A. and Shue, V. (eds). *State Power and Social Forces*. Cambridge University Press: Cambridge.

Kohn, H. 1965. *Nationalism, Its Meaning and History*, Van Nostrand: New York.

Krader, L. 1976. *Dialectic of Civil Society*. Prometheus Books: New York.

Kurland, P. and Lerner, R. (eds) 1987. *The Founders Constitution*. University of Chicago Press: Chicago, IL.

Lafargue, P. 1884. "A Few Words with Mr Herbert Spencer," in *To-Day*, January–June, 416–27;

Lane, J. and Ersson, S. 2003. *Democracy: A comparative approach*. Routledge: London.

Larmore, C. 1996. *The Morals of Modernity*. Cambridge University Press: Cambridge.

Laski, H. 1934. *The State in Theory and Practice*. George Allen & Unwin: London.

Lasswell, H. and Lerner, D. 1965. *World Revolutionary Elites*. MIT Press: Cambridge, MA.

Lenin, V. 1961. *Collected Works*. Progress Publishers: Moscow.

Lenin, V. 1965. *The State and Revolution*. Foreign Languages Press: Peking (Beijing).

Lev, D. 2005. "Conceptual Filters and Obfuscation in the Study of Indonesian Politics," *Asian Studies Review*. 9(4), December.

Leys, S. 1997. *The Analects of Confucius*. W.W. Norton and Co: New York.

Liebman, M. 1975. *Leninism Under Lenin*. Jonathan Cape: London.

Linz, J. 1993. "The Perils of Presidentialism," in Diamond, L. and Plattner, M. (eds) *The Global Resurgence of Democracy*. The Johns Hopkins University Press: Baltimore, MD, 108–26.

Lijphart, A. 1999. *Patterns of Democracy*. Yale University Press: New Haven, CT.

Locke. J. 1960. *Two Treatises of Government*. Cambridge University Press: Cambridge.

Lukes, S. 1974. *Power: A Radical View*. Macmillan: London.

Lukes, S. 1993. "Five Fables About Human Rights," in Shute, S. and Hurley, S. (eds) *On Human Rights: Oxford amnesty lectures*. Basic Books: New York.

Lyotard, J.-F. 1984. *The Post-Modern Condition: A report on knowledge*. Bennington, G. and Massumi, B. trans. University of Minnesota Press: MN.

McCloud, D. 1995. *Southeast Asia: Traditional and modernity in the contemporary world.* Westview Press: Boulder, CO.

Machiavelli, N. 1963. *The Prince.* Pocket Books: New York.

Mack, A. 2005. *The Human Security Report: War and peace in the 21st century.* Oxford University Press: Oxford.

MacIntyre, A. 1981. *After Virtue.* Duckworth: London.

Malefakis, E. 1982. "Spain and Its Francoist Heritage" in Hertz, J. (ed.) *From Dictatorship to Democracy.* Greenwood Press: Westport, CT.

Marker, S. 2003. "Effects of Colonization," in Burgess, G. and Burgess, H. (eds) *Beyond Intractability.* Conflict Research Consortium: University of Colorado, Boulder, CO. http://www.beyondintractability.org/essay/post-colonial/ posted November 2003.

Marx, K. 1959. *Economic and Philosophic Manuscripts of 1844.* Progress Publishers: Moscow.

Marx, K. 1967. *The Essential Writings of Karl Marx.* Caute, D. (ed.). Macmillan: New York.

Marx, K. 1970. *Critique of Hegel's Philosophy of Right.* Jolin, A. and O'Malley, J. trans. Cambridge University Press: Cambridge.

Marx, K. and Engels, F. 1969. *Selected Works*, Vol 1. Progress Publishers: Moscow.

Marx, K. and Engels, F. 1970. *The German Ideology.* C. Arthur (ed.). International Publishers: New York.

Maxwell, K. 1982. "The Emergence of Portuguese Democracy," in Herz, J. (ed.) *From Dictatorship to Democracy.* Greenwood Press: Westport, CT.

Michels, R. 1959. *Political Parties: A sociological study of the oligarchical tendencies of modern democracy.* Dover: New York.

Migdal, J. 1994. "The state in society: an approach to struggles for domination," in Migdal, J., Kohli, A. and Shue, V. (ed), *State Power and Social Forces. Domination and Transformation in the Third World.* Press Syndicate of the University of Cambridge: New York.

Mill, J. 1910. *Utilitarianism, Liberty, Representative Government.* J.M. Dent and Sons Ltd: London.

Miller, D. 1993. "In defence of nationality," *Journal of Applied Philosophy*, 10(1): 3–16.

Miller, D. 1995. *On Nationality.* Oxford University Press: Oxford.

Miller, M. 2006. PhD thesis. *Reformasi and Rebellion on the Verandah of Mecca: The Indonesian State's security and autonomy policies in Aceh Province, May 1998–May 2003.* Charles Darwin University: Darwin.

Mills, C. Wright 1951. *White Collar: The American Middle Classes.* Oxford University Press: New York.

Mills, C. Wright 1956. *The Power Elite.* Oxford University Press: New York.

Mittelman, J. and Othman, N. 2001. *Capturing Globalization.* Routledge: London.

Moertono, S. 1981. *State and Statecraft in Old Java*: Modern Indonesia Project Monograph Series no. 43, Cornell University: Ithaca, NY.

Moore, J. 2003. *Zimbabwe's Fight To The Finish.* Kegan Paul Ltd: London.

Morris, C. 1998. *An Essay on the Modern State.* Cambridge University Press: Cambridge.

Mosca, G. 1939. *The Ruling Class.* Livingstone A. trans. McGraw-Hill: New York.

Motyl, A. 2001. *Imperial Ends: The decay, collapse, and revival of empires.* Columbia University Press: New York.

NATO 1999. *NATO's role in Kosovo.* Basic Documents, NATO, Brussels, 10 June 1999.

Neustadt, R. 1960. *Presidential Power: The politics of leadership*. John Wiley: New York.

Nietzsche, F. 1968. *Will To Power*. Kaufmann, W. (ed.).Vintage Press: New York.

Nisbett, E. and Shanahan, J. 2004. *MSRG Special Report: US war on terror, foreign policy, and anti-Americanism*. Media and Society Research Group, Cornell University Press: Ithaca, NY.

North, D. 1990. *Institutions, Institutionalism Change and Economic Performance*. Cambridge University Press: Cambridge.

Nuremberg Trials 1947–9. *The Trial of Major War Criminals Before the International Military Tribunal, Proceedings*, vols I–XXIII, Nuremberg Trials, Nuremberg.

Oakshott, M. 1939. *The Social and Political Doctrines of Contemporary Europe*. Cambridge University Press: Cambridge.

Ober, J. 2000. "Quasi-rights: Political boundaries and social diversity in democratic Athens," *Social Philosophy and Policy*, 17(1): 27–61.

O'Donnell, G., Schmitter, P. and Whitehead, L. (eds) 1988. *Transitions from Authoritarian Rule: Comparative perspectives*, The Johns Hopkins University Press: Baltimore, MD.

O'Donnell, G. and Schmitter, P. 1986. *Transitions from Authoritarian Rule: Tenative conclusions about uncertain democracies*. The Johns Hopkins University Press: Baltimore, MD.

O'Donnell, G. 1996. "Illusions and Conceptual Flaws," *Journal of Democracy*, 7(4): 160–8, October.

Ogburn, W. 1964. *On Culture and Social Change*. University of Chicago Press: Chicago, IL.

Ong, W. 2002. *Orality and Literacy*. Routledge: London.

Ortega y Gasset, J. 1964. *The Revolt of the Masses*. W.W. Norton and Co: New York.

Orwell, G. 1946. *Animal Farm*. Brace Harcourt and Company: Orlando, FL.

Packer, J. 1998. "Autonomy within the OSCE: The case of Crimea," in Suski, M. (ed.), *Autonomy: Applications and implications*. Kluwer Law International: The Hague.

Packer, J. 1999. "The Implementation of the Right to Self-Determination as a Contribution to Conflict Prevention," in Praag, M. and Seroo, O. (eds) *Report of the International Conference of Experts*. UNESCO: Barcelona.

Packer, J. 2000a. "Self-Determination and International Law," "West Papua and the Quest for Self-Determination," *Self-Determination and International Law*. Utrecht, 6–11.

Packer, J. 2000b. "The Origin and Nature of the Lund Recommendations on the Effective Participation of National Minorities in Public Life," *Helsinki Monitor*, 11(4): 29–61.

Paine, T. 1969. *The Rights of Man*. Pelican Classics: Harmondsworth.

Parekh, B. 1994. "Cultural Diversity and Liberal Democracy," in Beetham, D. *Defining and Measuring Democracy*. Sage Publications: London.

Pareto, V. 1968 (1901). *The Rise and Fall of Elites: An application of theoretical sociology*. Bedminster Press: Totowa, NJ.

Pareto, V. 1984. *The Transformation of Democracy*. Ed. C. Powers. Transaction Books: New Brunswick, NJ.

Parkinson, C. 1957. *Parkinson's Law*. Houghton Mifflin Company: Boston, MA.

Pemberton, J. 1994. *On the Subject of "Java"*. Cornell University Press: Ithaca, NY.

Petit, P. 1999. *Republicanism: A theory of freedom and government*, 2nd edn. Cambridge University Press: Cambridge.

Philip, G. 1985. *The Military in South American Politics*. Croom Helm: London.

Ping-chia Kuo 1965. *China*. Oxford University Press: London.

Plamenatz, J. 1968. *Consent, Freedom and Political Obligation*, 2nd edn. Oxford University Press: London.

Plamenatz, J. 1973. "Two Types of Nationalism" in Kamenka, E. (ed.) *Nationalism: The nature and evolution of an idea*. Edward Arnold: London.

Plato 1955. *The Republic*. Lee, D. trans. and intro. Penguin Books: Harmondsworth.

Pompe, S. 2005. *The Indonesian Supreme Court: A study of institutional collapse*. Cornell Southeast Asia Program: Ithaca, NY.

Psomiades, H. 1982. "Greece: From the Colonels' rule to democracy" in Herz, J. (ed.) *From Dictatorship to Democracy*. Greenwood Press: Westport, CT.

Putnam, R. 1993. *Making Democracy Work: Civic traditions in modern Italy*. Princeton University Press: Princeton, NJ.

Pye, L. 1985. *Asian Power and Politics*. Belknap Press: Cambridge, MA.

Rawls, J. 1971. *A Theory of Justice*. Harvard University Press: Cambridge, MA.

Rostow, W. 1960. *Stages of Economic Growth*. Cambridge University Press: Cambridge.

Rostow, W. 1971. *Politics and the Stages of Economic Growth*. Cambridge University Press: Cambridge.

Rothstein, B. 1992. *Just Institutions Matter: The moral and political logic of the universal welfare state*. Cambridge University Press: New York.

Rousseau, J-J. 1973. *The Social Contract and Discourses*. J.M. Dent and Sons: London.

Rousseau, J-J. 1953. *The Confessions*. Penguin Classics: Harmondsworth.

Sapir, E. 1955. *An Introduction to the Study of Speech*. Harcourt Brace and Co.: Orlando, FL.

Sar Desai, D. 1997. *Southeast Asia: Past and present*. Westview Press: Boulder, CO.

Schumpeter, J. 1976. *Capitalism, Socialism and Democracy*. Harper & Row: New York.

Schurman, F. and Schell, O. (eds) 1977. *Imperial China*. Penguin Books: Harmondsworth.

Schmitter, P. and Schneider, C. 2003. *Exploring a New Cross-Regional Data Set on the Key Concepts in Democratization: Liberalization, transition and consolidation*. Paper to the 2003 Annual Meeting of the American Politican Science Association: Florence, 28–31 August 2003.

Sen, A. 1999. *Development as Freedom*. Oxford University Press: Oxford.

Sen. A. 2002. *Rationality and Freedom*. The Bellknap Press of Harvard University Press: Cambridge, MA.

Sen. A. 2006. "Democracy isn't Western," *The Wall Street Journal*, 24 March 2006.

Seymour, M. 2000. "On Redefining the Nation," in Miscevic, N. (ed.) *Nationalism and Ethnic Conflict. Philosophical Perspectives*. Open Court: La Salle and Chicago, IL.

Singer, P. 1979. *Practical Ethics*. Cambridge University Press: Cambridge.

Singh, B. 2001. *Civil-military Relations in Democratising Indonesia: The potentials and limits to change*. Strategic Defence Studies Centre Australian National University: Canberra.

Sitrampalam, S. (Unpublished paper) *Nationalism, Historiography and Archeology in Sri Lanka – A Perspective*. University of Jaffna: Thirunelvely.

Smith, A. 1986a. "State-making and Nation-building," in J. Hall (ed.) *States in History*. Basil Blackwell: Oxford.

Smith, A. 1986b. *The Ethnic Origins of Nations*. Blackwell Publishers: Oxford.

Smith, A. 1998. *Nationalism and Modernism*. Routledge: London.

Smith, A. 2003. *Chosen Peoples: Sacred sources of national identity*. Oxford University Press: Oxford.

Snow, R. 1999. *The Militia Threat: Terrorists among us*. Plenum Trade: New York.

Sophocles 1947. *The Theban Plays*. Penguin Classics: Harmondsworth.

Sorel, G. 1970. *Reflections on Violence*. Collier Books: New York.

Steadman, J. 1969. *The Myth of Asia*. Macmillan: London.

Steinmo, S. 2001. "Institutionalism," in Polsby, N. (ed.) *International Encyclopedia of the Social and Behavioral Sciences*. Elsevier Science: Surrey.

Stepan, A. 1976. "The New Professionalism of Internal Warfare and Military Role Expansion," in Lowenthal, A. *Armies and Politics in Latin America*. Jolmes and Meier Publishers: New York and London.

Stepan, A. 1985. "State Power and the Strength of Civil Society in the Southern Cone of Lain America," in P. Evans, D. Rueschemeyer and T. Skocpol (eds) *Bringing the State Back In*. Cambridge University Press: Cambridge.

Stiglitz, J. 2003. *Globalization and its Discontents*. Norton: New York.

de Ste Croix, G. 1987. *The Class Struggle in the Ancient Greek World from the Archaic Age to the Arab Conquests*. Duckworth: London.

Strayer, J. 1970. *On the Medieval Origins of the Modern State*. Princeton University Press: Princeton, NJ.

Stuart-Fox, M. 1997. *A History of Laos*. Cambridge University Press: Cambridge.

Suh, S. 1997. "No Easy Answers: Is the individual supreme? Or should country and community come first?" *Asiaweek*, 31 October 1997.

Supriyadi, W. 2006. "West Papuans are Happy to be Indonesians," *The Age*, 10 April 2006.

Tambiah, S. 1976. *World Conqueror and World Renouncer*. Cambridge University Press: Cambridge.

Tamir, Y. 1993. *Liberal Nationalism*. Princeton University Press: Princeton, NJ.

Thoreau, D. 1993 (1849). *Civil Disobedience*. Dover Thrift Editions, Mineola, NY.

Todorov, T. 1986. ""Race," Writing and Culture," Mack, L. trans. in Gates, H. (ed.) *"Race," Writing and Difference*. University of Chicago Press: London.

Trotsky, L. 1937. *The Revolution Betrayed*. Pathfinder Press: New York.

UN 1945. *Charter of the United Nations*, New York.

UN 1976. *International Covenant on Economic, Social and Cultural Rights*. UN General Assembly Resolution 2200A (XXI) 16 December 1966, entry into force 3 January 1976.

UN 1986. *Declaration on the Right to Development*. UN General Assembly Resolution 41/128, 4 December 1986.

UNDP 2005. *Human Development Report 2005*. United Nations Development Programme, New York.

UNTC 2002. "Declarations and Reservations," *International Covenant on Civil and Political Rights*. United Nations Treaty Collection, 5 February.

Voltaire 1979, *Philosophical Dictionary*. Besterman, T. trans. Penguin Books: Harmondsworth.

Wagner, D. 1971 (1938). *Ein Reich, Ein Volk, Ein Fuhrer: The nazi annexation of Austria*. Longman: London.

Walker, G. 1988. *The Rule of Law: Foundation of constitutional democracy*. Melbourne University Press: Melbourne.

Walzer, M. 1988. *The Company of Critics: Social criticism and political commitment in the 20th Century*. Basic Books: New York.

Watson, D. 2005. *Death Sentences: How cliches, weasel words and management-speak are strangling public language*. Random House: Melbourne.

Weber, M. 1946. *Social and Economic Organization.* Ed. Parsons, T. Oxford University Press: New York.

Weber, M. 1948. "Politics as a Vocation." Gerth, Hans H. and Mills, C. Wright, trans. (eds). *From Max Weber: Essays in sociology.* Routledge & Kegan Paul: London.

Weber, M. 1958. *From Max Weber: Essays in sociology.* Gerth, Hans H. and Mills, Wright C. trans. (eds). Oxford University Press: New York.

Weber, M. 1968 (1922). *Economy and Society.* Roth, G. and Wittich, C. trans. (eds). Bedminster Press: New York.

Weber, C. and Bierstaker, T. (eds) 1996. *State Sovereignty as Social Construction.* Cambridge Studies in International Relations: Cambridge.

Weingast, B. 1996. "Political Institutions: Rational choice perspective," in Goodin, H. *A New Handbook of Political Science.* Oxford University Press: Oxford.

Weinstock, D. and Nadeau, C. 2004. *Republicanism: History, theory and practise.* Frank Cass: London and Portland, OR.

White, M. 2002. *Historical Atlas of the 20th Century.* http://users.erols.com/mwhite28/20c-govt.htm accessed 23 November 2005.

Whorf, B. 1956. *Language, Thought and Reality: Selected writings of Benjamin Lee Whorf.* Ed. Carrol, J. The MIT Press: Cambridge, MA.

Wilson, D. 1969. "Thailand" in G. Kahin (ed.), *Government and Politics in South East Asia,* 2nd edn. Cornell University Press: Ithaca, NY.

Wolff, E. 2004. *Changes in Household Wealth in the 1980s and 1990s in the US.* Working Paper No 407, Levy Economics Institute, Bard College: Annandale-on-Hudson, NY.

Wolters, O. 1999. *History, Culture and Region in Southeast Asian Perspectives.* Southeast Asia Program Publications, Cornell University: Ithaca, NY.

World Bank 2005. *Governance Indicators: 1996–2004.* World Bank: Washington, DC.

World Bank 2006. *Engaging with Fragile States.* Independent Evaluation Group, World Bank: Washington, DC.

World Conference on Human Rights 1993. *Report of the Drafting Committee, Regional Meeting for Asia (Bangkok Declaration)* 29 March–2 April.

Wright, D. (ed.) 1974. *The French Revolution: Introductory documents.* University of Queensland Press: Brisbane.

Young, de. K. 2006. "Court Told it Lacks Power in Detainee Cases." *The Washington Post,* 20 October.

Index